MARKETING MANAGEMENT STRATEGY

Contributors

CLINTON A. BAKER, *Indiana State University,* Cases 13, 53

JOHN J. BRASCH, *University of Nebraska,* Cases 9, 78

JOHN ROBERT FOSTER, *University of South Carolina,* Case 6

WILLIAM M. MORGENROTH, *University of South Carolina,* Cases 16, 17, 18, 36, 49, 59, 76

WILLIAM R. THOMAS, *University of South Carolina,* Cases 3, 10, 22, 30, 32, 37, 38, 39, 50

ARCH G. WOODSIDE, *University of South Carolina,* Cases 4, 5, 34, 35

MARKETING MANAGEMENT STRATEGY
CASES AND PROBLEMS

STEVEN J. SHAW
JOHN F. WILLENBORG
RICHARD E. STANLEY
University of South Carolina

APPLETON-CENTURY-CROFTS
Educational Division
New York   MEREDITH CORPORATION

*HF
5415.13
S5
1971*

Acknowledgments

PAGE 3 and EXHIBIT 1, PAGE 6. Adapted with permission from "Progressive
Grocer Colonial Study," *Progressive Grocer* (October 1964), pp. 102–103.
PAGES 4–5 and EXHIBIT 2, PAGE 6. Adapted with permission from the *14th
Annual Study of Supermarket Shoppers*, 1967, Burgoyne Index, Inc., Cin-
cinnati, Ohio.
PAGE 5. From "Women Sound Off About Grocery Stores," *Changing Times*
(September 1968), pp. 7–11. Excerpted by permission from *Changing Times*,
copyright 1968 by the Kiplinger Washington Editors, Inc.
PAGES 25–27. Based on material provided by The James L. Tapp Company,
with permission.
PAGES 39–42. Based on material provided by Harvey A. Kresge, Director of
Public Relations, S. S. Kresge Company, Detroit, Michigan, with permission.
PAGES 55–61. Reprinted with permission from *Investornews* (July 1969), pp.
6–14, a publication of Francis I. du Pont & Co., One Wall Street, New York,
N.Y.
PAGES 74–76. Adapted with permission from "On All Shelves at Once,"
Business Week (October 5, 1963), pp. 127–128.
PAGES 76–79. Adapted with permission from "How a New Item is Born,"
Progressive Grocer (August 1967), pp. 54–59.
PAGES 80–88, 116–117, 118–120, 149–150. Based on material provided by
Texize Chemicals, Inc., with permission.
PAGES 112–114. Based on material provided by Thomas & Howard Com-
pany, with permission.
PAGES 121–125. Based on material provided by Volkswagen of America,
Inc., with permission.

PAGE 163. Reprinted with permission from the June 23, 1969 issue of *Advertising Age*. Copyright 1969 by Advertising Publications, Inc.

PAGES 164–165. Adapted with permission from "Selling Capitalism," *Barron's–National Business and Financial Weekly* (July 7, 1969), a publication of Dow Jones and Company, New York, N.Y.

PAGES 204–208. Based on material provided by Shaw Nursery and Landscape Company, with permission.

PAGES 209–210. From Perrin Stryker, "Auto Insurance: Battered by Its Own Boom," *Fortune* (October 1960), pp. 142–146 ff. Reprinted by permission; © 1960, Time, Inc.

PAGES 211–215. Adapted from a report by Matthew Godek, Ali C. Najjar, Kenneth H. Rossen, and Jean Woods. Based on material provided by Patrone's Cleaners and Laundry, with permission.

PAGES 224–225. From *Marketing Insights,* April 8, 1968, Copyright 1968, Advertising Publications, Inc., Chicago, Ill. Reprinted with permission.

PAGES 229–230. Excerpted from "The Automobile Industry: A Case Study of Competition, A Statement by General Motors Corporation," in *Planning, Regulation, and Competition: Automobile Industry–1968,* U.S. Government Printing Office, Washington, D.C., 1968, pp. 617–728. The statement was presented at hearings before subcommittees of the Select Committee on Small Business, United States Senate, July 1968.

PAGES 280–288. Edward H. Vogel, Jr., "Creative Marketing and Management Science," *Modern Brewery Age* (November 1968), pp. 34–39. Reprinted with permission.

To our patient and understanding wives, Aracelis, Martha, and Ann

Contents

II. CAPITALIZING ON OPPORTUNITIES THROUGH THE MARKETING MIX

Product Planning and Development

Development of Marketing Channels

x

Pricing Strategy

The Promotion and Selling Effort

III. MARKETING IN SPECIALIZED AREAS

Marketing of Consumer Services

The Legal, Social, and Ethical Environment

IV. COORDINATION OF THE MARKETING EFFORT

APPENDIX

Preface

In a nation characterized by an abundance of products and services, business enterprises of all sizes and interests compete vigorously within a complex market system. To be successful in selling to today's discerning customer, a business must carry out the activities of marketing in the most efficient way possible. These activities must be guided by objectives and implemented through strategies designed to increase the well-being of the customer as well as the firm. Successful businesses today are market-oriented and judge their marketing programs on how effectively they meet the needs of their markets.

Marketing strategies must be designed to fit particular situations, and these situations are subject to frequent and often rapid change. A firm must be ready to make decisions based upon short- and long-term considerations. Marketers must continually seek to increase their knowledge of the marketing environment and remain flexible in the use of strategies —for if there is one thing that marketers can be certain about, it is the constancy of change.

This book, *Marketing Management Strategy: Cases and Problems,* presents a wide variety of situations dealing with the broad range of problems confronting marketers and other decision-makers. The cases and problems involve businesses ranging in size from the small proprietorship to the giant corporation. The firms described are in a variety of industries, including the often-neglected service industry. Material also is included which relates to the social, legal, and ethical environment within which marketing activities take place.

It is our contention that a book intended for classroom use must first serve the student. Therefore, this volume has been prepared for the student who will soon put his textbooks behind him and take a position in the world of business. We have designed the book with several thoughts in mind: (1) Most students will never work in giant corporations, but rather in businesses of smaller size. (2) In the classroom, the learning experience is enriched through presentation of a variety of topics to be studied and discussed. (3) The gap between the textbook and problem-solving in the outside world can be partially bridged by the effective introduction of realism in the form of cases and problems.

Based on the preceding contentions, we have included in the book cases which place the student in varying decision-making situations. The cases also vary in length and complexity, providing the instructor with much-needed flexibility. Each section provides a balanced combination of situations. The short problems are designed to elicit ready answers to certain questions as well as to stimulate extensive discussion of important issues. Many of the cases are particularly intended to develop the analytical abilities of the student by forcing him to identify problem areas, weigh alternatives, and recommend solutions. Although some of the company names are fictitious, all cases are based upon actual marketing situations, and the problems are "up-to-date" in order to introduce the realism which will guarantee student "involvement."

Marketing Management Strategy: Cases and Problems should be particularly suitable for use as the principal text in courses in marketing management which utilize the case method at both the undergraduate and graduate levels. It also will prove useful as a supplement to standard marketing textbooks in marketing management courses in which an instructor wishes to expose students to realistic business situations and to provide them with practice in decision-making and problem-solving.

The authors gratefully acknowledge the assistance rendered by many persons in the preparation of this book. Without the willing cooperation of Dean James F. Kane of the College of Business Administration, University of South Carolina, and Associate Dean, William F. Putnam, the volume would not have been feasible. In addition, the contributions of several of our colleagues, listed on a separate page, were indispensable.

We are deeply indebted to the business firms which have allowed us to use materials from their files. A special note of appreciation is due William J. Greer, Chairman of the Board, Texize Chemicals, Inc. and his sons Richard and Tommy Greer, who furnished us materials for four cases.

Finally, we are also appreciative of the efforts of many of the secretaries at the College of Business in typing the early drafts and grateful to Mrs. J. Wayne Goff, who did an excellent job of typing the final manuscript.

S. J. S.
J. F. W.
R. E. S.

I.
ANALYZING
MARKET OPPORTUNITIES

CONSUMER
AND MARKET RESEARCH

1.
Collegiate Marketing Surveys
Evaluating Research Proposals

Noting the growing demand for small research studies throughout the state, several marketing students at a large state university organized a company to make surveys and other studies for moderate fees. The university campus is situated in the state's capital city, and the partners know that they can solicit considerable research work from the downtown businessmen. Also, since the five partners are from hometowns in different parts of the state, they feel they can do statewide surveys economically by using their homes as bases for fieldwork.

The five men are marketing majors, and they all have completed the marketing research phase of their formal academic training. Their main interests at this time are to make some money to pay a part of their college expenses and, more importantly, to gain valuable experience in practical research work. They have excellent relations with the marketing faculty of the College of Business Administration, and they know they can get professional advice when they need it. In fact, the idea for organizing Collegiate Marketing Surveys came from a lecture given by the marketing research instructor who stated that there were scores of research problems that needed to be tackled but that the potential sponsors either did not have or were reluctant to allocate enough funds necessary to engage the services of a professionally recognized commercial marketing research company. Sizable funds are often necessary to insure reliable results for the client and a reasonable profit for the research agency.

The students publicized the formation of their marketing surveys company through the campus newspaper, which is read by many alumni. Also, local chambers of commerce and such leading community organizations as the Sales and Marketing Executives were pleased to announce the availability of the survey organization.

Within two weeks of its formation, the student organization received three requests for research assistance. Before the students could decide

1

which of the proposals to accept, they had to think through the work involved in designing the sample and the questionnaire and the cost of the fieldwork. The three requests for survey help were as follows:

1. One of the leading candidates for governor wanted a statewide survey that would predict how he stood in his forthcoming close race with the candidate of the opposition party. He wanted an analysis of each of the sixty counties in the state. Since the vote in many counties would be split quite evenly, the survey percentages could not be off more than 3 percent either way. One thousand dollars was available for this study.

2. A national franchising organization wanted to know whether they should open one of their restaurants next to the university campus. Their specialty is fish and chips, and they wanted to know how much interest there is among students for this type of specialty food and what price students would be willing to pay for various specialty plates. At this time, there were four nationally franchised organizations operating successfully near the campus. Two specialized in hot dogs and other plates, while two others sold mainly king-sized hamburgers and beef sandwiches. The management of the franchise organization offered $200 for a study to determine if there was enough demand for an additional specialty restaurant of this type.

3. The merchants of a nearby city with a population of 50,000 wanted the students to come in and make a study to determine what improvements needed to be made by the main street merchants to make the entire downtown shopping area more attractive for city and suburban customers. For years, the downtown merchants had a virtual monopoly on the trade of the city. However, there were now plans for a sizable shopping center to open up in one year within three miles of the downtown area. No great precision in survey results was required, but the downtown retail association felt that a consumer survey might be helpful in pointing the way to needed improvements. Two thousand dollars was available for this survey.

QUESTIONS

1. What type of sampling procedure would you recommend for each of the studies? Your answer should take into consideration both the accuracy of results needed in each case and the cost of making each study.
2. Which of the studies would you accept and why?
3. For each of the studies accepted, describe in some detail the design of the sample, what universe lists might be used, and what maps and other tools might be helpful for the survey teams.

2.

Consumer Analyses
Comparing Findings from Different Studies

Progressive Grocer Colonial Stores Study

The management of Colonial Stores, Inc., an Atlanta, Georgia, based supermarket chain which operates close to 440 stores in ten states, co-operated with *Progressive Grocer,* a leading trade magazine, in conducting a customer survey in order to develop a statistical profile of the habits, opinions, and behavior of the typical Colonial Stores customer. Six Colonial supermarkets were selected by Colonial management to participate in this research project. The stores were chosen by Colonial management so that equal representation of income levels, occupational activities, and urban versus rural locations were obtained. The six stores in the sample ranged in size from 13,000 square feet to 35,000 square feet of selling area. Their average weekly sales amounted to $44,380.

The survey covered the twelfth and thirteenth Colonial operating periods, November 4 to December 29. Due to merchandising activities built around Thanksgiving and Christmas, this period represents one of the most active ones during the retailing year. Yet, according to U.S. Department of Commerce figures, this period accounts for only 18 percent of annual food sales.

One part of the research consisted of extensive observations of consumer purchases and consumer interviews at checkout counters on Thursdays, Fridays, and Saturdays. In all, over 12,000 customers were interviewed. Customers interviewed were asked, "Why do you shop at this Colonial Store?" Their responses are shown in Exhibit 1.

Finally, the study revealed that the typical Colonial shopper has seen the week's Colonial advertising but only "sometimes" buys the advertised specials (61 percent said they bought the advertised specials "sometimes" or "rarely"). She is not aware of the actual price of even the most heavily promoted item. She has been shopping at this store for a little over two years.

3

Burgoyne Study of Supermarket Shoppers

According to the 14th Annual Study of Supermarket Shoppers published by Burgoyne Index, Inc. and based on more than 3,500 interviews in August 1967, 84 percent of the respondents said they shopped in more than one supermarket during the previous month. The study also revealed, however, that 46 percent of supermarket shoppers have a "favorite" supermarket where they buy most of their food, and that they have been trading there for over five years.

Interesting facts revealed in this study are listed as follows:

1. Low prices are uppermost in many shoppers' minds when determining which supermarket to patronize. Without being asked, many shoppers complain that food prices are too high, indicating a great awareness of food prices by shoppers.
2. Three out of four supermarket shoppers shop for advertised specials every week; only 12 percent say they seldom or never shop for specials.
3. Quality and freshness of meats continue to be major factors in the selection of a favorite supermarket.
4. Health and beauty aids purchases in supermarkets show a declining trend; whereas chain drugstores and discount stores show an increase in the sale of these items.
5. Analysis of shoppers' complaints reveal that many supermarkets are tolerating lower standards of store housekeeping, probably in an effort to curtail operating expenses.
6. Less interest in saving trading stamps and greater interest in lower prices is indicated by the answers to trading stamp questions.
7. One out of two supermarket shoppers say that they are not interested in games or promotions and would prefer that supermarkets discontinue them.
8. Discount store food shopping is gaining in certain areas. While lower prices are the principal reason for shopping for food in discount stores, the element of one-stop shopping under one roof is also of almost equal importance.
9. Discount stores have upgraded their quality image, especially on fresh meats, fruits, and vegetables.
10. Consumers don't care too much for packaged meats. Almost half state they bought them but would prefer to buy fresh meat that had not been cut and packaged. Twenty-three percent state flatly they seldom or never buy them.

The six items most important to consumers interviewed are shown in Exhibit 2.

Consumer Dialogs

In September 1968, housewives in fifteen cities around the country told food industry representatives what they liked and disliked about grocery shopping, offering opinions regarding stores, advertisements, packaging, and stamps. They did this in a series of panel discussions called Consumer Dialogs, sponsored by the Coca-Cola Company and the National Association of Food Chains.

For each dialog, about a dozen housewives, representing a mixture of neighborhoods, ages, races, and income levels, were gathered together and discussed their food-shopping habits for three hours. William C. Nigut, president of a Chicago marketing research firm, moderated the talk among the panel. The audience, made up of chain store executives, food manufacturers, and distributors, listened to the housewives' views and asked them questions.

Early in the group discussion, each housewife was asked where she bought most of her food in the last week. Usually, the stores mentioned by the panel participants were of many types: small independent groceries, small local chains, large supermarket chains, convenience stores, discount food stores, and fresh produce stands and markets. The reasons for choosing a particular store varied, also, but typically involved prices, service, and convenience of location.

Do women shop the grocery advertisements in newspapers before going food shopping? In all fifteen cities, the answer was an overwhelming "yes." In Washington, most of the housewives read the newspaper ads every week and compared prices at different stores. Eleven of the twelve panelists in St. Louis read the ads of more than one food store to compare prices, and most of them read circulars received in the mail. On the other hand, the panelists were skeptical about national advertising claims, especially television advertising. When asked what effect television ads for new brand-name products had on their shopping, some of the panelists admitted they would purchase them occasionally.

The housewives were critical of the way meat and vegetables are packaged. The general feeling was that prepackaging frequently hides "bad produce" while the stores package meat with the best side up, hiding a wad of fat or a big bone on the bottom. The consensus in St. Louis was that service with a butcher on duty meant better quality and fresher meat.

Stamps, games, and coupons created heated discussions. Some liked them while others felt that stamps and other gimmicks only raised prices.

QUESTIONS

1. The Colonial study concludes that price is the least important factor in determining customer store patronage. On the other hand, both the Consumer Dialog research and the Burgoyne study indicate that low prices are uppermost in many shoppers' minds when choosing a supermarket. Suggest several possible explanations for these opposite conclusions.
2. You are the marketing research director for a large food manufacturer who sells more than 150 items through supermarkets. In which of the three studies would you place the most confidence? What items of information would be the most useful to you from each of the three studies?
3. Is there a consensus as to the principal reasons why consumers pick a particular store for shopping? Why?

EXHIBIT 1
Customer Survey Results

Response	Percent
Store personnel and services	73
Wide selection of products and brands	52
Trading stamps	50
Meats	44
Produce	36
Prices	18

EXHIBIT 2
Factors Desired by Grocery Shoppers

Factor	Percent
Low prices on groceries	31.9
Quality and freshness of meats	23.2
Convenient location	14.5
Attractiveness and cleanliness of store	10.0
Variety and selection of grocery items	6.8
Quality and freshness of fruits and vegetables	2.7

3.

American National Bank

Consumer Analysis as a Basis For Marketing Strategy Decisions

For the past several years, American National Bank, one of five major banks in a large Midwestern city, has taken a "back seat" position relative to its competition in supplying consumer banking services. The bank's steadily decreasing competitive position has created much unrest among the members of the Board of Directors. As a result, a new president was hired, and further organizational changes in upper management were being considered.

The new president, Mr. Robert Fuller, has called for a redesigning of the bank's marketing strategy in an effort to improve its status in the city's banking circles. These changes would begin with a completely new and intensive promotion program, with other service and organizational changes following soon afterwards.

Mr. Fuller, who considers himself to be a marketing-oriented business-man, recognizes the importance of customer satisfaction to the bank's success. Consequently, before embarking on any major marketing strategy, Mr. Fuller has instructed the bank's Research Department to gather and analyze information concerning the consumers of banking services.

Specifically, Mr. Fuller wants to know more about the bank's customers and the services (checking accounts, credit cards, personal loans, auto loans, savings accounts, etc.) they desire. In addition, the president has indicated a need for information about the customers' "buying" and usage habits regarding the bank's various services; that is, he would like to know what person or family member determines the services to be used and how frequently and to what extent they are used.

In connection with the pending advertising and promotion programs, Mr. Fuller feels it highly desirable to ascertain the characteristics of a "typical" bank customer as well as those of the competitors' customers. Moreover, the president wishes to determine the public's image of the American National Bank. Specifically, Mr. Fuller wants to know if people view American National as a conservative institution or as a pacesetter. In addition, he wants to determine if people are aware of how long American National Bank has been in existence or if they consider it to be a relatively new institution. Finally, the president wants to know if American National Bank comes to mind when banks and banking services are mentioned to the consuming public.

The Marketing Research Director is charged with the responsibility of providing the president with the information he needs to make sound marketing strategy decisions.

QUESTIONS

1. What information, in addition to that indicated above, do you feel should be acquired before management commits itself to any specific marketing strategy?
2. Specifically, what are the best sources for the desired information?
3. Explain how the information you derive will be useful in making marketing strategy decisions.
4. Based on your knowledge of competitive strategies among banks and other financial institutions, design a research study which you feel will obtain the information the president needs as a basis for sound marketing strategy decisions.

4.

Living Care Company

Determining the Advertising-Sales Relationship

Robert French, the market research director of Living Care Company, was attempting to evaluate the effects of advertising on the company's sales of mouthwash. Living Care successfully marketed one of the seven leading mouthwash products in the United States. Executives of the company estimated that promotional expenditures for their mouthwash were higher, in relation to sales, than any of their competitors'. The advertising to sales ratio had been maintained at the same level during the past eight years. Presently, promotional expenditures were 35 percent of total sales of $10,780,500. Living Care's Vice-president of Marketing wanted to know if the advertising/sales ratio could be reduced to 20 percent without incurring major reductions in total sales. Therefore, French was requested to examine the effectiveness of advertising and provide estimates of any possible losses due to reductions in advertising expenditures.

French first tried to determine what relationship did exist between the company's advertising expenditure and sales volume. He divided the company's market into eighteen geographic areas according to advertising coverage. Living Care promoted only through radio and spot television media. A total of 126 wholesalers distributed Living Care's mouthwash.

Through company data, French was able to determine that each of 112 distributors sold the product entirely within one of the eighteen advertising areas. The other 14 distributors were contacted by phone and their sales distributions were broken down by volume between areas. Exhibit 1 was prepared by French to show the relation of sales volume to advertising expenditures for 1969.

French also obtained data from a telephone interview study of the respondents in two cities: Rochester, New York, and Boulder, Colorado. The purposes of the study were to determine the relationship of radio listenership to product and brand usage and to obtain other information on the market using Living Care mouthwash. Telephone numbers were selected randomly from listings in Rochester and Boulder. A total of 1,600

9

persons answered the telephone calls from which 1,000 usable results were obtained. Respondents were asked if they listened to the radio on a daily basis. If the answer was "yes," the name of the station selected was requested. All respondents were asked how often they listened to the radio, if they could recall any mouthwash advertised on the particular station, if they used mouthwash, the brand used, other brands recently tried, and demographic questions. This study was completed one month prior to the company's request for an advertising evaluation. Radio advertising expenditures were kept constant during the past twelve months in the two test cities. Exhibits 2 and 3 present the results of the product and brand usage survey for listeners and nonlisteners in Rochester and Boulder. Listenership in the tables refers to the number of respondents listening to stations that advertised Living Care's mouthwash.

QUESTIONS

1. How should French analyze all the data before him?
2. What results are significant from an analysis of the data?
3. What should French recommend?
4. What are some limitations of the data gathered?

EXHIBIT 1
Living Care Advertising Expense and Sales for 1969
by Advertising Coverage

Area	Sales Total (000)	Sales Per 10,000 Adults	Advertising Expense Total (000)	Advertising Expense Per 10,000 Adults
1	$ 564.8	$102.70	$240.8	$43.78
2	713.2	80.40	250.4	28.28
3	224.9	76.85	71.0	24.26
4	117.6	48.12	40.6	16.61
5	1,322.4	99.50	380.6	28.64
6	129.6	51.65	38.5	15.34
7	453.0	91.80	121.6	24.64
8	645.6	149.50	119.0	27.56
9	231.6	46.00	68.5	13.61
10	1,147.0	102.25	450.2	40.13
11	541.0	80.55	116.0	17.27
12	1,247.5	107.50	405.0	34.90
13	1,436.0	109.30	506.0	38.51
14	311.0	68.50	88.0	19.38
15	229.5	60.85	71.6	18.98
16	439.0	82.15	151.0	28.26
17	146.0	39.50	62.7	16.96
18	940.0	85.60	316.5	28.82

EXHIBIT 2
Product and Brand Usage by Radio Listenership
in Rochester, N.Y.

	Total	Listeners	Nonlisteners
Total respondents	600	132	468
Use mouthwash	360	80	280
Do not use mouthwash	240	52	188
Use Living Care	42	17	25
Use Brand X	54	14	40
Use Brand Y	87	30	57
Other brands	177	19	158

EXHIBIT 3
Product and Brand Usage by Radio Listenership
in Boulder, Colorado

	Total	Listeners	Nonlisteners
Total respondents	400	94	306
Use mouthwash	310	74	236
Do not use mouthwash	90	20	70
Use Living Care	54	23	31
Use Brand X	61	18	43
Use Brand Y	36	12	24
Other brands	159	21	138

5.

Simpson's Bookstore
Seeking the Causes of Declining Profits

Background

Henry Simpson founded a college textbook store at Eastern University in 1933. The bookstore was a profitable operation from the start, and Mr. Simpson expanded it in 1948 by building an additional floor. With the additional space, Simpson's Bookstore was also able to sell sporting goods, university souvenirs, greeting cards, and greater selections of school supplies.

In 1963, a new competitor, the University Bookstore, was founded one block from Simpson's. This new bookstore was the third textbook seller to locate next to Eastern University. The other bookstore was founded during the 1920s. All three stores were nonaffiliated with Eastern University or with student groups.

Simpson noticed that his sales volume declined the very year University Bookstore opened its doors (see Exhibit 1). He felt that Eastern's student body, with 12,500 students, could not support three stores specializing in textbooks. Student enrollment had been increasing by 8 percent a year since 1955, but Simpson did not feel this growth would continue or be enough to allow profitable operation of three stores.

During the past three years, Simpson's Bookstore has been unprofitable (see Exhibit 2). Simpson had never experienced this situation before and in 1965 decided to lower prices on used textbooks during a midterm period of two weeks. He reduced prices on used textbooks by 5 percent below competitive prices during this two-week period every school term. He has followed this policy since 1965. New book prices have been maintained and are no different than the other bookstores.

Store Employees

Last year, 1967, Simpson hired an additional three students to work part time at the bookstore. He now employed seven students on a part-time basis to stock shelves, wash floors, and work at the cash register. Each student worked an average of two hours a day. Simpson felt it would help to increase sales by showing student customers that he employed students at the store. There were no other full-time employees besides Simpson.

Promotion

Heathley Advertising Agency has been employed by Simpson since 1960 and was responsible for all advertising done for the bookstore. Tom Garrett, the account manager at Heathley in charge of Simpson's advertising, had been responsible for suggesting the used book sale. Tom thought this would be a good advertising appeal and attempted to persuade Simpson to hold the sale at the beginning of each school term. However, Simpson vetoed this idea because of the potential loss to income.

All advertising for Simpson's Bookstore is done through newspaper and radio media. Typically, promotion is centered on Simpson's years of service to Eastern students and the store's central location relative to the University.

Market Research

Tom Garrett decided to do a brief buyer behavior study of students buying books at Eastern University. In October 1968, he developed a survey instrument containing socioeconomic and buyer behavior questions. Without approval from Simpson, Tom administered this survey to 160 students from various colleges at Eastern. He received permission from a number of professors to ask their students to fill in the questionnaires.

Tom employed a standardized company image profile test in his survey to determine student attitudes toward the bookstores at Eastern. Students completed the test for all three bookstores.

Results of the Survey

Few socioeconomic differences were found between students buying at the three bookstores. All three stores had proportionally the same student customer by family income, year in college, sex, and social class. However, Tom noticed that only fourteen of the 160 respondents purchased books at Simpson's for their courses in the fall term.

The Standardized Company Image Profile Test produced nearly identical results for Simpson's two competitors. Both of these stores had more positive attitude images than Simpson's for all eight attitude dimensions in the test (see Exhibit 4).

Simpson's Bookstore was believed by the respondents to be less friendly,

14

warmhearted, reliable, square-dealing, fair in pricing, modern, progressive, and dynamic in comparison to either competitor.

Using the t-test, Tom found these results to be statistically significant at below the .10 level (Exhibit 5) in all dimensions.

Tom was about to show his survey results to Simpson, but first wanted to decide on some specific promotional recommendations to help Simpson's sales.

QUESTIONS

1. What is the problem at Simpson's Bookstore?
2. When did Mr. Simpson's problems begin?
3. What should Tom Garrett say to Mr. Simpson?
4. How can Simpson's Bookstore recover from its present difficulties?
5. Evaluate the image profile test as a measure of attitudes toward the bookstore.

EXHIBIT 1
Simpson's Bookstore Sales 1955-1965

Year	Book Sales	Non-book Sales	Total
1955	$388,000	$ 2,800	$390,800
1956	410,200	3,000	413,200
1957	411,600	8,500	420,100
1958	421,300	10,700	432,000
1959	406,600	12,500	429,100
1960	401,100	11,500	412,600
1961	395,500	11,100	406,600
1962	375,900	8,500	384,400
1963	350,200	6,000	356,200
1964	320,000	7,100	327,100
1965	290,800	5,000	295,800

EXHIBIT 2
Net Earnings for Simpson's Bookstore 1963-1967

Year	Net Earnings After Taxes
1963	$ 9,100
1964	4,500
1965	(12,000)*
1966	(14,000)*
1967	(18,500)*

*( ) Losses

EXHIBIT 3
Standardized Company Image Profile Test
for Simpson's Bookstore

Simpson's Bookstore

Please check (✓) the appropriate space that expresses your feelings on Simpson's Bookstore. Beginning from left to right the four spaces are: Strongly Disagree, Disagree, Agree, and Strongly Agree.

Simpson's Bookstore is:

1. friendly, shows goodwill in its dealings.
   Strongly Disagree ____ ____ ____ ____ Strongly Agree
2. warm-hearted, has a deep interest in the welfare of others.
   Strongly Disagree ____ ____ ____ ____ Strongly Agree
3. reliable, merits confidence or trust, can be counted on to fulfill its promises with certainty.
   Strongly Disagree ____ ____ ____ ____ Strongly Agree
4. square dealing, fair and just in its transactions.
   Strongly Disagree ____ ____ ____ ____ Strongly Agree
5. fair pricing, charges prices that represent the true value of its products or services.
   Strongly Disagree ____ ____ ____ ____ Strongly Agree
6. modern, up-to-date, and belongs to the present time.
   Strongly Disagree ____ ____ ____ ____ Strongly Agree
7. progressive, accepts and uses new ideas and methods in order to move forward.
   Strongly Disagree ____ ____ ____ ____ Strongly Agree
8. dynamic, energetic, forceful, and enthusiastic in the conduct of its business.
   Strongly Disagree ____ ____ ____ ____ Strongly Agree

16

EXHIBIT 4

Image Profile Dimensions: Simpson's and Competitors'[*]

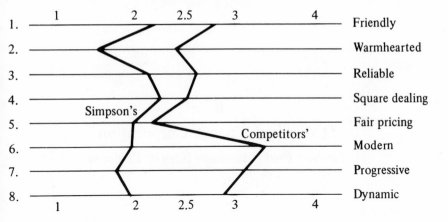

*Scores are averages of all responses. The higher the average score, the more favorable the response.

EXHIBIT 5
Significant Image Profile Dimensions
Simpson versus Competitors

Attitude	Simpson's	Competitors'	t	P<
1. Friendly	2.19[a]	2.82[a]	7.33	.001[b]
2. Warm-hearted	1.67	2.47	10.13	.001
3. Reliable	2.10	2.68	6.95	.001
4. Square dealing	2.40	2.55	1.86	.10
5. Fair pricing	1.91	2.06	2.24	.05
6. Modern	1.93	3.20	12.68	.001
7. Progressive	1.87	3.00	11.59	.001
8. Dynamic	1.90	2.82	5.65	.001
Overall	15.82[c]	21.48[c]	11.13	.001

[a]The average value assigned by the 160 subjects. The higher the average the more favorable the subject's attitude for the particular personality dimension.
[b]For example, the resulting t value of 7.33 in testing the difference in means between Simpson's and Competitors' friendliness could have occurred by chance less than one time in a thousand.
[c]The average of the total of the subjects' overall scores on the profile test.

6.

Diversified Finance Corporation
Seeking Profits through Repeat Business

Introduction

Diversified Finance Corporation (DFC) is one of the largest independent finance companies in the United States, although only about 18 percent of the firm's total net income is derived from its consumer and business finance operations. Its manufacturing operations alone contribute approximately 25 percent of the firm's total net income. Diversification into such nonfinance areas as manufacturing, retail merchandising, insurance, and computer leasing not only has proven to be profitable but also has enabled the firm to weather some of the periods of stress in the finance industry.

Diversified Finance Corporation was founded in the early 1930s at a time when the United States was in the throes of a serious economic depression. Retail automobile financing was the firm's basic activity in its early years, but with increasing competition from banks and manufacturer-owned finance companies, DFC shifted away from financing automobile paper. Currently, the financial operations are divided between the predominant consumer finance division, the retail finance division (which specializes in mobile home and marine credit), and three business finance divisions.

Consumer Finance Operations

The consumer finance division is the largest segment of DFC's finance operations. This division specializes in personal loans made directly with the consumer through approximately 600 branch loan offices located in thirty-seven states, Puerto Rico, and Canada. Currently, the total volume of loans outstanding amounts to $296,000,000. The average loan balance per account is approximately $570. Within the next five years, the management of the consumer finance division hopes to increase the number of loan offices to 800 with a $400,000,000 total loan balance outstanding by acquiring smaller loan companies and opening new branch offices. In addition to the $296 million in direct loans to consumers, DFC has approximately $11 million outstanding in conditional sales contracts, a type of retail financing for low-priced consumer purchases conducted with consumers through the personal loan offices. The average loan balance outstanding on these conditional sales contracts amounts to $192 per account.

The direct loan business is divided into three categories: new business, present borrowers, and former borrowers. New business represents personal loans initiated within the past six months with consumers who either have borrowed previously from DFC or consumers who have no record of previous business with the firm. Currently, approximately 12 percent of the loans outstanding represent new business acquired since the beginning of the year. Diversified Finance Corporation annually spends approximately $950,000 for newspaper, radio, and transit advertising designed to attract credit-worthy new customers. Present borrowers represent 74 percent of the total volume of loans outstanding. A customer is classified as a present borrower if his account was opened more than six months before and he still is making payments. Present borrowers are contacted regularly for additional business through counter solicitations whenever the customer visits a branch office to make a payment and by direct mail sent four or five times a year from a central mailing facility at the home office. Former borrower business represents customers of DFC who have a previous history of borrowing from the firm but who are not presently customers. Approximately 14 percent of the total loan balance outstanding at any one point in time represents former borrower business.

The management of the consumer finance division is concerned about the fact that while the finance industry has a 40 percent customer retention rate on personal loan business, DFC's record of customer retention is not as high. Customer retention is regarded as an important source of additional income for the firm because each former borrower typically renews his loan an average of four times before it is repaid. This repeat business often yields four to five times the interest income, while incurring little additional branch operating expense. Former borrowers are encouraged to borrow again through frequent telephone solicitation from branch office personnel and periodic direct mail pieces sent from the central mailing facility. Diversified Finance Corporation annually spends $400,000 on direct mail to present and former borrowers and an additional $250,000 annually on point-of-sale promotional and display material.

The Conditional Sales Program

In 1956, DFC initiated the conditional sales program as an experiment to attract new loan business. Conditional sales contracts are installment credit arrangements made through retail merchants and service establishments with their customers. The retailer sells his merchandise or service and offers to finance up to 90 percent of the purchase price up to twenty-four months for the consumer. The consumer signs an installment credit contract with the merchant who turns the contract over to the local DFC branch office and receives payment. The consumer then discovers that, instead of owing the merchant, he must make payments directly to the local DFC office until the obligation is paid. The program is attractive to the small retail merchant or individuals offering professional or other services and who have limited capital resources. They usually operate strictly on a cash-and-carry basis. Diversified Finance Corporation's conditional sales program offers the small businessman the benefit of helping to create sales which might otherwise be lost while relieving the merchant of the potential loss on delinquent accounts receivable. The Corporation also handles the credit investigation of every conditional sales contract application as well as providing point-of-purchase display material to help the small businessman promote the credit sales of his merchandise or service. The conditional sales program even appeals to small merchants and service establishments who are in a position to acquire local bank financing at the lowest prevailing rates. Locally borrowed funds can better be used to finance purchases of larger and more varied quantities of merchandise or to allow the merchant to take advantage of quantity or cash discounts.

In order to solicit conditional sales business from small business establishments, DFC employs forty-six sales representatives who work under ten district sales managers. They call on retail and service establishments in the cities where DFC has branch offices. A total operating budget of $600,000 annually is allocated to support this sales force. Of this amount, $562,800 is used to support field operations. This field budget is allocated each month on the following basis:

Payroll	$30,000
Meals and Lodging	11,500
Transportation	4,200
Point-of-Purchase Material	1,200

The sales representatives regularly call on merchants and service establishments in the various cities to explain the conditional sales program. Salesmen also maintain a constant liaison with merchants already participating in the program to make sure that the local DFC branch office is providing satisfactory service. Sales representatives also have the responsibility of verifying that the financial status and reputation of participating businesses and the quality of merchandise sold by them satisfies DFC's standards. Diversified Finance Corporation's approved conditional sales include:

Automobile repairs and accessories
Awnings, blinds, and storm doors
Bicycles
Camera and camera equipment
Dental and medical bills
Eyeglasses and contact lenses
Floor covering material
Gas, oil, and electric heaters
Home improvements
Home furnishings
Kitchen sinks and cabinets
Lawn and garden fences
Musical instruments
Nursery furniture
Outboard motors and boats
Playground equipment
Power lawn mowers
Radios and tape recorders
Sporting goods
Typewriters
Water heaters

While the conditional sales program is promoted ostensibly to provide small merchants with the means to extend installment credit to their customers, DFC's primary objective in engaging in the program is to convert as many sales contract customers as possible into regular loan customers for a DFC branch office. Although conditional sales accounts are usually profitable in themselves when properly handled, these accounts are aggressively and persuasively solicited for conversion into the more profitable direct loan accounts. Whenever a conditional sales customer visits a branch office to make his first payment, the branch personnel seek to make the customer's acquaintance and to express their appreciation for the opportunity to finance his purchase. This is followed by an explanation of the loan services available from DFC and a direct statement, based on a credit investigation, of how much money can be borrowed immediately, if desired. Diversified Finance Corporation's management feels this direct approach is particularly helpful when debt consolidation opportunities present themselves. If the customer pays by mail, he is contacted through telephone calls, personalized notes, and direct calls to the customer's home if state laws permit. In addition, current mailing pieces and envelope stuffers are used in returning payment receipts. If the customer requests that his business not be solicited, DFC branch personnel are instructed to respect the customer's request by discontinuing efforts to sell the customer on a direct loan.

The rationale for soliciting conditional sales accounts is based on DFC's experience that many such customers have additional needs for cash, and many can gain the benefits of debt consolidation which enable them to enjoy a higher standard of living within their budgets. The solicitation of such accounts is intended to provide these customers with a more complete financing service while providing additional avenues for repeat business for DFC. However, the management of the consumer finance division has not been satisfied with its performance in converting conditional sales accounts into direct loan customers. Only about 2.5 percent of the conditional sales customers actually have been converted into direct loan customers.

Survey of Conditional Sales Customers

The management of the consumer finance division was increasingly concerned about the relatively low conversion rate associated with converting conditional sales accounts, particularly in view of the amount of effort which the company puts forth to obtain conditional sales accounts. To explore the attitudes of conditional sales customers toward DFC's efforts to convert them into direct loan business, the firm authorized its local branch office in a large Southeastern city to conduct a research study of its customers. A list of 150 conditional sales contract customers was selected from the branch office files. One-half of these customers had completed one transaction with DFC while the other half had made six or more payments on a single transaction. From this list, twenty-nine names of people living outside the metropolitan area were deleted. Interviews were attempted with the 121 names remaining on the list. Seventy-five people agreed to be interviewed and seventy-two usable interviews were obtained. A combination of personal and telephone interviews were undertaken to reach the selected sales contract customers. Exhibit 1 presents a summary of the findings from the survey.

QUESTIONS

1. What can DFC do to improve its rate of conversion of conditional sales accounts into direct loan customers? Evaluate DFC's present policies.
2. How much "faith" can be placed in the survey taken?
3. What information of importance can be derived from Exhibit 1?

EXHIBIT 1
Summary of Findings

Attitudes Toward Conditional Sales Contracts

1. Fifty-four percent (39) of the total respondents said they remembered buying goods "on time" where the merchant sold the credit paper to a finance company. Forty-six percent (33) either did not remember or answered "no" to the question. A "no" answer indicates that the respondent was not aware of the fact that the credit paper was sold, did not remember it, or simply did not want to admit such knowledge.

2. Of the respondents remembering the sale of the credit paper, only 36 percent (14) identified DFC as the finance company handling the transaction. A variety of banks and other finance companies were mentioned by the respondents.

3. Of the thirty-nine respondents remembering the transaction, two-thirds said that it did not matter whether they owed money to a finance company or bank. Among people who said they objected, the most common reasons were the high cost of borrowing, the reluctance to deal with a finance company, or the belief that they should have been consulted beforehand.

4. Twenty-five respondents (64 percent) believed that it was all right for the merchant to sell the credit paper to a finance company or bank. The fact that they should have been told ahead of time about the credit arrangement, the belief that the transaction should be strictly between the merchant and the customer, and the cost of borrowing were cited most often as reasons for objecting to the arrangement.

5. Musical instruments, photographic equipment, TV, appliances, and furniture were the most commonly mentioned items bought under conditional sales contracts. Seventy-two percent remembered the transaction as occurring in the past year.

6. Fifty-one percent of the respondents who remembered dealing with a finance company reported that someone from the financial institution contacted them about what was owed. These contacts included being sent a payment book or being called to have the terms of the credit transaction explained to them.

Attitudes Toward Lending Institutions

7. Seventy-five percent (55) of all respondents interviewed said they would go to a bank to borrow. Eighteen percent (13) said that a credit union was the likely source for borrowing. Only two respondents (2.8 percent) mentioned a finance company as the place they would go to borrow.

8. Twenty-five percent (18) of all respondents reported borrowing money in the last six months. About 60 percent of these (10) dealt with a bank. The amount varied, but 28 percent borrowed less than $300. Automobile loans and home improvement loans were the most frequently mentioned purposes for borrowing, but a number of other reasons were also given, such as bill consolidation, buying tools, purchasing an airline ticket, paying for automobile repairs, and paying taxes.

Recall of Advertising

9. Seventy-seven percent of the thirty-nine respondents who remembered the credit transaction also recalled receiving direct mail advertising from a bank or finance company. The majority of the respondents who did not remember the credit sales transaction answered "yes" to remembering the receipt of direct mail advertising encouraging them to borrow.

10. Thirty-two percent (23) of the respondents recalled seeing advertising from a bank or finance company. Eight of the twenty-three respondents said that the advertising was done by a local bank. Only four identified a finance company as the source of advertising. Nearly two-thirds of those recalling advertising said it was direct mail, and an equal number could not remember what the advertising said.

Use of Retail Credit and Credit Cards

11. Seventy-seven percent of all respondents (56) reported having a charge account with a retail merchant. Seventy-two percent (52) said that they had a retail credit card. Twenty-one percent reported two or three charge accounts while another thirty-two percent had six or more accounts (including those who simply reported several accounts).

12. Eighty-four percent (61) of all respondents reported having bought goods on a monthly installment basis. Furniture, appliances, and clothing were the most commonly mentioned items. Forty-two percent of the installment contracts were twelve months or less in duration, and twenty-three percent of the monthly payments were $10 or less per month.

Attitudes Toward Credit

13. Many respondents believed that it was acceptable to borrow money for purposes of buying automobiles (85 percent), paying for education (62 percent), paying for home repairs (61 percent), and to buy appliances (54 percent). Seventy-four percent of the respondents said it was more appropriate to pay for clothing out of current income and savings while 80 percent believed in paying for a vacation out of current income. Sixty-nine percent felt that automobile repairs should also be paid out of current income.

EXPLORATION
OF GROWTH OPPORTUNITIES
AND STRATEGIES

7.

Tapp's Department Store
A Shopping Center Opportunity

Jim Tapp, who owns and manages Tapp's Department Store in downtown Columbia, S.C., a furniture annex across the street, and a small branch unit in the Trenholm Shopping Center called Tapp's Twig, was given the opportunity to open and operate one of three large department stores that are to be a part of the new fully air-conditioned and enclosed regional retail complex called the Dutch Square Shopping Center. This center is near a number of the residential areas which are springing up and growing rapidly to the northwest and southwest of Columbia. Moreover, the new regional center is to be located close to the point where Interstate 20 and Interstate 26 intersect. With this strategic location, the developer is confident that the shopping center will draw customers from within at least a twenty-mile radius.

While Jim Tapp has one middle-aged son, two nephews, and other managers who are fully trained and can help with managing the new unit, he is uncertain as to the decision to make since two national department store chains have already signed contracts to operate competitive units in the new center. One large competitor will be Mercantile Stores, which operates the local White's Department Store in the city's Richland Mall Shopping Center. The Woolworth chain is the other competitor, which will operate a Woolco Discount Department Store. At least a dozen smaller specialty shops will provide some added competition.

Finally, a large GEX Membership Discount Department Store will open its doors several months before the planned opening of Dutch Square, not far from the shopping center. Jim Tapp is afraid that the competition will be so intense in the area for a long time that none of the four department stores will be able to realize a reasonable return on investment.

To help him appraise the market opportunity and reach a decision, Tapp retained the services of a well-known New York consulting firm. After a thorough market analysis of the area, the firm strongly recommended that the Tapp family open a department store unit in the new shopping center. The move not only would be a defensive measure but also would enable the retail firm to take advantage of the intermediate and long-run profit opportunities the situation presents. The research findings indicated the downtown store, with current sales at the $5,000,000 level, would lose about 20 percent of its sales volume upon the opening of the new regional shopping center.

The consulting firm's study indicated that the operating expenses of the new unit would be much lower than those currently borne by the downtown parent unit, and that a break-even point could be reached at an annual sales volume of $2,000,000. Tapp has trained management personnel whose services are not fully utilized by the present three operations and who could perform the important buying function. Also, much of the warehousing cost could be borne by the downtown unit. Finally, the newspaper and television advertising budget would need to be increased, but only slightly.

The consulting firm's analysis of market potential confirmed the developer's belief that families residing within a twenty-mile radius would shop quite regularly in the Dutch Square Shopping Center. The consulting firm's report went even further and predicted that anywhere from one-fifth to one-fourth of the families in the state of South Carolina would find the shopping center an easy place to reach, and that these families would shop there occasionally due to its strategic location at the intersection of the two interstate highways. Interstate 26, already completed and heavily traveled, runs from the Greenville-Spartanburg area to Columbia and southeast to Charleston. The nearly completed I-20 connects with the north-south bound I-95 near Florence and will run in an east-west direction by Columbia to Aiken and on to Augusta and Atlanta, Georgia. Interstates 20 and 26 intersect just northwest of Columbia, and the giant "X" they form cuts the state into four parts.

If the Tapp family does not sign the lease, some other out-of-state firm will probably set up the third department store in the Dutch Square Shopping Center, and the loss of sales volume for the downtown Tapp store will be permanent. Finally, it was learned that the giant Sears, Roebuck and Co. chain was studying the areas to the north and west of Columbia in the hope of finding a site to place either one of its A- or B-sized stores within the next five years. Its present B-store has been losing volume over the last two years and, with the opening of the Dutch Square Shopping Center, further inroads into its sales are anticipated.

Based on the positive recommendations of the consultant and the new information on prospective Sears' strategy, Jim Tapp decided to sign the lease. Much time in late 1968 and early 1969 was spent in working with the developer on the blueprints for the design of the exterior and interior of the new Tapp building. The remainder of 1969 was spent finalizing and implementing numerous other pre-opening and merchandising plans. The opening of the Dutch Square Shopping Center was set for February, 1970.

QUESTIONS

1. List and describe the growth factors which the New York consulting firm had to analyze before it could reach its decision to recommend the opening of a Tapp's unit in the Dutch Square Shopping Center.
2. If you assume that the conclusion drawn regarding the potential of the market surrounding the shopping center is currently accurate, what possible conditions might arise in the future to make the site less attractive?
3. Make a list of the operating expenses that would be lower for the new Tapp unit in the regional shopping center. Are there any expenses which would be higher?

8.

The Merger Movement
Boon or Bane?

Background

It is estimated that 4,400 companies—small, medium-sized, and giants—were swallowed up in mergers and acquisitions in 1968. This was a 50 percent increase over the previous peak of 2,975 in 1967. The value of cash and securities involved in the 1968 transactions is calculated at $50 billion.

Mergers have multiple attractions to corporations. A company with a considerable supply of cash and securities sees the possibility of increased profits through the acquisition of a smaller firm with a superior technology or one with a promising product but little cash for the development of markets. For instance, the cost of setting up a national distribution organization that could compete effectively against IBM, the number one marketer of computers, was the moving force behind the merger of Control Data Corporation and Commercial Credit Corporation in the spring of 1969. This conglomerate merger put several billion dollars worth of credit in the hands of Control Data, which lacked the financial resources to market its new line of small computers.

The first major merger wave at the turn of the century resulted in the foundation of such industrial giants as U.S. Steel Corporation, U.S. Rubber Company, and American Can Company. In these horizontal types of mergers, two or more companies selling substantially the same product come together to form a larger production and marketing firm. In the second wave, during the 1920s, companies such as Bethlehem Steel Corporation, Republic Steel Corporation, and Allied Chemical & Dye, extended their operations into allied fields of supply and distribution. When companies such as these three reach back to merge with suppliers and/or reach forward to gain ownership and control of companies distributing their products, the resulting merger or acquisition is referred to as a vertical merger.

The current wave of mergers, which began in the 1950s, has spawned the conglomerates—huge corporations which expand by acquiring companies in diverse fields of products and services. Specifically, a conglomerate merger is one in which the acquiring firm is neither a supplier, a customer, nor a competitor of the acquired firm. It is of neither the vertical nor horizontal types in which the products of the acquiring and acquired firms are substantially alike.

Textron, Inc., is considered by some to be the grandaddy of conglomerates. In 1952, Royal Little, its president, realizing that the markets for his New England textile company were shrinking, set out on a diversification program through acquisition and merger unparalleled at that time. Today, Textron no longer manufactures textiles. Its operations are in aerospace, consumer, industrial, and metal products. It has thirty-four divisions, 170 plants, 72,000 employees, and $1.6 billion annual sales. Some of the more recently formed giants among the conglomerates are Gulf & Western Industries, Ling-Temco-Vought, Litton Industries, and International Telephone & Telegraph.

Merger and Acquisitions, a publication devoted to this field, reports that about one out of every five proposals for a merger is killed each year. Their demise is attributed to antitrust activity, legal snarls, wide price swings, clash of managements, impossible product mixes, regulatory problems, and other extraordinary developments.

Over the years, the government has successfully challenged certain mergers of the horizontal and vertical types under the antitrust laws on the grounds that the mergers stifle competition. However, government is having difficulty in moving against some of the questionable conglomerates because the elimination of competition, or potential elimination of competition, is more difficult to prove.

The Clorox Case

In 1967, the federal government won its first victory over a conglomerate merger when the Supreme Court ruled that the 1957 acquisition of the Clorox Chemical Company by Procter & Gamble Company was illegal. The grounds for the decision were largely based on marketing considerations. It was ruled that the advertising power of the two combined companies was upsetting some of the promotional efforts of Purex, the second largest manufacturer of household liquid bleach in the United States. In 1966, a federal court ruled against the Federal Trade Commission and in favor of Procter & Gamble.

However, the FTC evidence led the highest tribunal to overrule the federal court. Statistics showed that following the merger, Procter & Gamble substantially increased the amount of promotional appropriations for Clorox. For instance, from July 1958 to July 1961, $1,550,000 had

29

been spent on the promotion of Clorox over and above the $400,000 originally budgeted at the time of the merger. In addition, retaliatory promotions against competition had been used, unlike the previous policy of the Clorox Chemical Company.

In the New England region, during the four years since the 1957 merger, Clorox increased its market share by 11.5 percent from 56 percent to 67.5 percent of total sales of household liquid bleach in the region. The Federal Trade Commission charged that this was due to Proctor & Gamble's financial and economic strength as well as its advertising and promotional expenditures, which were high when compared to expenses of competitors in the liquid bleach industry.

In its competition with Purex, the second largest producer of liquid bleaches, the Procter & Gamble Company had been able to systematically counter promotional activities with even larger promotions of its own. Since P & G's advertising budget for the entire corporation amounted to close to $100,000,000, it could organize effective retaliatory promotions. Due to its great volume of advertising, P & G could offer cooperating retailers promotional discounts of up to 30 percent. It was further claimed that in one market area, Erie, Pennsylvania, Purex was unsuccessful in its attempt to conduct a market test due to P & G's disruptive counter-promotions.

Due to the advantage of its advertising power, Clorox, under Procter & Gamble ownership, had increased its market share. Exhibit 1 shows the changes in market shares among the three leading manufacturers of liquid bleach between 1957 and 1961. The facts tended to support the claim of Procter & Gamble advertising power.

Further Government Action

In April 1969, the Department of Justice followed the successful lead of the Federal Trade Commission and filed a complaint against Ling-Temco-Vought. The complaint, filed under Section 7 of the Clayton Act, charged that LTV's acquisition of Jones and Laughlin Steel threatened to diminish its potential independent competition in the steel industry and other metals markets, to diminish its potential independent competition in other diversified industries, to enhance its power to engage in reciprocal dealing, to increase substantially the concentration of control of the nation's manufacturing assets, and to encourage the trend to further concentration of economic power by merger.

The Justice Department, under its new chief, Richard W. McLarner, is presently attacking LTV on what he calls the superconcentration concept. On the basis of this concept, he is determined to stop any merger between two companies ranking in the top 200 largest companies in the United States—regardless of how disparate their lines of commerce may be. His theory is that any such merger would affect competition through the enhancement of the surviving company's economic power.

On the issue of aggregate concentration, the LTV suit looks like a strong case for the government—at least from the Justice Department's view. Both Jones and Laughlin Steel and LTV were among the 100 largest corporations, and their merger created an enterprise which is the fourteenth largest. Moreover, LTV has lifted itself to this lofty position in only three years by leapfrogging 242 other companies, some of which it bought out in the process.

QUESTIONS

1. What criteria should be used to decide whether a merger or acquisition is for or against the public interest?
2. List five reasons why mergers and acquisitions are so attractive to corporations as methods of expansion.
3. How important are marketing considerations in conglomerate mergers?
4. Do you agree with the FTC and the Justice Department that conglomerate mergers can stifle competition through the concentration of economic power? Explain your position in detail.

EXHIBIT 1
Percentage Shares of Household Liquid Bleach Sales
in the United States

	June-July 1957	June-July 1961
Clorox	48.8%	51.5%
Purex	15.7%	14.2%
Roman Cleanser	5.9%	4.1%

Source: Figures presented at the hearings before the Federal Trade Commission in *FTC Complaints, Orders, Stipulations, 1961-1963.*

9.

The Chicken Palace

Evaluating Small Business Opportunities

Background

The Chicken Palace, Inc. is a small (about 1,000 square feet) carry-out restaurant located in a well-to-do suburban area of St. Louis, Missouri. A few tables are available for customers who prefer to eat their food on the premises. Any comparison with similar restaurants would have shown the Chicken Palace to be exceptionally clean and attractive. The restaurant's speciality is broasted chicken. Simply stated, this is chicken that is deep-fried under pressure, taking seven or eight minutes to cook. Along with chicken, shrimp and jack salmon are on the menu, and prepared in the broasting equipment.

The Chicken Palace is owned and operated by Phillip Allen and Robert Tyler. These men had purchased the restaurant as a going concern from Frank Pointer. Allen and Tyler were unable to determine why Pointer had sold the business, but they did know that he owned another noncompeting restaurant about two miles away and had not been giving the Chicken Palace adequate attention for some time. The restaurant's sales at the time of the change of ownership were at about the break-even point. After six months of operation, the new owners were reevaluating their business.

In the time since their take-over of the restaurant, Allen and Tyler have been aggressive in trying to increase business volume and profits. One of the first things the new owners did was upgrade and stabilize the quality of the product. Under Pointer's ownership, chicken had been purchased sporadically, therefore, it was often in storage for too long a period of time. Taste and texture deteriorated if the chicken was not sold in two days. This situation was changed through a system of daily delivery of fresh chicken. Furthermore, an inferior brand of shortening had been used in the preparation of the chicken. After testing several qualities of shortening, Allen and Tyler decided on an expensive, but definitely superior, shortening for their purposes.

Promotional expenditures were increased. A portion of the back page of the direct mail piece sent out by a neighboring grocery store was purchased on a biweekly basis for $75 a month. A contract was made with Welcome Wagon, an organization calling on new residents in the general area, for their representatives to pass out coupons for free dinners. The Chicken Palace had always had a "marquee-type" sign on which a variety of messages could be presented. It had not, however, been used very extensively. The new management began to use the sign in ways it felt would be beneficial.

The owners also examined their pricing policy and found that they were charging about ten cents less for a dinner of one-half a chicken than were their competitors, whose chicken dinners included only three pieces of chicken. Therefore, they raised the price to the level of competition, believing that the increased profit would more than offset the small drop in sales that might result.

Consideration of Expansion Opportunities

From the time of the change of ownership, Allen had felt there was a strong opportunity for increased sales if a wider product line were provided. Specifically, he believed that barbecued ribs, barbecued beef, and barbecued pork sandwiches would be desirable additions. Unfortunately, the addition of barbecue equipment would have required capital investment beyond immediate capabilities; thus, the idea was temporarily shelved.

In recent months, several salesmen who called upon the restaurant presented new product ideas. Because of special deals on trial runs, the restaurant had been able to experiment with several of these ideas. One was a rack for fried fruit pies. The device utilized two 250-watt bulbs and heated fried pies which were bought from an outside salesman. The pies were purchased for ten cents each and were sold for twenty cents. On Fridays and Saturdays these pies sold reasonably well, about twenty to thirty. On weekdays, however, sales were discouraging. Occasionally, only three or four might be sold in a day. Pies left unsold at the end of the day had to be thrown away. The owners were considering dropping this idea although they had made an investment of about $40 in equipment. A possible alternative was to use the equipment in keeping french fries warm; however, they already had two french fry warmers which were adequate for present volume.

Another idea with which they had experimented was a gas broiler that charcoal-broiled steaks and hamburgers. The meat salesman had encouraged them to try this machine free of charge to see if they would want to

33

use one permanently in their operation. A used machine of the type they would need would cost between $300 and $400. On a trial basis, they used a new machine to cook two dollar steaks and seventy-five cent hamburgers. They realized a gross profit of about 50 percent. Over a two-month period, an average of thirty steaks and fifty hamburgers were sold per week. The products themselves were not heavily promoted during this period because of the trial nature of the product addition.

After considering the various expansion opportunities available to them, Allen and Tyler decided to go ahead with their barbecue idea. With the help of friends, they designed a pit that could be built with moonlight labor at a cost of about $1,500. Although the cash was not immediately available, the owners felt that they could borrow it from their credit union. Fire and city officials gave their tentative approval.

After the decision to build the barbecue pit was made, Tyler suggested that it would be desirable to change the name of their restaurant. Their present "Chicken Palace" marquee sign originally had cost $3,000, and they were still making payments at the rate of $100 a month. They still had five payments to make. Their hope was to find a name to which the existing sign could be adapted. They received suggestions from many parties, and the name they finally decided upon was Chic n' Rib Palace. This would entail changing only a few letters at an estimated cost of $300 to $400.

Plans were to complete the barbecue pit and change the name of the restaurant during the month of December when the owners felt the sale of ribs would be slow. They hoped that this plan would allow them time to become familiar with the problems they would have in the barbecue business before the main seasonal rush of barbecue sales would begin in the late spring. In April or May, they planned a major promotion of their new products, which would be fully perfected by that time.

At this point, Allen and Tyler felt that, although they had some problems, things were going well. They felt confident about the future they had planned. Since their take-over, sales had increased 10 to 15 percent per month over the previous year's sales. Although they were not taking home a salary, their operation was showing some profit. It would have been returning a greater cash flow to its owners were it not for the time payments on capital equipment, including the sign. Most of these payments would be completed in the next six to nine months.

A Franchise Opportunity

Matters were then complicated by the unexpected presentation of the idea of a franchise, by a man named Tom Turner. Turner was seeking a pilot operation for a franchise system, and he had approached the original owner of the Chicken Palace, Frank Pointer, who had referred him to Allen and Tyler.

Although Turner had experience in real estate, insurance, and construction, he apparently had no experience in the franchise business. It seemed that his interest in the venture he was proposing developed from conversations with a woman who had recent franchising experience. Turner believed that he could make a substantial amount of money by selling franchise rights.

Turner proposed to Allen and Tyler that, in return for use of their establishment, he would pay for the planned alterations in their sign and for a promotional campaign to kick off the sale of their ribs. Thus, he was proposing an investment of approximately $500. Furthermore, he would pay for the initial printing runs of bags and boxes for the carry-out orders. In return, he expected the owners to allow him to use their operation to show to potential franchise customers. If the franchising was successful, Allen and Tyler also would receive 3 percent of all royalties paid to the franchisor, Turner. They would not receive any part of the initial sale price of a franchise. The franchise corporation, headed by Turner, would take control of the name Chic n' Rib Palace. When questioned in depth, it appeared that Turner had no intention of trying to swindle them.

In spite of the apparent benefits for doing very little, Allen and Tyler were concerned with several matters. First, they did not know much about Turner; information received through outside sources was not conclusive. There was no indication that Turner was dishonest, although some people believed him to be a sharp operator who typically was trying to make the fast buck. Another reason for their suspicion was that when Turner was asked about his financial ability to handle such a franchise project, he sidetracked the question by talking about how costly such an operation was, but that he knew full well what he was getting into. He went on to talk about the architect he was employing at the time to design franchise structures who was "costing him so much." This comment was in conflict with what Tyler had heard from the architect himself. When the architect had stopped by the restaurant, he had stated that he was doing the work for nothing in exchange for the promise of doing all the work, for compensation, should the franchise succeed. Finally, Tyler and Allen were skeptical because Turner seemed to have only a hazy notion of the type of operation he intended to franchise. Other than it would be the same operation as the proposed Chic n' Rib Palace owned by Allen and Tyler, Turner seemed to have given little thought to the strategies regarding product line, price, type and extent of promotion, and so forth.

Allen noted that most of these negative aspects did not directly involve their operation. If anyone was to get hurt by these problems, it would be the new owners of the franchises. As far as Allen and Tyler were concerned, it appeared that they could obtain a relatively easy $500 by accepting this man's offer. They also felt that, if they put pressure on Turner, they could persuade him to put in the barbecue pit for them, raising his investment in their operation, with no ownership rights, to $2,000. In return for the money, it seemed that their responsibilities would be minimal. Therefore, they were very interested in the offer, but did not want to act without further deliberation.

QUESTIONS

1. Were the decisions reached by Allen and Tyler after taking over the business sound ones? What was the condition of the business at the time of the franchising proposal?
2. What decisions would you make regarding the proposed capital expenditures for the barbecue pit, gas broiler, and sign alteration?
3. Discuss the pros and cons of accepting Turner's franchise offer.

10.
Johnson's Restaurants, Inc.
Choosing Sites for Expansion

W. H. Johnson and sons operate a chain of restaurants in Indiana, Illinois, Ohio, Wisconsin, and Missouri, with headquarters in Cincinnati, Ohio. At present, their twenty-one restaurants are located in cities with populations of 100,000 or more, and with the exceptions of St. Louis and Kansas City, all the restaurants are located east of the Mississippi River.

The decor of Johnson's Restaurants provides an attractive atmosphere in which upper-middle and upper class families can enjoy dining without paying the high prices of more lavishly decorated restaurants. Meals are moderately priced and are served either at counters or at dining tables. The restaurants average about $2.50 per person for dinner, $2.00 for lunch, and $1.10 for breakfast.

Over the years, the company has expanded gradually by adding restaurants in cities where Johnson's establishments already exist and by slowly entering cities not previously served by the firm. In keeping with this conservative policy, management has plans to open three additional restaurants, but cities for the locations of these facilities have not been selected. Information about existing restaurant locations indicates that none of the new restaurants should be located in these cities. Thus, management intends to choose new cities which are not presently served by the firm.

With these expansion considerations in mind, the company has established criteria that will aid them in selecting possible sites for their new restaurant facilities. Since the firm desires to move in new directions, management has decided to examine those sites lying west of the Mississippi River and south of the Ohio River. However, because of the problems associated with locating too far from the main office, no site in this region will be chosen if it is more than 800 miles from Cincinnati. Moreover, a city will not be considered if its overall potential is less than is available at the presently occupied sites.

Company management realizes that some of the cities in this western region are saturated with restaurant facilities while others are virtually undeveloped. An objective of the company in its expansion is to use these three facilities as "pilot operations" around which other facilities will be developed later. Thus, management desires the most fertile markets for these three facilities in the hope that the favorable reputation built up through the pilot restaurants will give the company a competitive advantage when it opens restaurants in less fertile surrounding markets. Based on past experience, it is estimated that it takes at least two years to establish the Johnson image in new areas.

QUESTIONS

1. What specific data would you consider useful in determining the cities for new locations?
2. Where would you obtain these data? Are they readily available?
3. What specific recommendations would you make as to the sites for the three new restaurants? Why?
4. How would you go about selecting specific sites *within* each of the three cities you selected? What information would you need? Where and how would you get it?

11.

K-mart

Merchandising and Service Policies

K-mart stores are in 190 cities across the United States, Canada, and Puerto Rico. They make up the largest discount department store chain in the world. K-mart is still the fastest expanding chain in the field.

Twenty-eight new K-mart department stores were opened during the first six months of 1968 with floor space equivalent to fifty-six football fields, more than the total existing volume of 90 percent of the companies in discounting. Plans are set for K-mart to continue expanding at the rate of more than fifty stores a year through 1973.

K-marts are only part of the business of the S. S. Kresge Company. Kresge also operates 566 Kresge variety stores and 120 Jupiter discount stores. Jupiters are limited-selection discount stores, each very small when compared to any of the 343 K-marts presently in existence. More than half of the sales volume of the Kresge Company now comes from K-marts.

The success of K-mart discount department stores is the result of merchandising and service policies developed before the first K-mart became a reality in March 1962. During his two years as general vice-president (1957–1958), Harry B. Cunningham traveled across the United States investigating the operations of all types of retailers. The main purpose of his research was to determine what future course of action should be taken by the S. S. Kresge Company to increase its profitability.

Shortly after Mr. Cunningham was elected to the chief executive post in 1959, the decision was made to move into discount retailing. The first major objective was to study all major discounters in the United States and to analyze their strengths and weaknesses in order to develop standards upon which a Kresge-operated discount chain could live and grow on a sound basis.

When the first store opened in 1962, the K-mart blueprint was firmly established. Although experience and research continually result in improvements, there have been no important deviations from the original specifications. A testimony to the sound planning of the company management is the amazing response of consumers to the K-mart concept. Their acceptance has been responsible for the growth of the K-mart chain.

It is impossible to identify the single most important K-mart policy since all policies contribute to the success of the operation. However, the policy most rigidly enforced by top management requires K-mart selling prices to be truly competitive. A manager may lower recommended prices, but he does not have the right to raise them. In addition, all K-mart merchandise must meet rigid quality standards; there are no imperfects, irregulars, or substandards on K-mart counters.

K-mart stores are publicized as true discount department stores. To gain complete customer acceptance, K-mart must be just that. Only when unusual demand requires K-marts to carry certain "fair trade" lines do customers find a few items that are not discounted. Company policy requires the replacement of such merchandise as quickly as other items of equal or superior value and selling merit can be developed. K-mart merchandise assortments generally are limited to the best sellers. The profitability of every line is judged by its sales volume, selling costs, and the number of times it turns over annually. The only really important measure of overall K-mart success is the rate of return on total investment.

In the early days of discount retailing, many leading advertised brands carried by discount stores had to be obtained from jobbers or wholesalers, which made it difficult to reduce selling price dramatically. Realizing that repeat traffic depended on satisfied shoppers who could be assured of buying quality and leading brand merchandise at discount prices, the Kresge Company was determined to break down this barrier. A concentrated effort was launched by the company to prove to manufacturers that K-marts were reputable discount stores, founded on the Kresge Company's seventy-one year tradition of quality, economy, and service. Today, there are few manufacturers who will not sell directly to K-mart.

Part of the company's continuing effort to give K-mart customers quality merchandise is its private label program. The K-mart Division is gradually creating its own brands of exceptional values in staple lines. Private label merchandise is manufactured under strict controls of quality, packaging, and customer appeal. Every item is laboratory-tested to assure quality equal or superior to that of the leading competitive nationally advertised brands and which can be placed on K-mart counters at lower prices.

With an eye toward improving merchandise quality while maintaining discount prices, the company has an active import program. Buying representatives in European and Asian markets work closely with the home office import department. The Kresge Company buyers frequently travel abroad in search of quality merchandise and K-mart exclusives. All imported merchandise is required to equal or surpass the quality specifications of its domestic counterpart and be available at lower cost.

The customer who goes to a K-mart in response to a newspaper advertisement will find advertised items at advertised prices prominently displayed. The company's advertising policy, perhaps more than any other standard, was designed to gain the customer's complete confidence in the integrity and credibility of K-mart.

Long before K-mart came into existence, the Kresge company followed a policy providing for "satisfaction always or your money cheerfully refunded." This policy was incorporated into the operating standards of every K-mart and is proclaimed by prominent signs throughout the sales floor. Every K-mart newspaper advertisement repeats this statement. Proof of the sincerity of the claim is the ease with which a customer obtains a refund. The K-mart service desk is conveniently located at the front of the store where attendants are always available to refund shopper's money, exchange merchandise, or credit charge accounts. The only requirement is that the customer show the purchase receipt.

K-mart's image-makers conceived K-marts as one-stop centers where customers could conveniently park and complete all of their shopping, including grocery purchasing. Therefore, the majority of K-mart stores are designed to accommodate food markets, generally operated by qualified supermarket firms licensed as "K-mart Foods" under an agreement providing for the same merchandising and service standards required of all K-mart departments.

K-mart executives claim that their most important asset is quality personnel. The men chosen to manage K-mart stores are experienced career managers with proven executive ability and demonstrated qualifications as promotion-minded merchants. The strongest possible emphasis is placed on the maintenance of consistently high standards for department heads and sales people.

Top management realized from the outset that successful implementation of K-mart policies would depend entirely on quality standards established and maintained at all organization levels. The K-mart experience has been beneficial to the entire organization, particularly in terms of its contributions to the effective operations of the Kresge and Jupiter stores.

QUESTIONS

1. Plans call for K-mart to continue its expansion at the rate of more than fifty K-marts a year through 1973. What combination of factors has contributed to this rapid growth?

2. Describe and evaluate K-mart's merchandising policies in the light of changing consumer patterns.
3. What features contribute to making a K-mart discount department store a one-stop shopping center? Are there any potential future threats to the concept of a one-stop shopping center?

12.

Sherman Company

An Opportunity in Mobile and Modular Homes

All through his high school years and while attending a nearby college, James Hamilton was employed by Allen Sherman, a general contractor who built conventional homes, small offices, and other buildings for banks, beauty parlors, barber shops, sales offices, and specialty stores. Immediately upon his graduation from college, Hamilton was offered a job by Sherman, who had just set up Richland Homes, Inc., a new plant for the manufacture of mobile and modular homes. "With your building experience, education, and an investment of $50,000 you can get in on the ground floor of a new business with unlimited possibilities," Hamilton was told. "Both low-income families who cannot afford conventional housing and a growing number of affluent higher-income families who need a second home for a lake or beach house want economical housing," Sherman continued. "Think it over, investigate the potential of this industry, and if you like what you find, an investment of $50,000 will get you in as a partner."

Hamilton liked working with Sherman and, throughout his years of close association, had come to respect him as a hard-working, shrewd businessman. The $50,000 investment posed no great problem for Hamilton, and he had been looking around for a small business investment opportunity. He was tempted to agree at once to the offer but decided to investigate the opportunity carefully before making up his mind. Hamilton's first research step was to write to the Mobile Home Manufacturers' Association in Chicago. From this source, he learned that, as of mid-1969, over five million American families throughout the United States were living in mobile homes in some 25,000 parks or trailer courts. In three out of four instances, mobile homes were occupied by couples without children. Approximately one-half of the occupants were over thirty-nine years of age. Most of the existing trailer parks were located in such weather-favored states as Colorado, California, and Florida. Moreover, the Mobile Home Manufacturers' Association predicted that there would

43

be at least ten million families living in mobile homes by 1980 if the present rate of growth persisted.

Next, Hamilton's research efforts turned to the southern state in which he lived, where the mobile home industry seemed to be picking up momentum. He found that there already were fourteen companies manufacturing mobile homes, and that this new industry employed more than 1,000 persons. In addition, the state had over 100 companies which were listed as mobile home retailers. Personal interviews with some of these dealers revealed that business was good.

The largest manufacturing and assembly plant in the state currently employs more than 300 persons, has two assembly lines in continuous operation, and has recently been expanded to include its own lumber-cutting operation. Average daily production is ten homes. The firm markets a 12′ x 60′ model with luxurious appointments which sells for $10,000.

Selling prices of mobile homes range from $3,000 to $12,000. One dealer told Hamilton that a family could purchase a home complete with draperies and appliances for as little as $3,000. At the other end of the scale, deluxe models are available in many floor plans, with up to four bedrooms, two full bathrooms, living room, kitchen, dining room, and den.

Everyone to whom Hamilton talked within the industry attributed the popularity of mobile-home living to the tremendous rise in costs of building materials and skilled labor and to the high interest charges demanded by banks and even the Federal Housing Administration on real estate mortgages. An increasing segment of the population apparently is unable to afford the high prices of permanent housing which meets their needs. More and more, these people are turning to the mobile-home industry for housing. From data supplied by the state Real Estate Association, which represents the conventional home industry, Hamilton came to the conclusion that 20 to 25 percent of the families who want to buy homes are kept out of the market for permanent homes of the conventional type by high prices.

Finally, Hamilton contacted an official of the U.S. Department of Housing and Urban Development and learned that this agency was experimenting with a plan to utilize mass-produced housing units, either of the mobile or modular type in slum-cleared areas. Agency officials thought that it would be possible to replace an entire slum area with attractive homes at very modest prices. Problems which are holding up immediate implementation, according to HUD Secretary George Romney, are obsolete housing and building codes, restrictive zoning and land-use ordinances, and government red tape.

A check of ordinances and regulations in Hamilton's home-city revealed that local zoning prohibited mobile homes except in trailer parks, and there was only one such trailer park in the city. Obviously, it would take some time before this restrictive zoning could be removed.

After completing this research, Hamilton called Sherman to discuss his findings. He found Sherman fully aware of the possibilities of modular homes. Modular homes could be built in the same plant that was used for the assembly of mobile homes and with little extra cost. Sherman's initial plans called for the production of a few modular homes for public display and publicity purposes. Both men are in agreement that modular houses are basically mobile homes, except that they are installed on permanent foundations instead of resting on wheels and pillars. "You won't be able to tell a modular house from one that was built on the site," Sherman stated. "But we'll cut out a lot of the delays and costs of putting up the house on the lot. The house will be supplied with a metal platform and will be lifted off the platform onto a brick or concrete foundation by a crane. It takes a conventional home builder eight to ten weeks to build a home. With the factory-built house, the on-site work will take less than nine hours to make it livable," Sherman continued. "Use of assembly-line techniques will keep the factory costs down. For one thing, the plant crew will be working under better conditions. In the wintertime, the factory building will be heated, and they won't have to work in the rain. We can put materials and labor together better and cheaper than can the small conventional home builder who works with a crew of six on the site but who is frequently delayed by weather and other construction bottlenecks."

QUESTIONS

1. Distinguish between modular, mobile, and conventionally built homes.
2. What are the differences in the marketing of conventional homes and factory-built mobile homes?
3. List as many reasons as you can for the popularity of the relatively economical mobile and modular homes in an economy that has experienced such a great rise in income and consumer affluence in recent years.
4. What are some of the potential negative aspects to entering the industry described in the case?
5. What additional research should Hamilton undertake before making his final decisions?

13.
Modern Builders Supply Company
Entering a New Market

Background

William C. Johnson, who has had a substantial amount of experience in the home contracting and building supply industries, has contemplated opening his own building supply business for several years. He has concluded that an opportunity exists for such a business in a Southwestern city with a population in excess of 150,000. Preliminary research indicates that the city has great potential for growth. In a more extensive follow-up study, interviews with thirty leading home builders in the area yielded information which Johnson intends to use in establishing Modern Builders Supply Company and in developing his marketing strategies.

Sources of Building Supplies

Of the builders interviewed, most appeared to be in favor of shopping around the various supply companies in order to meet their needs. In fact, only five of the builders indicated that they dealt principally with one major supplier. The other builders stated that they spread their purchases around. Exhibit 1 provides evidence of this practice. Several other remarks which were made by builders were judged to be significant. First, several mentioned that they look for a price-quality relationship on each item and buy from the supply company which offers this combination in its best form. Second, one builder indicated that he buys from four different suppliers. He stated that he attempts to play one against the other on price and acknowledged that each gives good service and high quality work. Third, several builders mentioned that building material is a "price item"; therefore, one must spread purchases around to obtain the best price.

Two of the supply companies also operate in the home-building business. One supply house is actually a cooperative and is owned by a number of local builders. In general, builders have widely divergent opinions on whether to deal with a building supply company which also competes as a builder. Approximately one-half of the builders dislike buying from a "competitor," and one-third of the builders commented that it makes no difference. Other comments included the following: "They are large and powerful companies and could really take it out on the builders if they wanted"; "Their tie-in with land, building, and supplies places them in a position of strength which could be used as a weapon in bad times. One can never forget, they are competitors." Therefore, although some builders seem not to care whether building supply companies are in the building business or not, others voiced strong opinions to the contrary. Most of the builders, who said that they dislike the idea but who still buy from these supply companies, qualified their statements by saying that they would continue to do so only so long as there are no restrictions involved and the builders who are involved remain fair competitors.

Competition for the Builders' Business

Most of the builders described the building supply companies as "strong competitors" for the builders' business and noted that the majority of the suppliers compete on the bases of personality, price, service, and quality. A few, including Town Lumber, Ready Builders Supplies, and Compton Supply Co., compete primarily on price. Exhibit 2 presents the competitive factors which the builders believe to be most important in competing for their business. Price and service lead the list. Johnson felt that "quality" and "delivery" might be understated in the ranking because most builders take these supplier characteristics for granted. Both factors must be present before builders will even deal with a supplier.

When questioned about the performance of suppliers, the builders said that high quality of the products and credit availability are the only two factors which were satisfactory to all builders. Regarding each of the other factors, one or more builders commented that his supplier(s) are doing a poor job. Dissatisfaction is particularly evident regarding the quality of technical data and assistance made available to the builder. Also, although there were a high number of favorable comments regarding delivery, inventory availability, and breadth of product line, the number of dissenting opinions indicated that suppliers leave something to be desired in these areas.

Product Line Considerations

Generally, builders have a high opinion of the products which are handled by suppliers in the area. Those builders who said that the lines are not wide and fresh referred either to a very poorly managed supplier or to the failure of a supplier to stock a specialty item. Most of the builders commented that there are no specific omissions from their suppliers' line, with some minor exceptions. Several builders wish to find a "gadget" wholesaler who would have a wide variety of "gadgets" on display and in stock; these builders contend that many homes are sold because of the "gadgets" they contain rather than on the basis of the home's overall quality.

In analyzing the opinions of the builders, Johnson concluded that they favor an emphasis on ready availability of new products. However, the builders do not place the blame for not providing new products completely on the suppliers. Some builders feel that the local market is not ready for the newest products since the public is slow to accept new ideas. Others add that since innovation is slow to catch on, the suppliers cannot go out on a limb by adding these innovations to their inventories. However, builders did characterize the suppliers as unwilling to stick their necks out on new products and to take some chances. "The suppliers handle only good, tried and tested products; they want other suppliers to take the chance," stated one builder. Another noted that he cannot obtain new items which are pictured in the magazines. Since the local builders only carry the "run-of-the-mill" type item, they must often special-order merchandise.

Pricing Practices

Although there is some divergence of opinion regarding supplier pricing practices, the prevailing sentiment is that suppliers are not interested in competing on a price basis. An exception is pricing for the cash-and-carry business of the Ready Co., Town Lumber Co., and Compton Supply Co. A few builders indicated that price is highly competitive. However, these builders use the word "competitive" to mean "be in line." Generally, prices appear to be set on a "follow-the-leader" basis and firms do not deviate from this practice very often.

The builders strongly criticized the suppliers' failure to notify them of price changes. They stated that immediate notification of a change in price is of fundamental importance. In fact, the builders would like to be warned of price changes before they occur. Twenty builders complained either that notifications are not made or are furnished only on a builder's request. Of the builders who are satisfied with the practices of suppliers regarding notification of price changes, most are large-volume builders. Johnson interpreted this to mean that the price notification service is given only to preferred customers.

Delivery

Most builders think that delivery is performed "fairly efficiently." Some of the favorable comments include: "suppliers are cooperative; competition has brought good delivery; the area has excellent delivery conditions; delivery is one reason Allan gets our business; Allan will deliver in two hours, but the others—you can't tell; radio trucks sure help." The following comments made by certain builders are less favorable:

1. "The problem of delivery is with small amounts. No builder can order the exact amount that he needs. Many times the builder is short and cannot get fast enough delivery on the emergency items";
2. "Drivers dump at the wrong place, especially at five o'clock. This causes labor problems and personal inconvenience at the site";
3. "Inexperienced warehousemen foul up the order or damage the merchandise";
4. "Trucks get lost and many times delay the job";
5. "Damaged or incorrect items are delivered";
6. "Delivery at the wrong location causes inconvenience and time consumption";
7. "Delivery depends upon the help—a good dispatcher could remedy the situation";
8. "Suppliers can make use or better use of small trucks for small deliveries and emergency items. In the opinion of several builders, this service could be a tremendous assistance to the builder";
9. "A set schedule is important for delivery";
10. "Drivers seem to dump haphazardly and have an indifferent attitude toward the needs of the builders."

Personnel

Although builders initially rated most of the salesmen who call on them as "excellent representatives," further questioning of the same builders elicited a number of relevant comments. These comments relate to three major points of interest: (1) the relationship between the builders and the personal representatives of the supply company, (2) the sales ability of the salesman, and (3) the personal qualities of the salesman.

A common opinion is that the salesman should help out on the job by giving suggestions on products, quality, and quantity. Builders like a salesman to keep an eye on the job and to be on hand when needed, especially when the builder is ready to place an order for a product. One builder stated the salesman performs a great service when he estimates how much of a product is needed and assists the builder in ordering that amount. In addition, builders appreciate the salesman's efforts to keep the builder supplied so that he does not run out of a needed item. To do this, a salesman must follow the job well and be close to the supplier's operations. A few builders commented that some salesmen ought to make a special effort to "see the job more regularly."

Builders described most of the area salesmen as "order-takers" with little technical or sales ability. Builders commented that they favor salesmen who know what they are talking about, but that there are very few of these in the building supply trade. Generally, all salesmen should know more about the products they handle and should work more in the builder's behalf. It was a common complaint that most salesmen have no imagination or determination. Although salesmen tend to have ready answers to standard questions, they must call the office for information on specialty items. Also, they are not really professional salesmen. Too many salesmen make mistakes which have to be corrected. Builders generally commented that a salesman should know the building trade better. In fact, one builder stated that the suppliers' salesmen "do not contribute anything" and that he "would just as soon call in his order to the supplier."

"Salesmen talk too much," is a comment which was heard on a number of occasions. Several of the builders complained that salesmen substitute quantity of sales talk for quality. On the other hand, certain salesmen are described as being friendly, casual, courteous, gentlemen, loyal, and not overbearing.

Providing Information to Builders

The general comment as to the types of information or technical assistance which suppliers are able to give to the builder was that the supplier is not particularly knowledgeable. The counter clerks and telephone men in particular were described as not being able to supply information without asking someone else. Although the more experienced men are able to help the builder most of the time, even these have to call in the manufacturer's salesman for help on "sticky" problems. Several builders mentioned that if the builder asks (and only if he asks), the supplier can provide information on staple items. However, on items other than staples, the salesman might attempt to reply but is not always able to answer correctly. Because of this shortcoming, builders generally would rather talk to the specialist. One builder commented that salesmen do not always know as much as they think they know about the fine points of the trade. Another stated that the builder is not always sure that the information he receives from a salesman is correct.

Some builders are less critical regarding the suppliers' abilities to provide technical information, noting that the necessary information is provided by the literature and by representatives of the manufacturers. In contrast, other builders state that, although information received from the supplier is not now sufficient, technical assistance from them could be of great benefit to the builder.

Other Considerations

All of the builders commented that credit terms are sufficient for their needs. Also, very few comments were made relative to ordering and billing procedures. In fact, ordering and billing service is taken for granted and seems to be provided equally well by each supplier. Most builders also answered that exchange privileges are adequate. However, many stated that there is too much "red tape" in exchanging materials. These builders also commented that, although this service is not "too" important (since they don't use it often), a driver should have the authority to pick up merchandise to be returned without obtaining prior office approval. These critics, however, commend the use of the radio truck as an attempt to answer this problem.

Builders differ in their opinions of cash-and-carry dealing and cash-and-carry houses. Although eighteen of the builders said they bought cash-and-carry, only two of these indicated that cash-and-carry constitutes a major portion of their purchases. Price was the motivating circumstance listed by eleven cash-and-carry customers. Although these builders listed price as being important, many combined the price element with other factors such as emergency purchases, convenience, "small stuff," specialty items, and "to inspect the item before purchase."

Nine builders said that they *never* pick up any of their own purchases and do not ever intend to do so. On the other hand, twenty-one builders do pick up some purchases. Most of those who refuse to pick up their purchases reason that the activity is too costly for the builder. Also, most who buy cash-and-carry expect the cash-and-carry supplier to deliver at cash-and-carry prices. The normal practice is for cash-and-carry to be delivered if the purchase is $150 or more. However, the minimum requirement is waived for preferred customers. Eleven builders stated that they pick up their own purchases for emergency reasons, and seven said that pickups are made on "small stuff."

QUESTIONS

1. Based on the results of his interviews, evaluate Johnson's decision to compete in this market.
2. What types of services should be emphasized by a competitor in this city?
3. Should Johnson establish a cash-and-carry trade? Why?
4. Evaluate the validity of the research which Johnson has carried out and his conclusions. Are there any potential problems in accepting the comments of the builders?
5. What other suggestions for developing marketing strategy can you make based upon the information provided by the builders?

EXHIBIT 1
Building Supply Companies Listed by Builders
as Regular Sources of Supply

Building Supply Company	Times Mentioned
Allan Builders Supply Co.	13
Compton Supply Co.	12
Town Lumber Co.	11
Strong Lumber Co.	10
Johnstown Roofing & Supply Co.	10
Becker Lumber Co.	9
Ready Builders Supplies, Inc.	5
Capitol Lumber Co.	3
Builders Lumber Co.	2

EXHIBIT 2
Suppliers' Competitive Factors Mentioned
as Being Important to Builders

Factors	Times Mentioned
Price	17
Service	17
Delivery	5
Product line	5
Quality	5
Pleasant attitude	5
Product guarantees	4
Return policy	3
Keeping up with job	3
Being up to date	3
Credit	2

14.

J. C. Penney Company, Inc.
Expansion Activities of a Retail Chain

The J. C. Penney Company, capitalizing on its ability to undertake new activities efficiently, has recently added several innovations to its fast-growing business. Included are expanded catalog sales, a chain of drugstores, discount stores, and a general merchandise and food chain in Europe. The following sections relate how J. C. Penney Company management accomplished this expansion.

For the past few months, consumers in the northeastern part of the United States have been getting for the first time an 800-page merchandise catalog with a modishly dressed young lady on the cover staring happily at the words "1969 Penney's Spring & Summer."

This is the beginning of the assault by J. C. Penney Co., Inc. on the nation's most populous and best-spending retail area as it seeks to expand its catalog business, one of the fastest-growing branches of retailing.

Entering the populous Northeast with its catalog is made possible for Penney by the opening next month of its Atlanta distribution center, a multimillion dollar investment. Penney's catalog bears the subtitle: "Americans on the Go." Few companies have been more on the go in recent months than Penney.

Last October, it bought for $8.6 million a more than 20 percent interest in Sarma, S.A., a large retail chain based in Belgium but with outposts in Spain. In March, Penney acquired for stock the Thrift Drug Co., a ten-state operation of 157 units with annual sales of $76 million. In May, Penney announced a computer system which puts it a long step ahead of its competition in making the computer do a better job for both customers and store management.

All for the Customer

Each of these developments represents a significant new and forward step by Penney in moving toward the goal proclaimed a long time ago by

Chairman and chief executive William M. Batten: "We are in the distribution business for any and all kinds of goods and services the great mass of people want. We will sell them anything for themselves or for their homes, in any way convenient to them, and for cash, or credit if they wish."

Or, as President Cecil L. Wright put it more bluntly just last month: "We try like the dickens not to miss anything that fits into our total plan of giving the customer all we can give in service and merchandise."

This effort last year brought Penney sales of $3.3 billion, 15.3 percent above 1967, and earnings of $109.3 million, 19.3 percent above 1967. That's more than $1 billion in sales and $40 million in earnings greater than five years ago before Penney began converting itself from essentially a small-town retailer of apparel, linens, and piece goods into the operator of huge shopping center stores which sell everything from bedsheets to automobile tires.

Many Changes Since 1963

Before 1963, such things as refrigerators and furniture were strangers to Penney stores; now they occupy as much as one-third of the floor space in the new stores. Before 1963, Penney did a cash-and-carry business; now 36 percent of its business is for credit. Even the traditional merchandise has changed. Soft goods still account for this great bulk of sales, but, says Wright, "80 percent of this merchandise did not exist five years ago or has been significantly changed due to product innovation."

At the recent annual meeting, Batten pointed out that it took Penney forty-nine years to reach $1 billion in sales, thirteen years more to reach $2 billion, but only an additional four years to reach $3 billion in sales.

Expanding in Europe

It also will be a year of adjusting new things to the "total plan" Wright mentioned. Part of that total plan for some years now has been to expand abroad. Europe's consumer economy is growing as fast as in this country. Incomes are rising and so, too, are consumer expectations. Yet, retail practices are perhaps some years behind those in the U.S. That's why such major U.S. retailers as Sears, Roebuck, & Co., Federated Department Stores, and the Jewel Companies have moved into Europe: Sears by building stores in Spain, Federated by buying an interest in a Spanish department store, and Jewel by buying interests in stores in Belgium and Italy.

The Sarma deal may give Penney the strongest position in Europe of any American retailer except F. W. Woolworth, which has been in England and Germany for more than half a century. Sarma gives Penney a tie-up with an established retailer with nearly 100 stores, including five in Spain, 280 franchised units and sales of $170 million a year.

Sarma stores range from 3,000 to 50,000 square feet in size and sell both general merchandise and food. But Sarma's experience is stronger in food than in soft lines, and Penney shines in soft lines. "I see a fit there," says Wright.

Drug Stores and Catalogs

The Thrift Drug acquisition is apiece with Sarma. Thrift is well-established and already operating leased departments in the Treasure Island stores of Penney. Penney has felt the need to strengthen its trade in health and beauty aids in the big new stores. The Thrift management knows how to stock and sell health and beauty items, nationally a $4 billion-a-year business.

"Anything we go into," says Wright, "we expect to cause to grow—or we wouldn't be in it." The story of how Penney's catalog now is ready to bump heads with Sears and Montgomery Ward in the Northeast shows exactly what Wright means.

Today's catalog business is decades away from the days of the farmer poring over the "wishbook" by the light of a kerosene lamp. The image of the catalog business today is a smart young suburban housewife—dinner dishes done, kids put to bed—picking up the phone to order her needs from a catalog center that may be manned by only a tape recorder.

Total retail sales in five years have increased 38 percent; the total catalog business in the same period, 53 percent. The catalog business accounts for about 22 percent of the total sales of Sears, the retailing pacesetter which Penney has used as a target since it began to accelerate its transformation in the early sixties.

To get a finger-hold in cataloging, in 1962 Penney bought General Merchandise Co., a small Milwaukee concern. It enlarged and modernized the warehouse, brought out a big, new catalog, and gradually expanded catalog service through thirteen states in the Midwest.

From the start, the plan was to sell nationally from the catalog—and do it right the first time. Penney executives frankly admit that they drew on Sears' experience and then improved upon it. Sears serves the nation with about a dozen catalog warehouses. Penney expects to do it with perhaps as few as four.

Beginning from scratch, it can use advanced physical distribution methods and computer inventory controls that were not available when Sears was building its catalog network.

Penney expects to complete its national expansion in the catalog business and be in the black within the early Seventies. It is moving deliberately and thoroughly. "Atlanta, for instance, could have been opened a year ago," Wright says, "but some problems arose in the Milwaukee operation on which Atlanta was patterned." Penney didn't want to proceed on the 2.1 million square foot Southeastern center until it was sure of what it was doing.

Meanwhile, Penney had begun to seed and fertilize the Southeast for the coming catalog. Beginning in 1966, it issued special Atlanta and Dallas editions of the catalog and set up catalog desks in its stores in the nine Southeastern states. Merchandise was shipped from Milwaukee to a Dallas or Atlanta "break-bulk" point and then to the customer, who paid shipping charges only from Dallas or Atlanta.

As far as the customers have been able to tell, they have been dealing with Dallas or Atlanta for three years. Penney was absorbing a lot of extra costs in that operation, but by the time the warehouse opens, Wright says, "We'll be starting from a solid base of 152 catalog desks in nine Southern states. And as soon as the center opens, our service to the area will improve."

That means cutting delivery time to forty-eight hours for many stores instead of up to seventy-two hours when everything had to come out of Milwaukee. The Atlanta warehouse also makes it possible to promise forty-eight to seventy-two hour delivery in the fifteen Northeastern states. Penney's next target is 1,000 catalog units in thirty-nine states.

Treasure Island Stores

Penney bought General Merchandise for the catalog business. But it found that General Merchandise had just started to enter discount retailing. It had one store named Treasure Island already open in Appleton, Wisconsin, another under construction at Madison, and sites for three more stores in Milwaukee. Penney completed the second store and sat back to watch the operation, which in concept as well as merchandising lines was foreign to it.

The Penney company had never had experience in food retailing. The Treasure Island stores had internal food operations, managed by an experienced food retail chain. Penney at that time was only beginning to enter hard goods, but Treasure Island sold these, too. And it was all done in a way unfamiliar to Penney people: largely self-service, with checkout counters.

Officially, Treasure Island became an "experiment." The Penney executives, from their glass-and-concrete tower in New York City, watched carefully what this strange breed was doing with those odd stores in Wisconsin—and learned. (One thing they learned, of course, was that selling health and beauty aids—very high-profit items—was a business Penney people did not know very well and the Thrift people knew very well indeed; and that led to the recent acquisition.)

The most important thing they learned was that Treasure Island could be a profitable operation in its own right, totally separate from the catalog business which spawned it, and from the Penney stores.

"There are Treasure Island customers and there are Penney customers," explains Oakley Evans, vice-president for corporate development. "In Milwaukee, we built a Treasure Island store right across from a Penney store and the business of both increased."

The consequence of all this is that Treasure Island no longer is an experiment. It now is an operating division of the Penney company and late last year four stores were opened in the Atlanta area to add to what are now six in Wisconsin. There are plans for further expansion, notably in Los Angeles.

Capitalizes on its Strengths

Treasure Island tells something about Penney's strength. Penney has the capital to open stores in clusters when it enters an area new to Treasure Island; it has a modern credit system which it can extend to Treasure Island customers; and it has an enormous pool of employees from which it can develop managers (men originally trained in Penney stores now are becoming Treasure Island managers). Clearly, Penney has the financial and manpower strength to get involved in new things in the most efficient way.

An example is the computer. Several years ago, Penney started to place special precoded sales tickets on year-round lines of both soft and hard goods. When an item was sold, one part of the ticket was torn off and mailed to a collection center. There, the information on the coded ticket was fed into a computer which kept records on such merchandise for each store, and issued orders to manufacturers or warehouses to replenish a store's stock when the inventory got to a predetermined level.

Innovation with General Electric

Now, based on that system and the experience with it, Penney has recently contracted with General Electric Company for a totally new and unique extension of computer controls right down to where the Penney person makes the sale. The system has been tried for a year in a Penney store in Glendale, California, and will be in approximately fifty more stores around Los Angeles by the end of 1970.

What happens with the system that Penney and GE call TRADAR is this: All Penney merchandise will carry a special sales ticket designed by Dennison Manufacturing Company. When an item is sold, say for credit, the special device (which supplants the cash register) reads the ticket and tells the computer what has been sold and to adjust the stock records for that class of item.

The device prints out a receipt for the customer and reads the credit card into the computer, which instantly verifies that the credit card is valid. (If a card has been lost or stolen and that fact has been reported to the company, the computer will reject the application to charge merchandise.)

All of this is done in about the time it takes to read this explanation. According to Kenneth S. Axelson, vice-president for finance and administration, customers are getting faster service than with the conventional "ringing up" on the register. "And," he says, "it gives sales people the information they need daily." Retailers generally have to settle for such detailed sales reports once a week, sometimes less frequently.

This on-line computer control (where the computer takes in information instantly and responds instantly) is costly. To equip the fifty Los Angeles stores is costing about $10 million, and Penney has more than 1,600 stores. It has about 20,000 cash registers, and one of the point-of-sale devices costs up to $3,000.

Penney has not yet made the decision to put every store on the TRADAR system; there are some real questions, such as whether it would be economical to hook up an isolated store in the great open spaces with a computer in a data center hundreds of miles away. But even when costs are formidable, Penney management does not balk at spending to keep moving ahead.

Store Expansion

Last year it spent nearly $127 million to add 6.1 million square feet of space in thirty-six new Penney stores (four of them Treasure Island stores), fifty automobile service centers, and thirty-two catalog desks. This year it plans to spend a greater sum on 4 million square feet for thirty-two new stores, thirty auto centers, 250 catalog desks, and on real estate for further expansion in the near future. "The reduction in total new store space," Batten explains, "is the result of delays encountered by developers in the building of shopping centers."

Since it began its break-neck expansion in 1963 with the opening of its first full-line store, Penney has put most of its stores in big shopping centers. ("That's where the people are," an official says succinctly.) That accounts for the fact that the average new Penney store now is 193,000 square feet, compared to 53,000 square feet in 1962. This year, the money squeeze has made it more difficult for developers to get these big shopping centers under way.

Although it has expanded in every direction—Penney sells life, health, and accident insurance by mail and is itching to get into mutual funds—Penney executives never let their eyes stray too far from the Penney store. Says Wright, "Penney's opportunity for growth depends on the public confidence in the Penney store and the Penney name. It's really that simple." Everything Batten, Wright, and Company do is designed to increase the sales and profits of the stores.

Take the catalog business. "Catalog sales are oriented toward the desk in the Penney store," says Donald V. Seibert, vice-president of the catalog operation. The whole idea is to get people to come into the store; even if a customer phones in an order, it has to be picked up at the store. "Anytime you bring people into the store," Wright emphasizes, "you sell more."

Seibert stresses that the catalog desk is essential in older Penney stores. These stock mostly soft goods, with limited selections in smaller stores, and the catalog extends the store's merchandise, enables it to compete in hard lines, and everything else.

Personnel Policies

The store, too, is where the Penney people—called "associates"—are nurtured. The J. C. Penney Company, since its founding in 1902, has been built on a partnership concept (originally, a store manager had to be part owner); generous profit-sharing and retirement plans have been designed to enlist people's interest and to hold it.

Over the years, a big part of any Penney executive's job has been to concern himself with personnel development, since Batten some years ago installed a program of five-year profit performance forecasts, with semiannual reviews to make people individually accountable for their performance.

Wright says he spends several hours a week in talking with individual officers about nothing but personnel. "One of the most encouraging things in my forty-one years at Penney," says Wright, "is to see these young people take these stores and make a success of them."

That success is not left to chance. In the words of Batten, "We provide the climate that will enable people to develop themselves." It's a good climate, to judge by the results. Penney is proud of the fact that it has never, in its long history, employed an outsider as store manager. All promotions to that coveted and highly profitable spot have come from within, a policy which has provided a continuing reservoir of trained and eager management material. It has also contributed, in a major way, toward the high morale and loyalty which exists throughout the organization—the most important factor of all, undoubtedly, in maintaining the "Penney Edge."

QUESTIONS

1. What type of merchandise did the J. C. Penney Company sell principally before 1963? What radical changes have been made since 1963?
2. For the most part, Sears, Roebuck, & Co. has accomplished its foreign expansions slowly over the past twenty-five years through the construction of its own stores. On the other hand, J. C. Penney has expanded quickly into Europe through the purchase of the large Sarma chain. What are some of the advantages and disadvantages of these two methods of foreign expansion?
3. Why has catalog selling become popular again? Is Penney's next target of 1,000 catalog units in thirty-nine states a worthwhile goal?
4. In what concrete way might the merchandising of the entire Penney organization be improved through the acquisition of the Thrift Drug Chain?
5. What other innovations has J. C. Penney management pioneered during the 1960s? Suggest some expansion possibilities that management should consider for the 1970s.

II.
CAPITALIZING
ON OPPORTUNITIES
THROUGH THE
MARKETING MIX

PRODUCT PLANNING
AND DEVELOPMENT

15.
Why Do So Many New Products Fail?
Some Facts and a Theory

We are told that over 80 percent of our economy is based on products that did not exist 100 years ago. Yet, the great majority of the new products that were placed on the market over the years have failed and have had to be withdrawn. For example, in the first two years following World War II, 98 percent of the new products entered into the market failed. Many of these were launched by energetic but inexperienced veterans who had little capital. Even so, about 80 percent of new packaged consumer goods placed on the market by the 200 leading firms (including companies like Lever Bros. and General Electric) were found to have ended in failure according to a study made by nationally recognized A.C. Nielson Company shortly after World War II. Certainly, these companies had plenty of capital and experience in new product introduction.

More recently, however, it appears that the failure rate has been reduced substantially. For example, in a *Printer's Ink* survey made in the 1960s, it was found that the failure rate was reduced to about 50 percent among companies that used test marketing before launching the new product on a full-scale basis.

Sociologist Everett M. Rogers published his life's research work in 1962 in a well-received book titled *Diffusion of Innovations*. In the book, Rogers claims that product developers have paid too much attention to the economic advantage factor and not enough attention to such other important consumer-perceived product attributes as compatibility with existing consumer values, complexity of understanding the innovation, its divisibility for trial use, and the ease of observing and communicating to others the benefits of the new product. Dr. Rogers contends that if product developers made a greater effort to determine and predict consumer reaction to new products on all five of these points, the failure rate could be reduced even more.

QUESTIONS

1. List and describe the reasons for the high failure rate of new products.
2. What factors do you feel are responsible for the progress made since World War II in the reduction of the failure rate from 80 percent down to 50 percent?
3. Explain each of Sociologist Rogers' criteria in some detail.
4. Do you agree with Rogers? Give several reasons for your support or nonsupport of the Rogers position.

16.

The Broom Vacuum (A)

Developing a Product to Satisfy a Need

John Livingston was vice-president of a large machine tool and die firm jobbing and subcontracting orders for other manufacturers. In his spare time, he tinkered with mechanical devices. In this, he showed a great deal of ingenuity and gained much personal satisfaction from solving intricate mechanical problems.

While watching his wife sweep the tiled kitchen one morning, he noted her awkwardness in trying to sweep crumbs into a dustpan and subsequently dispose of the debris. En route to work, his active mind chewed on the awkwardness and inconvenience. By the time he reached the factory, he had a tentative solution: a small vacuum, able to fit into a square the size of a kitchen tile. He recognized several potential problems: activating a vacuum cleaner built into the floor, finding scuff-resistant metals, coping with water seepage into the vacuum's motor, and disposing of the accumulated wastes. At dinner that night, he discussed it with his wife. She became enthusiastic immediately, seeing it as a boon to all housewives.

Livingston set to work feverishly in his spare time. At the shop, his men created a prototype according to his specifications. Motors from one-eighth to one-half horsepower were tried. Recognizing that subflooring under tile could be cement or wood, two models were developed: one which allowed for the bag to be removed from the floor level when the subflooring was cement and one which provided that the bag could be removed from the ceiling in the cellar. Potential water seepage was avoided by canting the motor 90° from the grill and sealing it.

A friend looked at the finished product and suggested that there might be a market for it. If there were, he should patent the device if possible and then test market it. Livingston thought it over. He already had invested $2,400 and was willing to invest more, and since he was a rather wealthy man, the expenditure was not critical to him. He found the product and its potential exciting and, therefore, was interested in pursuing the project further.

Livingston decided to go ahead. He hired a good patent attorney, who proceeded to Washington with blueprints and a working model. Livingston next developed options for activating the motor: either a wall finger-switch or a floor toe-switch would work. The toe-switch also presented options: one had to be installed when the tile was laid, as in a new home; a second switch could be installed in any circumstance, but there would be a slight indentation in the kitchen floor, posing a hazard to people walking over it.

Livingston was elated over having solved his problems, and rosy dreams of queues of housewives clamoring for his vacuum filled his mind as he drove to work that morning. His mood changed, however, when his morning mail was received at the office. The bill for the patent attorney's costs and fees was staggering. Now his total sunk costs were almost $20,000. He picked up the phone and called his friend, Bart Henry, who had suggested the patent. Henry wasn't surprised at the cost. He quickly recognized that his friend's next problem was to sell the vacuum, and he suggested obtaining a booth at an upcoming home builders show to demonstrate the model. Livingston decided to take his advice.

Contact with the show's sponsors wasn't fruitful—all the booths were leased. Livingston, however, found a friend who would be showing major appliances. The latter agreed to let Livingston demonstrate his new product on a temporary stand.

Livingston built two new prototypes in stainless steel. Both were of the toe-button type. He arranged to take orders for the product at the booth, promising shipment within three weeks.

In the first half hour of the show, Livingston demonstrated the vacuum himself. Pricing the vacuum for $35.00, he sold forty-two of them and proceeded to collect payment. At that point, the appliance dealer, due to an unforeseen event, was forced to ask Livingston to stop giving demonstrations.

At home that evening, Livingston began to calculate his costs per unit. Motor, frame, wiring, parts, and assembly would amount to $19.87 per unit on a production run of 1,000 per month for twenty-four months. Dies and special tools would be amortized in that two-year period.

QUESTIONS

1. Evaluate the steps taken by Livingston in the development of his product and in the planning of his marketing strategy.
2. What other costs should Livingston include in determining his total costs?
3. What basic price philosophies must he consider in determining the future selling price of the vacuum? Based on your knowledge of the

characteristics of the small appliance market, which pricing policies should be established?

4. What other factors should he consider in calculating his selling price?

5. What other problems, in addition to price determination, does Livingston now have?

17.

The Broom Vacuum (B)

Evaluating Sources of Product Information

John Livingston had invented and patented a vacuum cleaner to fit in a 9″ x 9″ tile on a kitchen floor. With an orientation toward job-shop manufacturing and not to marketing, he had invested over $20,000 before recognizing some of the additional problems facing him. His friend, Bart Henry, suggested he talk to a marketing consultant or one of the University's marketing professors. Henry had no idea what either would charge.

Livingston phoned Samuel Perry, a consultant. Over the phone, Perry advised that his rates were $35 per hour for discussing marketing problems, that the cost of field research would be $250 per day plus expenses for himself and $100 per day plus expenses for his field team. Livingston thanked him numbly and hung up. When he recovered, he called the dean of the business college, who referred him to Professor Peter Fragg, who had recently researched major appliances, and an appointment was made for lunch. Over coffee, they discussed the project; Dr. Fragg was interested in the product and envisaged other applications in addition to kitchen floors. Although his available time was limited by his teaching and committee assignments, he was willing to devote an average of one or two days each week to make a market study. Livingston asked what fees would be charged. Fragg thought a while and stated: "My price will be my out-of-pocket expenses plus $5.00 for each floor unit sold." Livingston thanked him, indicated he would be in touch with him shortly, and went home to consider the proposal.

QUESTIONS

1. What other alternative sources of assistance are open to Livingston? Evaluate each.
2. As an inventor, you might choose between Perry's and Fragg's bids.

What would each one's charges add to your product's ultimate selling price? Is the choice between the two proposals likely to be made on any other basis than cost?

3. As Professor Fragg, what alternate uses can you envisage for the floor vacuum? In what industries would you find the product to add value?
4. How would you test-market the product? At what price? Which factors must be considered in making decisions regarding test-marketing?

18.

The Broom Vacuum (C)

Seeking a Market for a New Product

John Livingston considered obtaining a marketing consultant to evaluate the market for his ingenious floor vacuum. The consultant's fee was $250 a day and expenses. Livingston had invested over $20,000 in perfecting and patenting his product. He also considered utilizing the services of Dr. Fragg, a marketing professor, who wanted a royalty of $5.00 for each vacuum sold, plus personal expenses associated with consulting.

Since Livingston did not want to invest much more capital, he chose Dr. Fragg. The professor proceeded to identify the various market segments for the product. Sixty-two different market segments were identified, some with widely different channels, each probably necessitating the use of different promotional techniques and different pricing methods.

Of the many market alternatives, Fragg felt that two should be tried first. The first possibility was to utilize the ready-made channels of other household appliance manufacturers marketing small items. These manufacturers might purchase the rights to the product and take over production as well as distribution. In such a case, the added cost for distribution of the single item would be minimal. To explore the first alternative, Fragg contacted three manufacturers. The first one, the Beaver Corporation, a vacuum cleaner maker with a prominent national brand, was not interested in any product its own Research and Development Department had not created. The second, the Fairtone Company, studied the product for several months, agreed that it would cost about $19.50 each to produce the item, but hesitated to commit itself without a thorough market test. Fragg agreed, figuring he could obtain evaluations from the forty-two customers Livingston had sold the product to during the home builders' show. Meanwhile, Fragg showed the prototype and the patent papers to the third manufacturer, the Johnson Company. The latter was interested in both items. After two weeks' study, the president tersely told Fragg the product was suitable for the new homes being built as well as for older homes. However, the president then indicated that he planned to build the product himself and that he believed he could beat the patent rights. That ended the discussion.

Fragg developed a questionnaire, sending it to all but one of the original purchasers. One customer had sent the vacuum back, stating her discontent and asking for a refund which was promptly sent.

While waiting for the Fairtone Company's decision, Fragg decided to investigate the second alternative and contact retailers. He got in touch with Sears' Chicago office, a Canadian firm which asked for a prototype, and a buyer for a large national department store chain. Sears did not reply. The Canadian company kept the vacuum for two months and returned it badly damaged. Fragg and Livingston were even more disturbed when the department store buyer stated that, while the product appeared useful, it needed market acceptance. "We sell Bibles, not religion" was the position taken by the buyer.

Fairtone was sent and subsequently reviewed the summarized replies of the original purchasers. The replies were essentially favorable but not enthusiastic. The company decided not to try to produce and market the vacuum until it could be proven that a market existed. It did, however, offer Fragg a job as marketing consultant, a position he declined with thanks.

Shortly afterwards, however, Fragg accepted a post as academic administrator for a new school on the West Coast. Since his new position precluded part-time consulting, he phoned Livingston. After a discussion, Fragg agreed to turn over his notes and ideas and to drop his rights to any future royalties in exchange for his out-of-pocket expenses of $1,320, plus $750 for his recent efforts which might result in a developed market and for his recommendations for Livingston's next steps.

QUESTIONS

1. Assuming that the principals in the case had been able to interest a manufacturer in the product, what price considerations would be involved in negotiations? If a chain retailer were interested?
2. If Livingston hired you as an additional consultant, what steps would you now recommend he take based on results obtained so far?
3. What other markets should be considered?
4. What factors were responsible for the cool reception the product received from the manufacturers and retailers?

19.
General Mills, Inc.
Contrasting Methods of Product Development

Gold Medal Wondra

Within a period of a few days, row after row of blue, white, and gold packages of a different kind of flour suddenly appeared on the shelves of 100,000 stores across the country. Simultaneously, television, newspaper, and magazine advertisements announced, "The first truly new form of flour in 4,000 years . . . Gold Medal Wondra." Thus General Mills, Inc., Wondra's maker, had performed a rare and complex maneuver. It had put a new consumer product on sale in every market in the country—attaining, for all practical purposes, simultaneous national distribution.

Simultaneous national distribution of a new product is used at times, but in the food industry it is uncommon because the costs of rapid build-up to volume production and of distribution and promotion are high. Moreover, if the product is not accepted by consumers, the losses can be so staggering that only a giant firm can survive. But General Mills, the world's largest miller with over half a billion dollars in annual sales, felt it could afford to take the chance. In Wondra, management had reason to believe they had a major innovation. It was felt that research had made a major breakthrough in that a way had been found to make flour granular in form without changing its other properties. The resulting new Wondra flour would overcome the homemaker's chief objection to flour. Wondra flour did not stick to fingers, and it poured like salt—even a novice could make gravy without lumps. Moreover, laboratory experimentation had discovered a way to produce Wondra competitively so that it would sell for only two or three cents more per two-pound package than ordinary flour. Economical production was the secret that had eluded competitors' researchers.

General Mills, believing it had a sure thing and wanting to get maximum lead time on competition, kept product research, development, and market testing under wraps. Marketing's task was especially difficult. The

74

research department could not run the usual tests to gauge consumer acceptance because of the danger of information leaking to competition. Thus, 98 percent of the acceptance testing of Wondra was done in the company's Betty Crocker kitchens and the remainder in the kitchens of a few of General Mills' highly trusted employees. Normally, consumer tests would be conducted for a six-to-eight month period in hundreds of homes.

By the fall of 1962, it was possible to plan production and distribution schedules, and the company's advertising agency, Dancer-Fitzgerald-Sample, Inc., was brought into the plot. This agency had handled Gold Medal for forty years. General Mills gave D-F-S the biggest advertising budget—running into millions for Wondra—that it had ever allocated for a single product. It was decided that the bulk of this budget would be spent on television because the product has such great visual demonstration properties. For a secret place to film the commercials, D-F-S went to a studio that had a Navy clearance and Brinks guards on the doors.

Advertisements were approved in January and February of 1963 and filming began. There was not much Wondra available at this time, so in the rehearsals salt was used (although Wondra was used in the actual filming). Meanwhile, General Mills had gone out of the feed business and had a plant available in Kansas City. The machinery for the production of Wondra was installed there and volume production was set for July with a mid-August introduction date. On June 10, the 700 members of the General Mills grocery products sales organization were told about Wondra. Within three days, they had called on every one of the approximately 3,000 flour buyers in the country for both chain stores and wholesale grocery houses, as well as some retailers who did not buy directly from General Mills, but who did have a pretty good idea of what the consumer likes. The response from this ordinarily hard-to-sell group was gratifying. They would give Wondra full shelf space.

With the secret out, General Mills could now do what normally would have been done months earlier. It immediately began test-marketing Wondra in fifty stores in Grand Rapids and Muskegon, Michigan. The company wanted to gauge advertising penetration and get some clue as to product turnover before Wondra hit the shelves nationally. Due to a worker's strike in the Kansas City plant, production was held up for a month and the well-conceived timetable upset. Finally, shipments were begun to General Mills' eighteen family flour warehouses in mid-August. Shortly after, shipments began from these warehouses to the stores. The object was to be sure every store had at least some of the flour by September 15 when the television advertising would begin. Distribution had to precede advertising. The meshing of distribution and initial advertising is considered to be vital in any new product introduction whether the company goes national in one campaign or takes the more cautious approach of one market at a time.

For several weeks the response to television and newspaper advertising of Wondra was gratifying. Shelves were quickly cleared of the initial stock; however, after the initial push, sales died down. For some reasons, housewives stopped buying, and initial purchasers did not repeat their purchases.

In the post-campaign research, one of the major reasons for Wondra's disappointing performance was quickly identified. Housewives had not read the instructions on the back of the package which stated the amount of flour that should be used. Instead, they used the same amount they had been accustomed to using, and the baked product came out heavy and soggy. The frustrated and disappointed initial consumers slowed down the sales of Wondra by their unfavorable word-of-mouth comments.

Entering the Snack Food Market

So many new items appear on supermarket shelves with such frequency today that many retailers and customers tend to take them for granted, not realizing the vast amounts of money and research which manufacturers put into these efforts to assure public acceptance of their products and added sales for the supermarket. Multimillion dollar expenditures on foreign aid, new roads, and other governmental activities have become common knowledge today. It would surprise many people to learn that similar amounts are also being spent by food manufacturers on the development of new food items which are appearing in increasing numbers in today's supermarkets. For instance, at General Mills the commitment to research is backed with a budget of approximately $9 million a year. As a result of its multimillion dollar expenditures on product research and development, General Mills is able to introduce products such as Bugles, Whistles, and Daisy*s. The following paragraphs give a behind-the-scenes look at the research, testing, and merchandising that went into the development of these very successful snack food items.

About five years ago, this opportunity in the snack field came to the fore in the company's continuing examination of eating habit trends. This research, which concentrated on evolving new markets, indicated that old habits of eating were changing with the modern way of life. "We know, of course, that the reason for three meals a day is historically based on physical needs related to the day's pattern of life," James P. McFarland, executive vice-president at General Mills explains. "Man got up in the morning with the sun and had his breakfast to get some energy. Then he worked until he and his animals needed nourishment again, so at noon they all stopped for lunch. At the end of the working day, supper became the natural thing. So there are three meals a day.

"But because of the basic changes in physical requirements related to our way of life, with greater affluence and greater automation, our patterns have changed. New recreational pursuits, the fact that people are frequently away from their normal eating environment of the home, and other factors have broadened the trend of eating between meals." Recognizing this changing pattern of consumption, the marketing research personnel at General Mills examined the various factors that would give the company the best opportunity for product participation in the new lifestyle, and the signs pointed toward snacks.

At this point, it was possible for the research and development team to establish certain criteria for product character and quality deemed necessary for entering the snack field:

1. The snack products should have shelf stability comparable to other products sold by General Mills, thereby making them available for distribution through chain and wholesaler warehouses.
2. They should have taste appeal superior or equal to the best-accepted, store–door delivered products.
3. They should have fundamental characteristics that would be identifiably different to the consumer, either through variations in shape, color, or texture.
4. They should afford the grocer adequate margins and, at the same time, be competitive in consumer pricing with items in the same category.

With these four product standards as guidelines, the company's research department went to work on developing the new snack foods. Four years of dedicated effort by technicians were required to move the products from the outlining of specifications to the completion of laboratory work. The starting point was the breakfast cereal grain, such as corn and rice. Processing of snacks was related to the process used for breakfast cereals but with the addition of such steps as frying in oil and similar processes to convert the grain into snacks rather than breakfast cereals. At the end of the first three years, it became evident that the company was going to be able to enter the snack field with a significant line. At this time, therefore, a product team was appointed to coordinate all elements required before the product could be put on the market.

For about eight months of the final laboratory development period, a consumer panel for in-home testing was used. Consumer taste tests were used to determine the proper salt and grease content for the new line of snacks.

At the same time, product packaging began to take shape. In this effort, General Mills' package design group worked with a New York designer on the snack line. Since it was felt that snack sales at the retail level were essentially of an impulse character, the aim in designing a suitable package was to come up with something that would shout from the retail shelf to the consumer about what the product was. When the designer submitted his concept of the basic package, a few changes were necessary, but the basic initial design was approved. The distinctive names of "Whistles," "Bugles" and "Daisy*s" were combined decisions made by the marketing people and the advertising agency.

The test-marketing program was concentrated in three pairs of cities. These locales were chosen with great care so that the consumers would be representative of demographics across the country. The choice of the three test-market areas not only considered consumers' income levels, ethnic backgrounds, and similar considerations, but also the predominant methods of merchandising of snack products by the trade. It was found that supermarkets sell their snacks primarily from wire racks on the West Coast, from gondola-type arrangements on the East Coast, and by a combination of methods in the Midwest.

General Mills kept a close watch on the results of the various display techniques in the test-markets. However, after several months of the rack venture, it became apparent that an exhaustive survey was necessary to arrive at a definite answer. Thus, a survey of over 1,000 supermarkets in about fifty areas was conducted. This study took only one week, and the survey information made it clear that the new line of snack items should be displayed from the permanent gondola-type shelving for the following three reasons:

1. It was found that a permanent gondola position was desirable in the store so that the shopper would always know where to find his snack items. In contrast, General Mills found that snacks on racks might be located in a corner of the store one day and on a gondola end the next.
2. It was found that store employees were more prone to restock items on shelving than those located on rack displays assuming, evidently, that wire racks were the assignment usually of wagon-jobbers rather than store personnel. During test-marketing, wire racks were out-of-stock 30 percent of the time.
3. There was also the feeling that the shopper has a definite mental concept of products displayed on wire racks. These racks are associated with potato chips and other perishable snacks which are packaged in the cellophane type of wrapper.

Whatever doubts General Mills may have had about the appeal of its new snack items to customers were dispelled by sales results of its marketing tests. If anything, the acceptance of the new items was too immediately successful. The test-marketing schedule called for advertising to begin six weeks after initial distribution of the products was made in the six test cities. Everything appeared to be going according to plan, but then the unexpected happened. Word-of-mouth advertising took over and consumers began to buy the new items faster than stock replacement could be secured for the store.

This inability to keep production in line with demand forced General Mills to drop the Des Moines and Omaha test areas. Even then, the company could not keep up with the remaining four test areas, so the Portland market was also dropped. To get retailers off the hook with their customers, General Mills ran advertisements in the areas where it had withdrawn from the test-market, explaining that the reception was just too overwhelming.

The proposed advertising program, which was scheduled to kick off the snack items' introduction into test-marketing, was not used during the initial campaign since it would only have added to the imbalance between supply and demand. The only advertisements used during this initial period were those apologizing for the inadequate supply.

Although the testing of Whistles, Daisy*s, and Bugles may have resulted in an embarrassment of riches, the future of the product was clear to General Mills management. The decision was made to go ahead with full-scale production. To make sure that factory output would be able to meet customer demand, national distribution was phased gradually into the company's twenty-one sales regions according to growing productive capacity.

QUESTIONS

1. List and describe briefly the steps involved in the development and testing of a new food product. Evaluate the procedures employed by General Mills for Wondra and the snack products.
2. Distinguish between laboratory consumer tests and test-marketing and explain how the differences affect interpretation of test results.
3. Wondra's failure to win consumer acceptance can be attributed to what principal cause or causes?
4. How might General Mills have avoided consumer dissatisfaction due to stock shortages?

20.

Texize Chemicals, Inc. (A)

Introducing a New Cleaning Product

Texize Chemicals, Inc., producers of a variety of industrial and consumer products, was considering the possibility of introducing a heavy-duty liquid household cleaning product. The product which the company executives were evaluating was somewhat unusual in that it was of the strength traditionally sold only for industrial markets. As a consumer product, it would be superconcentrated and designed for extremely difficult household jobs. The company anticipated selling the product through the same channels which handle much milder cleaning products. Company executives decided that the revolutionary product idea should undergo rather extensive testing.

Texize's Product Line

The company's first entry into the consumer market, after its beginning as a manufacturer of textile sizing, was an all-purpose liquid cleanser under the *Texize* label in 1948. Other consumer products followed: *Care*, a non-chlorine bleach; *Pine Oil Disinfectant;* and *Fluf* laundry rinse. The firm also manufactured rug cleaners, starches, and window cleaners. All of the products were sold on a regional level.

Several years ago, Texize introduced its first nationally advertised product: *K2r Spot Lifter*. The product was successful in revitalizing what had been a rather static spot remover market. Less than two years later, a second product was promoted nationally: *Fantastik* spray cleaner. The company considered both of these products successes.

Market Analyses

One of the earliest decisions that had to be made was whether or not a significant opportunity existed in the liquid cleaner market. In order to evaluate the extent of the opportunity, several types of market analyses were undertaken. Based on the replies of housewives who had used all-purpose cleaning products in the last month, it was determined that liquid cleaners were favored in the home. The data are presented in Exhibit 1.

At the time of this analysis, the market for household cleaners was divided, based on dollar volume, as shown in Exhibit 2.

The market analyses provided some interesting information. For example, liquid cleaners, based on dollar volume, held the greatest percentage of the total market. However, the most popular cleaner of all was a powder—Spic and Span. A significant competitive consideration was that the typical powder has to be dissolved in water before use, an obvious inconvenience. The Texize product, because of its great strength, would also have to be combined with water for most applications. Thus, it could be speculated that a liquid Texize product would have no great advantage over a powder—at least in terms of ease of application.

Obviously, profitability was an important consideration to Texize. The market analysis yielded these estimates. In terms of total tonnage produced, sprays accounted for 22 percent, powders for 29 percent, and liquids for 49 percent of total production. Based on dollar retail sales, sprays accounted for 29 percent, powders for 22 percent, and liquids for 49 percent. However, estimates of profit pointed to a weakness of powders. Sprays accounted for 36 percent, powders for 18 percent, and liquids for 46 percent of total retail profits.

On a unit sale basis, the leading powder, selling at fifty-nine cents, returned a profit of nearly ten cents to the retailer. The leading liquid yielded a profit per unit sale of twelve cents when selling at sixty-nine cents. It was estimated that the Texize product, if sold as a liquid for eighty-nine cents, would provide a profit per unit of 22.6 cents.

The company officials also noted that, in the year preceding, sales volume of liquid cleaners had dropped by over 12 percent. In the same period, sales of powdered cleaners had decreased by almost 3 percent. The most significant sales increase had been obtained by spray cleaners. Several officials worried that the figures indicated a growing consumer dissatisfaction with liquids which would adversely affect the new Texize product. Others, however, felt that the data indicated a weakness in the appeal of the other brands, thus leaving a substantial market opportunity for Texize.

Based on the above considerations, Texize decided that an excellent opportunity was present in the liquid cleaner market. Therefore, all further tests were undertaken with the product in liquid form.

The Concept Test

A variety of research procedures were planned to test certain aspects of the product and its probability of acceptance by consumers. Included was a "concept test," in which housewives were asked whether the concept of an industrial-strength cleaner for household use was attractive to them. The study was performed by an independent research organization.

For purposes of the test, the following description was presented to housewives:

> A superconcentrated liquid cleaner, formulated for heavy-duty industrial use, now is available to homemakers. It's for the difficult jobs like grease-soaked garage floors . . . even car engines caked with greasy dirt . . . as well as those tough cleaning chores inside the home, including wax stripping. Just mix with water as directed. No rinsing necessary. Ideal for preparing surfaces for painting. Gives your detergent a boost when laundry is heavily soiled. Rubber gloves recommended for prolonged use. This cleaner comes in a quart size and sells for eighty-nine cents.

The question was then asked: "Which of the following statements best describes how you would feel about buying this new heavy duty cleaner?" The results are shown in Exhibit 3. The company was encouraged by the fact that 41 percent expressed a strong interest in purchasing the product.

The data were then classified according to such demographic factors as age of respondent, economic status, race, and family size. The company felt that breakdowns of data shown in Exhibits 4 and 5 were of particular interest.

Performance Evaluations

It was apparent to company executives that competition in the household cleaner industry was strong. Consumers who sought a cleaning product which would handle the tougher household cleaning jobs would not be satisfied unless the product performed as they had anticipated. The major performance test utilized was the Gardner Scrubbability Test. The procedure involves three steps:

1. A standard soil is applied and dried on standard white tiles under strict laboratory conditions.
2. The tiles are equally machine-scrubbed with the test products mixed to use recommendations.
3. Light reflectance from the tiles is measured after drying. The greater the light reflectance number, the whiter the test tile—hence, *cleaner.*

Texize management considered the differences in the performances of the products tested, as shown in Exhibit 6, to be "significant."

In a further test, 501 housewives in five test cities (New York, Chicago, Dallas, St. Louis, and Los Angeles) received a 32-oz. size of industrial strength cleaner for use in their homes. They were to use the product over an extended period of time. Intentions of the housewives to buy an industrial strength cleaner were determined prior to and after the extended use.

Prior to use of the product, 57 percent of the housewives said they "definitely" or "most likely" would buy such a cleaner, 25 percent said "I think I might," and 18 percent expressed doubt or definitely had no intention to buy. After the cleaner had been used extensively, intentions were again solicited and positive intentions calculated. Those who then stated "definitely" or "most likely" are shown in Exhibit 7.

Therefore, although over 30 percent of the early "intenders" no longer were strongly in favor of the product after using it extensively, many who had expressed some earlier hesitation apparently had been won over by the product.

Further, it was found that the Texize product was preferred for certain types of cleaning jobs. For cleaning grease-soaked floors, 60 percent of the housewives preferred the product over their usual brand. Sixty-six percent preferred the new product over their regular brands for wax stripping jobs, and 40 percent preferred the industrial-strength cleaner for tough laundry jobs.

The Texize executives found it especially interesting that users of the leading powder cleaner (Spic and Span) were especially favorable in their opinions of the industrial-strength cleaner, as shown in Exhibit 8.

Test of Consumer Satisfaction with All-purpose Cleaners

It was felt that the degree of satisfaction provided by household cleaners currently in use by housewives was an important issue if the new product were to be accepted. Eighty-seven percent of all housewives interviewed were using household cleaners. The brands being used and the extent of their usage is shown in Exhibit 9.

The housewives who reported that they presently used household cleaners were asked: "Now speaking about the brand of cleaning product you presently use, how effective would you say this brand is as an all-purpose cleaner?" The results are shown in Exhibit 10. It appeared from the data that most housewives felt that the all-purpose cleaners performed satisfactorily. However, it was commonly accepted that consumers regularly changed brands and continued to look for the "perfect product." As a result, the questions of consumer satisfaction and brand loyalty were not completely resolved by the test.

Other Considerations

Certain other factors entered into the decision whether or not to proceed with the marketing of the product. For example, the effect of sales of the new product upon sales of the already successful Texize product—Fantastik—was uncertain. Although Fantastik was a spray cleaner and the new product would be a liquid, some competition was inevitable.

Another factor was the internal competition for the Texize promotion dollar. With several products in the consumer cleaner market, all in need of significant promotional effort, some expressed concern that promotional dollars would be spread too thin.

Finally, there was some question as to whether more tests ought to be undertaken before taking the next important step: test-marketing. The plans for test-marketing involved introducing the product in a test area which covered nearly 30 percent of the household cleaner market. Thus, even the test-marketing necessitated a major commitment of funds.

The Decision

Texize officials, after evaluating the test results, decided to enter immediately into test marketing of the industrial strength cleaner. The test-markets were to include nearly 30 percent of the household cleaner market. It was felt that there was sufficient evidence of consumer willingness to try the product and of the relative effectiveness of the product to justify taking this next step. At the same time, however, they recognized the inherent risks in the decision.

QUESTIONS

1. Evaluate the conclusions drawn from the market analyses. Did the data on market shares and profitability indicate a market opportunity for another liquid cleaner?
2. Do you agree with the company's decision to go ahead with test-marketing of the product? Were the test results favorable enough to justify the company's action?
3. Evaluate the data derived from the performance tests and the company's interpretation of them.

EXHIBIT 1
Type of All-purpose Cleaner Used

Type	Percent
Fingertip spray	18
Aerosol foam	7
Liquid	62
Powder	52
Other	1
	140*

*Total exceeds 100 percent due to multiple responses.

EXHIBIT 2
Market Shares by Brand and Product Type

Spray Cleaners	Share of All Cleaners (%)	Share of Sprays (%)
Fantastik	7.8	25.7
Formula 409	7.2	24.1
Cinch	4.1	13.5
All other sprays	11.1	36.7
	30.2	100.0

All-purpose Liquids	Share of All Cleaners (%)	Share of Liquids (%)
Mr. Clean	9.0	22.0
Top Job	10.6	25.9
Ajax Liquid	11.6	28.4
All other liquids	9.5	23.7
	40.7	100.0

Powdered Cleaners	Share of All Cleaners (%)	Share of Powders (%)
Spic and Span	18.0	72.4
All other powders	6.9	27.6
	24.9	100.0

EXHIBIT 3
Intentions to Buy Industrial-strength Cleaner

Statement	Percent of Housewives
I definitely would buy it	19
I most likely would buy it	22
I think I might buy it	20
I doubt that I would buy it	18
I definitely would not buy it	18
Don't know	3
Total	100

EXHIBIT 4
Comparison of Intentions by Family Size*

Statements	Family Size					
	1-2	3	4	5	6	7+
I definitely would buy it	14	22	24	16	23	23
I most likely would buy it	17	26	24	32	17	26
I think I might buy it	17	15	23	27	31	23
I doubt that I would buy it	21	22	15	12	17	14
I definitely would not buy it	28	13	12	11	11	11
Don't know	3	2	2	2	1	3
Total	100%	100%	100%	100%	100%	100%

*Of all housewives responding, 36 percent had one or two children, 17 percent had three children, 19 percent had four, 12 percent had five, 7 percent had six, and 9 percent had seven or more.

EXHIBIT 5
Comparison of Intentions by Age Group*

	Age					
Statements	Under 25	25-34	35-44	45-54	55-64	65 & over
I definitely would buy it	22	22	18	21	20	10
I most likely would buy it	26	29	26	19	20	10
I think I might buy it	22	22	25	20	18	15
I doubt that I would buy it	17	17	14	23	15	23
I definitely would not buy it	9	8	15	14	25	38
Don't know	4	2	2	3	2	4
Total	100%	100%	100%	100%	100%	100%

*Ten percent of the housewives interviewed were under twenty-five years old, 20 percent were 25-34, 22 percent were 35-44, 19 percent were 45-54, 14 percent were 55-64, and 15 percent were 65 and over.

EXHIBIT 6
Performance in Gardner Scrubbability Test

Product	Light Reflectance or Performance at 45 Scrub Cycles
Leading liquid	62.3
Leading powder	63.1
Texize industrial-strength cleaner	65.5

EXHIBIT 7
Change in Intentions to Buy after Extended Use

Purchase Intention Prior to Use	Intention Definitely and Most Likely After Use
Definitely and most likely (57 percent)	64%
I think I might (25 percent)	53%
Doubt and definitely not (18 percent)	42%

EXHIBIT 8
Preference for Industrial Strength over Usual Brand

Brand Currently Being Used	Percent Preferring Industrial-strength Cleaner
Spic and Span	41
Ajax	38
Top Job	36
Mr. Clean	36

EXHIBIT 9
Extent of Cleaner Usage by Brand

Brand	Percent Using Cleaner
Spic and Span	41
Fantastik	11
Top Job	20
Ajax	36
Lestoil	8
Texize	4
Mr. Clean	21
Formula 409	12
Crew Bathroom Cleaner	4
Dow Bathroom Cleaner	7
Comet	2
Pinesol	2
Other	10

EXHIBIT 10
Degree of Effectiveness of Household Cleaner

Answer	Percent Replying
Very effective	81
Somewhat effective	11
Moderately effective	6
Not very effective	1
Not effective at all	1
	100

21.
The "Lint-Caddy"
Marketing a Specialty Item

A partnership involving two men is considering producing and marketing a device for the removal of lint and other foreign matter from clothing. It makes use of a thin, smooth-surfaced tape, coated with a pressure-sensitive adhesive material. It has tentatively been decided that the product will be called a "Lint-Caddy" or "Valet Lint-Caddy." Other names are under consideration. Complicating the venture is the fact that the partnership is faced with the problem of limited finances with which to produce and market the device.

It is the present purpose of the partners to investigate the potential market for the product, establish a selling price, and determine the proper channels of distribution. A description follows of all known factors to date, including research into several possible marketing alternatives.

Background

For nearly two years, the partners, both residents of the same city, have been considering the possibilities for their proposed product. Neither man is able to devote full time to the project; rather, work has been done during the hours spent away from their regular full-time jobs. Neither partner intends to devote full time to it in the near future—barring phenomenal success of the sales effort.

The affluence of the American people and the booming economy in recent years have increased demand for both convenience and specialty items. It is the desire of the partners to capitalize upon that demand. Present plans call for marketing of the product to begin approximately nine months hence, in the last quarter of 1970.

89

Description of the Product

The lint removal device as a finished product will consist of two flat pieces of extruded plastic approximately 1" wide and 5" long. One piece will be about $\frac{1}{2}$ inch in depth and the other $\frac{1}{8}$ inch. The latter piece will slide into the cutout portion of the former so that the overall dimensions when carried will be 1" x 5" x $\frac{1}{2}$" (See Exhibit 1).

Attached to one side of the smaller piece (hereafter referred to as the "slide") will be the "pad" of tape used for picking up the lint. This pad consists of any number of laminations of a thin, flexible material coated on one surface with an adhesive. It is presently planned to include 20 laminations on each pad.

The first lamination will be coated with the adhesive on both surfaces. In this way, the tape will adhere to the smaller part (slide) of the handle. The remaining 19 laminations will be coated on one side only and stacked one on top of the other with the adhesive side facing outward. The top lamination will have a flexible, protective covering to be "peeled off" to make the device ready for use.

A small portion at one end of each lamination shall be without adhesive. This will provide a "tab" to be pulled downward to remove each lamination after use. Each successive lamination will pull off one at a time.

When not in use, the pad and the slide will fit inside the larger handle (See Exhibit 1). To use, the pad is removed, turned upside down, and re-inserted with the laminated tape facing outward for immediate use. The article of clothing is "brushed" of all foreign matter in this fashion.

Competitive Products

The proposed lint remover will be marketed in direct competition with several other models and will rely on the distinguishing features enumerated below for product distinctiveness. Some other products will compete more indirectly. Descriptions of some of these will be given for purposes of comparison.

The greater share of competing products are of the roller-adhesive tape variety; that is, they use similar tape, but wrap it around a cylindrical "roller" to which handles of various sizes and shapes are attached. Thus, the device is *rolled* easily over the clothing to be cleaned, rather than being used as a "brush," as in the "Lint-Caddy." The rolling principle allows the user to follow the contours of the body effectively when cleaning.

These products provide 240 square inches of adhesive surface compared to the "Lint-Caddy's" 100 square inches. However, they are more difficult to prepare for use—tape must be lifted from the roller and unrolled to a certain length; then the used tape must be cut or torn off. Refills are available and can be prepared for use by pulling apart the halves of the roller, inserting the tape, snapping together the roller again, and unrolling the tape through a narrow opening in the roller to the necessary length. Most of these devices are larger than the "Lint-Caddy" and less convenient for carrying on the person.

Lint removers of the type described above as direct competitors include the "Lint Pic-Up" (produced by Helmac Products of Flint, Michigan, and Santa Barbara, California); the "Pixall" Lint Remover (made by Maywood Industries of Newport Beach, California); and another Maywood product featuring a smaller handle. All of these devices are sold at retail for $1.00.

There are several other devices that perform the same functions but do not use pressure-sensitive tape. Some are electrostatic devices; others employ a sponge rubber or plastic surface. All of the competitive products will be evaluated in determining marketing and pricing procedures.

Special Advantages of the "Lint-Caddy"

The decision to produce the product is dependent on the availability of a market for it. It is felt that the product has several distinct advantages over competing devices:

1. The "Lint-Caddy" has the advantage of being smaller and less bulky than other types. It can more easily be carried in pocket or purse to provide instant good grooming.
2. It is easy to prepare the tape for use. It is necessary only to take hold of a "tab" and pull off a used lamination to expose a new one. No cutting of tape is necessary.
3. Refills are easily applied to the handle and can be made available with various numbers of laminations.
4. The products can be made in several attractive colors.
5. The adhesive qualities of the tape compare favorably with any other product presently on the market.
6. Lower production costs will make the product available to the consumer at a low price in comparison to competitive products.
7. The product may be used effectively for "reminder-type" advertising. Space is available on the flat surfaces of the handle for any desired message.
8. The plastic handles are durable and should not chip or crack with normal usage.

Production Process

The construction of the handle portion of the product is relatively easy. Any one of several plastic extrusion companies in the area can perform the necessary production. Dies are to be used for all successive production runs.

The partnership plans to invest in a machine which will assemble the tape into the pads of twenty laminations each. In addition, it will attach the pads to the slides as desired and insert them into handles. It is estimated that the machine will require a $5,000 investment. Its estimated life will be five years.

It is intended that, in the beginning stages of production, the assembly machine will be maintained and operated in the garage of one of the partners. The machine is designed to assemble 300 pads of lint removers per hour. A lot will include 2,100 of them. The machine can be loaded by one man with ease and allowed to run for seven hours until one entire lot is completed. Packaging will then be undertaken in the desired manner and distribution begun from the place of production.

Per unit cost of assembly will, of course, depend upon the units assembled. It is hoped that 500,000 lint removers ultimately will be produced to reduce the machine investment per unit cost to one cent. Estimated costs of the operation for various output levels, along with time required, are shown below.

Output Level (Units)	Cost Per Unit	Machine Hours
5,000	$1.00	17
10,000	.50	33
25,000	.20	83
50,000	.10	177
100,000	.05	333
250,000	.02	833
500,000	.01	1,667
750,000	.007	2,500
1,000,000	.005	3,333

Patent Rights

The partnership has obtained a patent on its method of laminating the tape and attaching it to the handle. The patent protects, therefore, the process of attachment of laminations to the handle for 17 years. However, stacked pieces of adhesives can be used if the method of attachment is different. The partners feel that the patent will result in a distinct competitive advantage for the "Lint-Caddy."

Pilot Production Run

At the present time, a sample run of 2,000 units is being produced. The plastic handles are being extruded at a cost of approximately six cents per foot—or six cents per lint remover. The pads will be assembled manually and the entire device put together in the same way.

The pilot run will be used for purposes of studying the market, appraising customer acceptance, evaluating methods of distribution, and promoting the product's usefulness. The methods to be employed have not yet been determined.

Financing the Venture

Estimates have been obtained regarding all relevant factors of production. After the initial pilot run, the following costs will be incurred per unit produced.

Item	Per Unit Cost (cents)
Raw Materials	
Plastic Handles (2 pieces)	1.666
Tape Pad (20 laminations)	2.777
Labor Estimate	1.000
Assembly (@500,000 u. production)	1.000
Packaging	0.500
Total	6.943

The variable costs listed above will apply to each unit produced in the future. Other variable costs include advertising, distribution, special packaging if desired, and printing of advertising on the handle or slide. These costs are dependent on the channels of distribution chosen and the desired appearance of the product when presented for sale.

The partners are operating on a limited budget of $10,000 for the entire project. It is intended to be a relatively short-term project (2 to 5 years) according to present plans, with long-run considerations depending on its success. The partners do not intend to invest more than $10,000; however, in the event of a very profitable project, additional financing would be considered. To help in determining any possible need for funds, costs incurred to date and a description of proposed future expenditures follows.

Expenditures To Date

Legal Fees	
Patent Search	$ 55
Patent Filing Fees	300
Pilot Run	
Extruded Handles	120
(2,000 @ 6¢)	
Tape	56
(2,000 @ 2.8¢)	
	$ 531

Future Expenditures

Assembly Machine	$5,000
Market Research (Pilot Run)	unknown
Initial Advertising	unknown
Distribution Costs	unknown

As shown above, costs-to-date plus anticipated outlays total $5,531, leaving $4,469 of the original $10,000 available. The amount of advertising, research, and so forth, undertaken will depend on how long the funds hold out—or the willingness of the partners to obtain more funds.

In the event that further financing is desired, several sources of funds are available—but at considerable cost. An investigation of several of these sources produced some useful information. Commercial banks expressed differing opinions; however, the most representative response is summarized below.

The bank would require collateral, either in the form of insurance policies, negotiable securities, or personal savings. It would be prepared to loan approximately 90 percent of the surrender value of the insurance policy, 65 percent of the market value of the securities, and nearly 100 percent of the savings. Interest rates would be between $8\frac{3}{4}$ and 9 percent per annum. The loan would be a six-month renewable term loan. To obtain the renewal, a payment must be made (approximately 10 percent) every six months.

Another alternative might be a long-term loan secured by real estate. It would involve a first-mortgage arrangement for 10 to 15 years. Up to 60 percent of the value of the real estate can be loaned at an interest rate slightly above the prime rate (around 8 percent). In addition, under both conditions, the bank would require personal financial statements of both partners plus endorsement of the note by both partners and their wives to protect against risk of default.

It is anticipated that funds could also be obtained from finance companies, savings and loan firms, and insurance companies at slightly higher rates. Further investigation is needed.

Pricing Considerations

Pricing techniques may depend, in part, upon the channels of distribution which are chosen. It is intended that the lower costs of the "Lint-Caddy" will enable it to be sold under the price of competitive products. However, the partners are considering both "penetration" and "skimming" pricing. Prices to wholesalers, retailers, or firms which would use the "Lint-Caddy" for promotional purposes would vary considerably. It is hoped that market research, using the pilot production run of 2,000 lint removers, will provide pricing information.

Market Research

Due to the unavailability of sample products, limited market research has been undertaken. However, it is estimated by a reputable advertising agency that between 80 and 90 percent of specialty items of this nature are purchased by women. Men do not, as a rule, seek out the items in a store. In addition, the advertising agency feels that the product would be somewhat seasonal in nature, due to the preponderance of heavy, dark clothing which is worn and picks up lint, and so forth in the winter.

Promotion and Packaging

The partners do not intend to advertise their product extensively. Point-of-purchase advertising, accomplished only by a paper-board card to which the Lint-Caddy is attached as a "package," is the only activity planned at this time. However, some promotion or test advertising may be considered for the pilot production run.

Channels of Distribution

It is the aim of the partners to market the product on a nationwide basis through yet to be decided channels. In addition, using the lint remover as an advertising specialty item and selling to industrial firms, etc., is being considered. Following is a description of alternative channels along with relevant research data.

The volume of production to be undertaken will vary according to distribution plans. In most cases, economies can be realized with higher volumes. The goal of nationwide distribution could be reached in several ways.

It is felt by the partners that extensive research is required before marketing can be undertaken. It is important that sales, costs, advertising, transportation costs, and market coverage be ascertained. Several channels of distribution under consideration are enumerated below.

1. Small-scale retailers
2. Chain stores
3. Department stores
4. Mail-order houses
5. Supermarkets
6. Specialty advertising vendors
7. Motel or hotel chains

In addition to the above channels, the partners are considering direct sales to industrial firms, service organizations, and so forth, for promotional uses. Thus, selling to wholesalers, jobbers, manufacturers' agents, or direct selling are all feasible channels.

QUESTIONS

1. What do you consider to be the most significant problems confronting the partners in the marketing of the "Lint-Caddy"?
2. Develop a complete marketing program for the "Lint-Caddy," beginning at the present "pilot stage" and carrying it through to eventual placement of the device for sale.
3. Evaluate the chances of success in marketing the product.

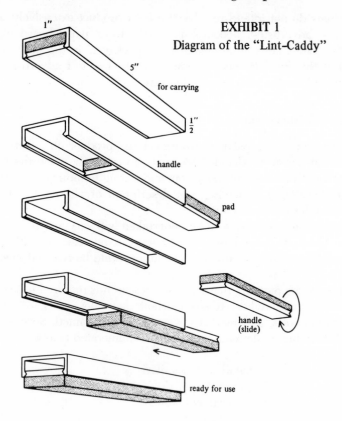

EXHIBIT 1
Diagram of the "Lint-Caddy"

22.

Melbestos, Inc.

Planning for a New Product Introduction

Background

In May 1967, a talented chemist and eight other local citizens obtained a $270,000 Small Business Administration loan for the purpose of manufacturing a new, decorative, customized wall tile developed by the chemist. The wall tile, called Ornatile, is a unique product that consists of an asbestos-based back fused with a decorated melamine surface. Melamine, the same material used for surfaces on Formica, Micarta, and Textolite, is very versatile in that it allows practically any combination of color and design to be "printed" on the surface of the tile. In addition to its many color and design combinations, Ornatile, unlike ordinary ceramic tile, is also considered break-resistant because of its melamine content. The break-resistant quality of melamine has been proven effective in other uses such as in Mel-mac dinnerware.

Ornatile had been in the process of development for nearly ten years and had proven itself through extensive product testing to be an outstanding building product. Over its testing period, Ornatile had been installed in bathrooms in place of the usual ceramic tile. The occupants of the "test homes" reported virtually no cracking of the tile squares over the years, which was not typical of most ceramic tile installations. In the kitchens of these test homes, Ornatile was applied to walls around electric and gas ranges, as well as on the walls between cabinets and Formica counter tops. Housewives of the test homes reported that Ornatile in the kitchen made cleaning much easier than when the walls were painted with ordinary gloss enamel. Moreover, because of its asbestos backing, walls covered with Ornatile were considered virtually fireproof.

Because of Ornatile's unique product advantages, the business partners felt that it would be a potential strong competitor in the wall tile market. Accordingly, the partners drew up detailed plans for beginning the production and distribution of Ornatile. The following paragraphs outline their plans.

Cost Projections

The small, experimental production facilities used to develop Ornatile and produce it in small sample quantities have provided the basis on which production plans and production cost estimates are made. These facilities, including materials and labor for samples of Ornatile, cost $20,000. Of the remaining $250,000 of the loan, the company plans to use $150,000 for plant production equipment (exclusive of a building) and $100,000 for operating funds to cover wages, raw materials, salesmen's salaries, and other operating expenses.

Cost projections for production and distribution operations are shown in Exhibits 1 and 2. Exhibit 1 shows the direct, variable costs of materials and labor associated with the production of Ornatile. For the most part, labor rates shown are for semiskilled labor. The only skilled labor required is for the printing operation. Material costs per 1,000 pieces are based on order quantities of sufficient size to take advantage of quantity discounts, but small enough to keep storage costs and capital invested in inventory at a low level. Exhibit 2 summarizes the various costs and projects the anticipated profit when the builder's price for the tile is $1.20 per square foot.

Production Process

The face designs for the various tiles are printed on a two-color press which yields nine prints per sheet. These sheets, along with the tile face covers, are impregnated with resin at moderate temperatures. The covers and face prints are then cut into nine individual tile facings. For the tile base, predetermined quantities of asbestos and resin are blended at moderate temperatures and pre-formed into rough-shaped tile squares. The molding process bonds the tile cover and printed facing to the body of the tile. The high temperatures used in this molding process not only provide an inseparable bond, but also harden the asbestos-resin tile body material. After removal from the molding presses, a pair of which produces 700 square feet of tile per eight-hour shift, the tiles are allowed to cool. After cooling, the tile edges are smoothed by a sanding operation which eliminates the rough edges and molding marks made by the molding presses. The tiles are then inspected for defects; and acceptable tiles are packed in boxes and labeled as to the tile face pattern and colors.

These techniques for producing Ornatile at price and quality levels comparable with other wall tile materials are based on twelve years of laboratory and pilot production experience. These production methods and a plant housing facility of 10,000 square feet will potentially allow the firm to produce 100,000 square feet of tile per month. The plant is designed to allow for rapid future expansion if consumer demand for Ornatile warrants it.

Inventories

Each of the items of raw materials is a standard commodity and has more than one large supplier close enough to the plant site to allow rapid and continuous delivery at competitive prices. Thus, virtually no inventory of raw materials will have to be maintained.

Except for a few patterns of Ornatile known to be fast-moving, no inventory of finished tile will be maintained. Only the printed stock or printed pattern sheets will be inventoried; and this will be at a carrying cost of $35 per thousand square feet. Without special effort and at no additional cost, the printed stock, which has an unlimited shelf life, can be converted into Ornatile and shipped within two days. With this type of operation the firm can maintain an unusually low inventory of finished tile and, at the same time, provide customized manufacturing and delivery of the product to the customer. This will allow the firm to minimize the amount of money invested in inventory stockpiles and to provide personalized service for each customer. The unique production capability provides for production of Ornatile in limitless patterns and without excessive cost. As a result of this unusual flexibility, the company expects to be able to supply special patterns for chains of restaurants, motels, and other such establishments.

Market and Competition

The national market for wall tile is some 400,000,000 square feet annually. Thus, Ornatile is a product that will be competing in a very large market; however, it can be a highly profitable one even if sold to a relatively small part of the market. Based on this market size, the projected maximum sales volume for Ornatile is only 0.2 percent of this total, or approximately 800,000 square feet. Keeping this in mind and considering the limited plant capacity, the partners considered it wise to sell Ornatile as a specialty product to carefully selected outlets. In anticipation of beginning production, missionary sales effort has already been expended with potential customers, so that the firm will be able to direct its early sales efforts to fruitful markets.

Competition consists primarily of ceramic tile manufacturers which, at present, dominate the market for wall tile and wall-covering material. However, management feels strongly that Ornatile's unique features will make it easy for the firm to enter the market quickly. First, the firm's

ability to match and repeat colors cannot be approached by even the best of ceramic tile manufacturers. Second, the capability of supplying special customer-designed patterns and unlimited decorative possibilities provide the company with a formidable competitive advantage that none of the other tile producers have. Third, most ceramic tile is priced at retail between $2 and $10 per square foot, depending on the color and decoration on the tile. Most tile applications sell for $2.50 to $3.50 per square foot. Ornatile, regardless of color or face decoration, will sell at a price somewhere in this range—probably around $3 per square foot. This price level does not apply to specially ordered, customer-designed tile which will be priced slightly higher because of the special work required for the duplication of the customer's art work on the firm's facilities. Because of the product's unique features, it is expected that Ornatile will have little trouble in carving its own competitive niche in the market for tile wallcovering.

A great deal of time has already been spent to determine the proper use for Ornatile and the most effective way to reach selected markets. About two years were required to convert the first molded Ornatile into a satisfactory building product and to learn how it should be presented to the builder. During this period, Melbestos developed the proper method of application, learned the proper base materials on which to mount Ornatile, and began to recognize the proper market group on which to concentrate the sales effort.

Though Ornatile has been used successfully in almost every tile application, including bathroom applications, experience indicates that the most logical place for Ornatile in the home is in the kitchen. There appears to be no firmly accepted product for use behind the kitchen range or between Formica counter tops and kitchen cabinets. The company's ability to coordinate tile patterns with a variety of kitchen decors should provide a strong sales appeal to potential customers.

The problem of establishing a quality image for a new product should be more easily solved for Ornatile because it has seen limited use for over ten years. Based on reports from product users, management has concluded that it is absolutely necessary to get Ornatile into the hands of potential users before any sales effort is made. The company's experience has been that once potential users have handled Ornatile, they need no further assurance of its quality. In addition, Miracle Adhesives Corporation, which supplies mastic and grout materials to Melbestos, has an outstanding reputation of its own. Melbestos' association with this reputable company has opened many doors for Ornatile and will continue to do much to establish its reputation for quality.

To build quality into Ornatile, the company has compiled building specifications and installation instructions based on its ten years' experience and with the help of many architects, builders, material suppliers, testing laboratories, and Formica personnel. The testimony and reputation of these professionals, along with the firm's association with the Miracle Adhesive name, should provide an early boost for the quality reputation of Ornatile.

Distribution Outlets

Eventually, the firm plans to distribute Ornatile through all of the outlets listed below; however, the initial sales effort will be concentrated only on those which will yield the most immediate results.

1. *Project Builders.* In every geographic area, there is at least one builder who takes the lead in selling attractive homes. The company contacted many of these builders, most of whom indicated strong interest in kitchen improvement. It is maintained by Melbestos management that if the key builders endorse Ornatile, other builders in the area will soon follow.

2. *Kitchen Specialists.* In most large metropolitan areas, there are concerns which specialize in kitchen modernization and new kitchens of superior design. These should represent a fertile market for the initial selling effort.

3. *Commercial Outlets.* Professional decorators and architects have shown much interest in Ornatile for commercial uses in lobbies and washrooms. In this respect, the negligible extra cost of special design for restaurants and motel chains gives the firm a unique sales position with these institutions. As a selling point to these institutions, the company will point to the Quality Courts Motels' ten-year experience with Ornatile.

4. *Tile Dealers.* In areas in which good tile dealers are available, they will be included in the sales effort on a "time available" basis. Although at some point in time these outlets will be a major sales factor, they will play little part in the early sales program.

5. *Furniture Dealers.* The company feels that a significant market for Ornatile exists with these dealers.

Initially, the firm's capabilities will not allow distribution to all of these outlets. Therefore, its immediate goal will be to make the easier sales first; later, it will attempt a deeper market penetration through additional outlets. Therefore, project builders will be the first of these distribution outlets contacted by the salesmen. Other accounts will be cultivated as Ornatile begins to take its place in the market.

Salesmen

In planning the sales program, Melbestos followed the lead of several successful concerns, particularly one very successful firm which sells kitchen cabinets and accessories. Although firms of this type are virtually unknown to retail consumers, they are among the most profitable in the industry. Essentially, their approach is to avoid advertising to the myriad of retail outlets and to concentrate instead on selling to the large, responsible users. Today, a small number of users are purchasing over 50 percent of the total volume of building products. Companies which sell to these large purchasers use a few, highly qualified salesmen to give close personal attention to these users.

The firm soon plans to use two salesmen who are highly qualified in the field of building products. Projected salary and commissions for each of them amounts to $20,000 for a projected monthly sales volume of 20,000 square feet. In addition, $13,000 is anticipated for travel and promotional expenses for each of them. Backing these men with sales promotion and sales presentation ideas will be a professional staff designer.

Only one salesman will be hired initially. He will be retained to call on large project builders and other prospects in order to generate immediate sales. As sales volume begins to build, the salesman will begin prospecting for new potential customers. The second salesman will be added when sales volume reaches a satisfactory level. Deeper market penetration will be required as the firm takes on additional sales personnel. Each salesman's territory will be adjusted in size so that his market penetration efforts can be focused on a smaller territory. Although their territories will be reduced over time, each man's sales volume will be expected to remain at least equal to past levels.

There are many experienced men available to fill these sales positions, and the firm is considering a few specific individuals. Currently, the market is slow for manufacturers' representatives in the building products market; thus, many of the good men who left corporate sales for "tenpercenting" are now available for selection.

Before any man is placed in the field to sell Ornatile, he will be required to understand thoroughly the properties and uses of Ornatile as described in the sales training booklet. He also is to be reasonably proficient in the actual installation of the tile.

Salesmen will sell Ornatile only if Miracle Adhesive mastic and grout are purchased along with the tile. This policy is set in order to insure top quality installations through the use of proper materials. Moreover, salesmen must oversee installations by each new installer to make sure they use proper techniques in applying Ornatile. Each salesman will be responsible for servicing both installations and complaints for every application of Ornatile within his territory regardless of how the tile got there or who was paid a commission on the sale.

Advertising and Sales Promotion

Initially, advertising will be limited to a frequently published catalog which will be printed as soon as the production facilities are completed.

This catalog will include full product description, architectural details for the proper use of Ornatile, specifications, installation instructions, and a full listing of standard design patterns and colors. Prospects will be mailed a catalog as well as samples of Ornatile prior to being called on by one of the salesmen.

It is believed that the best means of promoting the sale of Ornatile is to attractively install it where it will be seen by many people. With this in mind, the firm has budgeted a quantity of tile to each salesman to give away for display purposes in model homes, department store exhibits, and plumbing and other trade shows.

In addition, it has been found that Ornatile, when backed with a cork pad material, makes an excellent coaster for the coffee and drink cups of building and design personnel who occupy desks or drawing boards. On a continuing basis, Melbestos plans to furnish these coasters, which will have the Ornatile trademark on each face, free to all customers and sales prospects.

Ornatile will be sold F.O.B. plant on terms of 2 percent, 10–net thirty. A 5 percent discount will be given for firm orders delivered at the company's option within sixty days.

Sales will be accepted initially at base price for any increment of the standard package of ten square feet of Ornatile. Later, as sales volume increases, a system of quantity discounts will be introduced to encourage large quantity buying.

Analysis of Early Sales Results

In March 1968, the plant began production. The first salesman was hired and began generating sales volume as well as some new sales prospects. In June, a second salesman was hired.

In the first ten months of production and distribution, the company experienced some success, but also some problems. Overall, the business partners were disappointed. Sales lagged severely and sales personnel reported extreme difficulty in penetrating the market. In early 1969, one of the salesmen was released because the company could not generate enough volume to warrant keeping him on.

Other signs were present which indicated that the firm would be in danger of bankruptcy unless sales picked up dramatically. The managers were greatly concerned over the firm's future.

QUESTIONS

1. What explanation can you offer for Ornatile's poor sales performance during its first year of operation?

2. What do you consider to be the major and minor problems now confronting Melbestos?
3. Based on your own inquiry into the market for tile and other wall coverings, what do you think are the future prospects for Ornatile?

EXHIBIT 1
Variable Direct Costs

LABOR

Operation	Rate/hour	Time (in hours) /1,000 pcs.	Cost/1,000 pcs.	
1. Printing, 2-color, 9-up	$3.50	0.15	$ 0.53	
2. Impregnate and die-cut cover	2.20	0.30	0.66	
3. Impregnate and die-cut print	2.20	0.84	1.85	
4. Blending and pre-forming	2.20	1.44	3.17	
5. Molding (1 pair of 150-ton presses w/6 cavities each, 63 seconds)	2.20	1.44	3.17	
6. Sanding, inspecting, packing and labeling	2.20	1.44	3.17	
Rejects (estimated @ 5%)			0.63	
			$13.18	$13.18

MATERIALS

Paper, resin, etc., for cover sheet	$ 1.40	
Paper, resin, ink, etc., for print sheets	6.07	
Molding compound for 70 gram tile, 25% resin	15.70	
Packing material	3.75	
Rejects (estimated @ 5%)	1.35	
	$28.27	$28.27

Total Variable Direct Costs per 1,000 Pieces $41.45*

---

*Since there are eight pieces of 4¼" x 4¼" Ornatile to each square foot, $41.45/1,000 pieces equals 33.2¢/square foot.

EXHIBIT 2
Projected Costs and Profits

	Cents/sq. ft.
Labor and material	33.2
General plant	23.2
Administrative, sales & finance	36.8
Profit	26.8
Sales price*	120.0

*For ordinary full production operation, 80 percent of full capacity will be used or approximately 45,000 square feet per month or 540,000 square feet annually. Based on this figure, annual net sales are projected to be $648,000 with net profit estimated at $140,289.

DEVELOPMENT
OF MARKETING CHANNELS

23.

The Pichard Company
Considering Changes in a Distribution System

The Pichard Company is a relatively small distributor of a fine line of European china and glassware which it imports from Venice, London, Prague, and other continental cities. During its thirty-year history, the company has built up a reputation for handling distinctive merchandise. Its domestic customers include some china and glassware wholesalers, hundreds of gift buyers for department stores, and several thousand smaller neighborhood gift shops located mostly in the South, Southwest, and Midwest. Currently, about 60 percent of its sales are made to these smaller shops. These three types of customers have always been contacted and products sold directly through a company sales force which has gradually expanded to twenty men. The company's net sales volume for 1969 was over $1,000,000.

In February 1970, Fred Pichard, the founder and president of the company, called a meeting of his executive committee to consider: (1) the advisability of making some radical changes in the company's distribution methods, and (2) the long-run effect of accepting large orders for china and glassware from chain discount houses on total sales and profitability.

The search for a more economical channel of distribution was dictated by the rapidly rising costs of maintaining a sales force. In 1960, for instance, it cost Pichard $300 in expense payments per month to keep a salesman on the road. The salesman received a commission of 15 percent of sales, an average of $700 per month. By 1968, it had become increasingly difficult to recruit, train, and retain highly productive salesmen. Road expenses had jumped to $500 per month. Salesmen were still paid the same 15 percent commission rate, and total sales volume had increased by 40 percent from its 1960 level. However, much of this volume increase was due to price inflation.

Due to the declining effectiveness of direct selling, the president wanted his executive committee to consider the feasibility of handling at least a part of the company's sales volume through exhibitions of the company's products at trade shows. It was now possible for a company to exhibit its wares at thirty shows set up periodically in leading cities throughout the country.

A recent article in *Gifts and Decorative Accessories* had caught the attention of the president and led him to speculate whether his small company could afford to display its merchandise to potential store buyers at these exhibitions. The article, while obviously written by a proponent of this type of distribution, did show that trade shows were becoming increasingly popular with retail buyers, and that attendance at these exhibitions was increasing rapidly. When buyers are in their home stores, they spend much of their time planning promotions and waiting on customers. Consequently, they cannot give their full attention to the presentations of visiting salesmen. It is easier for the buyers to occasionally leave their departments in the hands of assistants to free themselves for a several-day trip to exhibition cities. At these shows, they can inspect and make their selections from a wide merchandise assortment made up of the offerings of many wholesalers and importers who display their wares in adjacent booths in a large auditorium or warehouse.

Another method of lowering costs, which was being considered, was to turn to jobbers entirely for physical distribution. There are china and glassware jobbers in most of the larger cities. These jobbers are primarily order takers, and they can easily contact the thousands of small gift shops located within a 150-mile radius of the warehouse city. Pichard tries to maintain selling expenses at 25 percent of net sales, but recently these costs have risen to nearly 30 percent. For a 15 percent margin, the jobber would relieve the Pichard Company of most of its selling costs.

The next item of business which Mr. Pichard wishes to put before the executive committee is a review of the firm's pricing policy. While approximately half of the states in which Pichard china and glassware are sold no longer have effective fair trade laws, the company has continued to protect its wholesale and retail customers by suggesting prices that allow everyone a reasonable markup.

However, in January 1970, the Pichard executives were approached by an executive from the Detroit buying headquarters of the S. S. Kresge Company, which wants to purchase the Pichard lines of glassware and china in large quantities for resale through its 400-unit, K-mart discount department store chain. The K-mart chain is expanding rapidly by adding about fifty new stores annually. While the acceptance of this order will revoke a long-standing policy of loyalty to its smaller customers, management is strongly tempted to accept the order. Selling costs have risen, and the profit margin is being squeezed to the point where it will soon disappear altogether unless some meaningful changes are made in the immediate future.

Kresge's initial order would be for $100,000 worth of merchandise at a price that is approximately 10 percent less than what the company harges for large orders to its regular customers. Moreover, if the door to iscount selling is opened, management can expect that sales in this cateory will increase to over $200,000. However, in order to gain this added olume, the Pichard Company will have to expect to lose some of its busiess from regular customers who buy and resell at higher prices than do le discount stores. Management is also aware of the fact that many of le families who patronize the small gift shops want novel designs and :e willing to pay a higher price for something distinctive.

QUESTIONS

What are the advantages and disadvantages of dropping direct selling and switching entirely to jobber distribution?

What are the advantages and disadvantages of using trade shows as a method of selling china and glassware? If you were a member of the Pichard executive committee, what decision would you recommend with regard to the use of trade shows?

Since Pichard Company is a small importer and distributor of china and glassware, one executive serves both as controller and marketing manager. Assume that you hold this position and are asked to analyze the long-run effects on sales and profitability of accepting large orders from chain discount houses. What recommendation would you make to the executive committee?

24.

Plantex Corporation

Changing Garden Supply Distribution Channel

The Plantex Corporation distributed its Plant-Gro line of garden supplie through 35,000 authorized retail dealers across the United States. Th Plant-Gro line was composed of Plant-Gro—plant food, Weedban—weedi cide, and Pestban—insecticide. These products made up a widely adver tised line of home garden supplies which was sold to consumers throug] garden supply retailers and nurseries.

At this time, supermarkets were diversifying rapidly into nonfood line: Supermarkets were becoming one-stop retail outlets where many house hold purchases could be made rather than just food items. As yet, no lin of garden supplies was handled by any of the major supermarket chains

Some Plantex executives suggested that supermarkets be added to th established authorized dealer distribution system. The proposal involve selling directly to large supermarket chains such as A&P, Kroger's, an Safeway, in addition to continuing to support the selling efforts of Plante dealers. Their reasons for suggesting the addition of supermarkets were (1) their belief that garden supplies would sell well through supermarket and tie in with the idea of "one-stop" shopping, and (2) their fear that an other garden supply manufacturer would enter supermarkets first and secure the best outlets since supermarkets would be unlikely to handl multiple lines of competing garden supplies. These executives though Plantex should immediately enter supermarkets with the 100-lb. bag o Plant-Gro plant food and the smaller sizes of Weedban and Pestban.

To determine the attitudes of authorized dealers toward Plantex addin; supermarkets to its distribution system, Plantex announced at the Na tional Garden Supply Show in Chicago that the company was thinkin about entering supermarkets with the Plant-Gro line. Immediately, ove 70 percent of the authorized dealers threatened to drop or discontinu pushing Plantex products if supermarkets were added to the distributior system. Their main objection was that supermarket chains would discoun the prices of products in the Plant-Gro line and make it less profitable for authorized dealers to handle.

Authorized Plant-Gro dealers have made substantial gross profits from sales of the Plantex line in the past. Although the markup percentage on the Plant-Gro line is no greater than on competing lines, Plantex spends about $1 million per year in promoting its line—more than most competitors.

QUESTIONS

1. Should the Plant-Gro line of garden supplies be marketed through supermarkets? Why?
2. What can be done to retain present authorized Plant-Gro dealers if the product line is distributed through supermarkets?
3. What type of distribution policy is Plantex presently following? What type would you recommend they follow in the future?

25.
Thomas & Howard Company
Operating a Voluntary Chain

Thomas & Howard Company operates a wholesaler-sponsored voluntary food chain with thirty-one large independent supermarkets organized under the Red and White franchise and forty-eight smaller stores organized under a special group designated as the Independent Neighborhood Stores (INS). Thomas & Howard also sells to about 200 nonaffiliated independent grocers. Their stores are serviced out of a centrally based warehouse in the capital of a medium-sized state. Thomas & Howard also operates Red and White and INS franchised stores in several southern states, but these are run as separate divisions by relatives of the family. By running them as separate businesses, certain tax savings are realized. Also, separate warehouses are operated in each state because the cost of delivery to all stores from one regional warehouse would be prohibitive.

In performing the buying function, however, the four divisions work together through the National Red and White Corporation. Some thirty wholesalers from various parts of the country are members of National Red and White, and this organization's combined purchasing power is roughly equivalent to that of any one of the larger grocery chains.

Thus, Thomas & Howard is able to give its member stores merchandise at prices that are comparable to those charged by chain stores. To enable the Red and White stores to operate at a competitive 17 percent gross margin, Thomas & Howard uses a simple cost-plus plan of selling merchandise. Under this plan, the retailer is relieved, to a great extent, of the time-consuming buying function, making it possible for him to concentrate most of his efforts on selling and merchandising. A printed order form which lists the cost, the suggested selling price, and the percentage markup on each item is sent weekly to each member grocer. After filling in the quantities desired, he returns the order form to Thomas & Howard, together with payment. This eliminates the cost of credit. Under this plan, the order-taking salesman is replaced by a merchandise supervisor who visits the stores and assists the Red and White merchant with merchandising plans, advertising, window posters, market information, and other retail management problems.

Another sizable reduction in store operating costs is effected through cooperative advertising. Since all the Red and White stores in one metropolitan area look alike, carry the same merchandise, and sell at the same prices, it is possible for them to imitate the chains by running full-page weekly advertisements. The cost is small when split among the cooperating stores.

Independent Neighborhood Stores is a special group, organized by Thomas & Howard to take care of the smaller independent stores that generally do not qualify for membership in Red and White. The member stores share in the purchasing economies generated by Red and White National, and they have their own joint advertising program. Half-page advertisements are featured weekly, and the names of the cooperating stores are listed at the bottom of the ad. However, Thomas & Howard sells to these stores at a price that is slightly higher than the price charged to Red and White members. This is due to the fact that the smaller INS stores have smaller delivery orders from the warehouse.

In February 1970, Howard Timberlake, the president of Thomas & Howard, called a meeting of his executive group to consider problems that had arisen with one of the Red and White stores and with one of the INS stores. These are described below.

Problem 1. The Red and White Store, located in the Forest Lake Shopping Center, has not produced an adequate return on investment during the past three years. This store was very profitable during its early years when the Forest Lake Shopping Center first opened. A unit of Colonial Stores located in the same center had been its principal competitor. In 1958, the Trenholm Plaza Shopping Center, with an A&P food store as one of its principal tenants, was opened within two blocks of the Forest Lake Shopping Center. Several years later, the Richland Mall Shopping Center was opened less than a mile away, along the same highway. Its tenants included two grocery outlets: another Colonial supermarket and a Winn-Dixie unit. Finally, in the mid-1960s, a Piggly Wiggly store was added to the Trenholm Plaza Shopping area.

The population of the surrounding residential areas has more than doubled during the past ten years, and the incomes of the families have increased substantially. However, with six major supermarkets and other small independent grocers within the Forest Lakes area, it is possible that the vicinity has become overstored with food markets. It does not appear that any of the six supermarkets are actually losing money.

Problem 2. One of the small INS stores served by Thomas & Howard is in danger of becoming insolvent. The owner is not adhering closely to the merchandising, promotional, and control policies recommended by the merchandise supervisor, and the store's cash position has become extremely tight. A year ago, the owner borrowed funds from Thomas &

Howard. Once or twice a week, a Thomas & Howard merchandise supervisor visits the store to help the manager with operating problems.

QUESTIONS

1. How does a wholesaler-sponsored voluntary such as the one operated by Thomas & Howard differ from a retailer-owned cooperative?
2. What research should be undertaken to determine whether the Forest Lakes area has actually become overstored with supermarkets?
3. Suggest several alternative courses of action which Thomas & Howard can take in regard to the financially distressed INS store.

26.

The Home Builder vs. the Appliance Dealer

Competing for the Major Appliance Market

Manufacturers of major appliances, as well as their retail dealers, have become concerned in recent years with the entrance of the home builders into the market for major appliances. This is particularly true with respect to major kitchen appliances.

The highly competitive situation was summarized in an article in *Merchandising Week:* "Years ago, a builder putting in a kitchen in a new home left holes for the appliances; the home buyer went to her neighborhood appliance retailer to fill those holes, or moved her old appliances and a few years later was ready to become a replacement customer— again, for her neighborhood appliance store. But in recent years things have changed. Now the builder is fully equipped to offer his new-home customer a complete selection of appliances to fill her kitchen, and the appliance dealer resents it." [1]

The appliance manufacturers, of course, are also becoming concerned about their dealers' unrest. Some of them suggest that the dealers try to compete with the builders for the "kitchen market" in other ways to offset the inroads being made by builders.

QUESTIONS

1. What can the appliance dealers do to compete with the builders for the kitchen appliance market?
2. Can the progress of the builders into the kitchen appliance market be halted?

[1] Cathy Ciccolella, "Builder vs. the Retailer: Still a Battle," *Merchandising Week* (January 19, 1970), pp. 1, 20.

27.

Texize Chemicals, Inc. (B)

Making Channel Choices

Background

In a recent year, Texize Chemicals, Inc. developed in the laboratory a product which, in the opinions of several executives, had strong potentia in any of several possible markets. The product was an aluminum cleane which could be produced either as a liquid or a paste. Preliminary, bu fairly extensive laboratory tests had shown the cleaner to be highly effec tive on a wide range of aluminum products.

Texize had considerable experience in the marketing of both consume and industrial products. However, company officials recognized that eacl product possibility was unique in certain respects. As a result, carefu analysis of all aspects of the marketing mix was necessary before majo decisions could be made.

It appeared that the overall effectiveness of the product warranted fur ther study into the alternative methods of marketing it. One key issu which had to be resolved at an early date was that of the proper channel through which to distribute the product. The answer to the problem, o course, could only be derived from serious consideration of the product' attributes and the various markets which could be served effectively b the product. Some of the channel alternatives open to the company ar described below.

Channel Alternatives

The first alternative was to develop the aluminum cleaner as an industria product for sale to Texize commercial customers. As such, the produc would bear the Texize label and be distributed through the company' sales representatives. This alternative had the advantage of utilizing ar existing, proven channel which would save wholesaler costs. It was alsc felt that such distribution would help to better establish the Texize repre sentatives with their customers and make future product diversification easier.

A second proposal involved selling the product as a consumer product under the "Simoniz" label. The Simoniz Division of Texize already produced a fairly wide line of consumer cleaning products. This line of products was distributed through wholesale distributors only. Such a distribution method saves storage, transportation, and certain other costs. It, of course, does not enable the firm to receive the profits which go to the middlemen.

Third, the aluminum cleaner could be sold as a consumer product but with the Texize label. In such a case, two possible methods of distribution could be used. In most of the Southeast region, sales are made through Texize direct representatives who, in turn, sell to retail outlets such as grocery stores. In other parts of the country, brokers (particularly food brokers) are the major type of middlemen. Each state has a Texize representative to work with the brokers; however, it is the broker who contacts the retail outlets and completes the sale.

A fourth channel alternative would be to offer the product to the trade as a private brand item. Such a channel would relieve Texize of much marketing responsibility. The company would act only as a manufacturer and would distribute the cleaner directly to the retailer. It was kept in mind, of course, that such a policy could be followed in combination with some other alternative, especially if Texize wished to broaden the potential market for the product.

Finally, Texize was considering the possibility of selling the product to the government. Distribution would be direct and the company would have to carry out its supply obligation according to the terms of a contract and often subject to strict federal regulations.

All of the alternatives described above have some merit. Theoretically, any of the five, or more than one in combination, present marketing opportunities. All have been previously utilized by the company at one time or another. It remains for Texize to evaluate its product and to consider carefully the pros and cons of each alternative.

QUESTIONS

1. Evaluate each of the alternatives in light of the characteristics of the product and its potential market. Be sure to enumerate the pros and cons of each.
2. What factor or factors are of the most importance to Texize in its channel decision? What, ultimately, must the company base its decision upon? What would you recommend the company do?

28.

Texize Chemicals, Inc. (C)

The Federal Government as a Channel Alternative

In recent years Texize Chemicals, Inc. has encountered several situations in which sales of its products to the Federal Government were seriously considered. However, no major contracts have been entered into. At this time, Texize is evaluating an opportunity to sell its aluminum cleaner, which had only been introduced as an industrial product six months previously, to the Federal Government.

The government would like to use the product as a cleaner for the many aluminum parts of its jet aircraft. Texize is reasonably certain that the product will prove acceptable to the government in terms of its performance. Although the initial order probably would not be large, the prospects for future contracts appear to be excellent. It is estimated that a contract would add 20 percent to forecasted sales of the cleaner in the next year.

Officials of the company, while always seeking wider markets for the firm's products, recognize that selling to the Federal Government involves certain considerations not applicable to normal selling operations. For example, one high-ranking Texize official noted that the government strives to obtain the lowest possible price on the highest quality merchandise. He also noted that it is required that each product be packaged and labeled in a specific manner for distribution through the governmental channels of supply; special care must be given to products destined for overseas shipment; and packaging quality must generally be higher in government selling than for shipping the same product to other consumers because of the strict federal regulations.

Because it had been several years since the firm had taken a close look at the advantages and disadvantages of selling to the government, it was decided to weigh the pros and cons carefully.

The major advantages of selling to the government are: (1) a contract adds certainty to sales forecasting, that is, if a bid is accepted, a forecast (in time and in units) can be accurately made; (2) sales can be used to take up any slack in production, often without incurring additional fixed costs; (3) contracts can help to smooth out production peaks and valleys; (4) additional raw material purchases necessary to increase production may enable the company to take larger quantity discounts and, therefore, offer lower prices to other customers.

Certain disadvantages are likely to be attendant with sales to the government. For example, the company is forced to commit itself to a definite contract price; thus, if costs rise during the period of the contract, losses may easily be incurred. This is particularly true since most government contracts are made on a very low margin basis. Another potential problem related to the time span covered by the contract is the possible increase in regular consumer demand. If the demand is greater than anticipated, the government contract work might require costly overtime hours. With the relatively low margin, losses are likely.

Other possible negative aspects derive from the need for the government to remain free from public criticism. For example, the Federal Government requires that each contract certify that the company is an equal opportunity employer. Although Texize meets all requirements, opening the firm's doors to extensive government inspection could be a time-consuming and costly proposition. In addition, the Federal Government requires that a minimum wage per hour be paid on all work done under their contracts. The obvious problems of increased costs and administrative difficulties would be present. There is also the potential labor relations problem of employees claiming favoritism for those allowed to work on the government contracts.

Other considerations pertaining to the methods of obtaining government contracts are involved. When a company develops a new product, it must take it to the applicable government agency. The agency tests the product for its potential value and then draws up a set of specifications. The product is then purchased for evaluation at a negotiated price. If the product meets requirements during the evaluation period, a contract will be drawn up and bids solicited. Ordinarily, the company has a good chance of obtaining the first contract with a healthy margin. In subsequent contracts, however, the margin often decreases. It becomes more difficult to beat the bids of competitors.

If the product is not new and specifications on it already exist, the firm may get the product qualified by an approved laboratory. This qualification process includes: (1) making certain that the product meets the chemical and physical requirements of the specifications; (2) checking to see if the product poses a pollution threat to waterways near the place of manufacture as well as in the locale where it will be used; and (3) field testing to ascertain whether or not the product will perform as required. The qualification process may cost the firm as much as $3,000. Of course, the qualification merely enables the company to bid on a contract. There is no assurance that any sales will be obtained.

The Texize Company has carefully forecasted production and sales of the aluminum cleaner according to its long-range plan for marketing the product through various channels. The plan had been established before the government opportunity presented itself. It was now necessary to consider the pros and cons of altering the plans, taking steps to qualify the product, and opening the bidding procedure.

QUESTIONS

1. Which factors or considerations should carry the most weight in Texize's decision-making process?
2. What additional information should the company generate in order to facilitate the decision-making?
3. What effect would entering into a government contract have on the marketing program and channel plans presently in existence?

29.
Volkswagen of America, Inc.
Channels of Distribution

Global Picture of the Parent Company

Volkswagen of America is the sales subsidiary of Volkswagenwerk of Wolfsburg, Germany. The factory at Wolfsburg is in its twenty-sixth year of production. From its mile-long assembly lines, VW beetles and the larger fastbacks and squarebacks continue to roll off in record numbers. See Exhibit 1 for annual production and worldwide distribution figures.

An economical product, a constantly improved product, an exceptional warranty plan, and an efficient repair service are some of the characteristics that account for Volkswagen's appeal throughout the world. In twenty-six years, sales have spread to the extent that customers are now served in 136 countries. This global export is accomplished economically through the use of a charter fleet of more than sixty vessels. The ships carry new Volkswagens across the oceans and bring back imported commodities. For example, VW vessels visiting the United States return to Europe with bulk loads of coal from West Virginia, grain from the Great Plains, chemicals from the Southeast and Southwest, and ore from other parts of the country. Ports visited in the U.S. on a regular basis include Boston, New York, Baltimore, Jacksonville, New Orleans, Lake Charles, Houston, Long Beach, San Francisco, Portland, Seattle, and Honolulu. During the St. Lawrence Seaway's navigational season, VW charter vessels also call at Toledo and Chicago.

With the purchase of Auto Union in Ingolstadt during the mid-1960s, Volkswagenwerk entered the medium-priced car market. This plant produced a new automobile, the Audi, which was introduced in America in 1970. Also, in 1969, a new VW factory located in Pueblo, Mexico, began to ship a wide range of replacement parts to the United States.

Volkswagen of America, Inc.

Three types of companies make up the Volkswagen organization in the United States: the importing company, fourteen authorized distributors, and over 1,100 authorized dealerships. Volkswagen of America (VWoA) in Englewood Cliffs, New Jersey, serves as the authorized importer of Volkswagens to the United States. A wholly owned subsidiary of Volkswagenwerk AG of Wolfsburg, the importing company coordinates many activities related to the marketing of cars in the U.S. Much of VWoA's effort is devoted to planning—VWoA plans the activities while the authorized distributors are responsible for implementing these activities. For example, personnel at VWoA are responsible for the following functions: (1) arranging for the periodic arrival of shiploads of new VWs at fourteen American ports, (2) developing and supervising training programs for service mechanics, (3) developing national sales programs, (4) preparing and distributing technical and sales literature, (5) maintaining precise inventory control over replacement parts, (6) assembling orders and transmitting them to Wolfsburg, (7) producing and publishing advertisements, (8) administering insurance programs, and (9) gathering market information for the distributor and dealer network.

From 1949 through 1968 VWoA enjoyed a record of nineteen straight years of rising sales, as shown in Exhibit 2. Finally, sales declined from 567,975 cars to 551,379 in 1969. According to Stuart Perkins, president of Volkswagen of America, the 3 percent decline in sales was primarily due to a crippling longshoremen's strike which tied up the ports. Coming at the start of 1969, it cut off the supply of new VWs to about 75 percent of the dealers for about three months, and sales during the first quarter of 1969 slipped 19 percent behind the comparable months of 1968.

Wholesale Distributors

Most of VWoA's activities are with the fourteen authorized distributors whose distributorships are located from coast to coast. Each distributor holds a one-year contract with VWoA, which is normally renewed at the end of each year. Each distributor has the overall responsibility for developing, maintaining, supplying, and servicing a network of dealerships in its assigned geographical area. For example, Volkswagen Southeastern Distributor, Inc., located in Jacksonville, Florida, covers the states of Florida, Georgia, and South Carolina. Like other Volkswagen distributors, Southeastern serves as a wholesaler of Volkswagens and Volkswagen parts for the authorized dealerships in its area.

A function of all authorized VW distributors in the United States is to operate a training school at its headquarters, and personnel from dealerships throughout each distributor's area regularly attend classes there. There are courses in service work, parts department procedures, dealership business management, office management, and a series of seminars attended by sales personnel. Perhaps the most important of the training activities is the schooling given new mechanics. Each man sent in by a dealer is given sixteen weeks of intensive training in the repair of Volkswagen vehicles.

Southeastern's quota of cars is shipped directly from Germany to the Jacksonville port. Volkswagen of America does not allocate the cars directly to the individual dealers but to the distributors. It is Southeastern's responsibility to divide the shipment among its eighty-eight dealers. Two main criteria are used by Southeastern and other distributors for the allocation of cars: one is the dealer's ability to service; the other is the dealer's ability to sell.

Generally, each Volkswagen distributorship in the United States represents an investment of more than $2,500,000 in administrative offices, parts warehouses, mechanic training, and other facilities essential to its proper performance as a wholesaler of VW products. Each distributorship maintains a parts stock equal to a five-months' supply for the VWs in its area. This supply, together with the three-months' supply in the parts departments of VW dealers, means that there are enough replacement parts on hand to keep all VWs in the United States in operation for at least eight months.

Selection and Supervision of Dealerships

Since VWoA is interested in increasing its dealer network from coast to coast, it is the responsibility of each distributor to find the most promising locations within his area for new dealerships and to select the best prospects for these new locations. To help each distributor with this important work of developing new dealerships, VWoA maintains a marketing research department. The final approval of dealer applications and "packages" takes place in the New Jersey home office of VWoA. However, before a decision is reached on an application, the VWoA sales department has a member of its field staff visit the area and interview the prospective dealer. To help with the selection process, VWoA publishes a detailed manual which lists the minimum requirements for sales, service, and office facilities as well as requirements concerning capital, equipment, and personnel. The manual serves as a guide for the field staff and distributors in appraising prospective dealers.

The dealer, once selected, is supervised closely in matters large and small to a degree encountered by few other car dealers, foreign or domestic. Under the franchise agreements, VWoA and the regional distributor prescribe the amount of land a dealer will purchase to house his agency (six times as much as the area under the roof), what kind of building he will erect (the "Volkswagen Standard Type Building"), determines size, layout, and appearance, how he will decorate it (one illuminated round sign, one illuminated lettered sign, one illuminated used-car sign), how many parking spaces he will allot for service-department customers (four times the number of work stalls), and even how he will treat the help (e.g., in a large dealership, no mechanic needs to eat a sandwich in the shop—a clean lunchroom off the shop floor must be provided).

The excellent reputation Volkswagen enjoys for service and availability of parts—refuting the classic arguments for not buying a foreign car—has been acquired through dealer supervision. Dealers are required, for example, to set up and staff service and parts departments adequate not just for the number of cars they sell, but for the total number of Volkswagens in their territory. VWoA has been able to enforce dealer discipline over the years both because the dealers are successful and because VWoA and its distributors have given sound guidance. On the "Beetle" which the dealer sells for $1,799, he can normally count on a sufficient gross profit to net from 4 to 5 percent.

In testimony before a Senate subcommittee investigating U.S. automakers' warranty policies and dealers' performance under them, a spokesman for the National Automobile Dealers' Association recently complained that, in the years 1965 through 1967, the average dealer's total operating profit (not just on sales of new and used cars, but on service and parts as well) was a thin 1.8 percent. Over the same period, the average Volkswagen dealer's operating profit was 4.4 percent.

The Volkswagen dealer network has been expanded aggressively during the past twenty years by VWoA and its distributors. In January 1970, there were over 1,100 dealerships in the U.S., and this network will continue to expand as VWoA tries to solidify its reputation for outstanding service. In line with the objective of giving the most efficient service possible, Volkswagen dealers in 1969 introduced a system of electronic diagnosis, the first in the industry. The electronic diagnosis service is free of charge at 6,000 mile intervals to buyers of new 1970 Volkswagens during the first 24,000 miles. The service is designed to discover minor ailments and to permit their correction before major problems develop. The new program combines the precise readouts from electronic equipment with the work of skilled diagnosticians to tell exactly what, if anything, needs adjustment or repair to keep a Volkswagen in top operating condition. A diagnostician checks each vehicle during an examination which takes about forty-five minutes. During the diagnostician's work, he performs up to ninety-six different tests, depending upon year and model of Volkswagen being examined. The engine gets an electronic check-up while the diagnostician goes over the rest of the car to test other important areas such as wheel alignment, brakes, tires, battery, electrical systems, and other vital parts.

It has been VWoA's policy to establish an organization of medium-sized dealerships and to avoid the extremes of either very large or very small operators. In 1969, each dealer delivered an average of 506 new Volkswagen vehicles to customers. A typical dealership may be organized along the lines described in Exhibit 3. Separate departments are maintained for the sale of new and used cars. A sizable parts department exists, with enough parts to service all the Volkswagens in the dealer's market area for a period of three months.

The service department is spacious and is manned by eighteen mechanics trained at one of VW's distributor schools. Each mechanic has his own large tool cabinet. All tools used are made in Germany. All replacement parts for repairs and many extras are shipped in from Germany through the Jacksonville port. In the service department, a special dust-proof room is maintained. This room is entered through a sliding door. In the room, a constantly churning fan sucks out the dust. The room is used for precision work such as the repair of transmissions.

QUESTIONS

1. Volkswagen of America renews distributor contracts annually. Five distributorships have been bought out by Volkswagen of America, while nine are still independent. What criteria should the company use to determine whether a distributor's contract should be renewed or not?
2. On what bases should Volkswagen choose its dealerships in the United States?
3. List and describe briefly the major reasons for Volkswagen's success throughout the world. Are there any potential problems?

EXHIBIT 1
Volkswagenwerk Worldwide Production*

Year	Total	Cars	Trucks & Station Wagons	Total Inside Germany	Total Outside Germany	Total Exported From Germany
1945	2	2	---	2	---	---
1946	10	10	---	10	---	---
1947	9	9	---	9	---	2
1948	19	19	---	19	---	4
1949	46	46	---	46	---	7
1950	90	82	8	90	---	29
1951	106	94	12	106	---	36
1952	136	114	22	136	---	47
1953	180	151	29	180	---	69
1954	242	202	40	242	---	109
1955	330	280	50	330	---	178
1956	396	333	63	396	---	218
1957	473	381	92	473	---	271
1958	553	451	102	549	4	316
1959	697	575	122	689	8	404
1960	866	726	140	841	25	489
1961	1,007	838	169	959	47	533
1962	1,185	1,005	180	1,113	72	628
1963	1,210	1,020	190	1,132	78	636
1964	1,411	1,211	200	1,317	94	797
1965	1,543	1,352	190	1,448	95	851
1966	1,583	1,392	191	1,476	107	965
1967	1,290	1,127	163	1,162	128	813
1968	1,707	1,452	255	1,549	158	1,105
Totals	15,090	12,872	2,218	14,274	816	8,557

*In thousands of vehicles.

EXHIBIT 2
U.S. Registrations of Volkswagens

Year	Cars	Trucks*	Total
1945	---	---	---
1946	---	---	---
1947	---	---	---
1948	---	---	---
1949	2	---	2
1950	157	---	157
1951	390	---	390
1952	601	10	611
1953	980	33	1,013
1954	6,343	271	6,614
1955	28,907	2,021	30,928
1956	50,547	5,233	55,690
1957	64,803	14,721	79,524
1958	79,038	25,268	104,306
1959	120,442	30,159	150,601
1960	159,995	31,377	191,372
1961	177,308	26,555	203,863
1962	192,570	30,170	222,740
1963	240,143	36,865	277,008
1964	307,173	36,090	343,263
1965	383,978	4,614	388,592
1966	420,018	3,627	423,645
1967	452,937	3,294	456,231
1968	563,522	4,453	567,975
Totals	3,249,764	254,761	3,504,525

*Volkswagen bus-like station wagons, which were included in truck registrations through 1964, have been included in passenger car statistics since then and accounted for 46,060 of the 563,522 VW passenger cars registered during 1968.

EXHIBIT 3

Organization Chart for the Typical Volkswagen Dealership

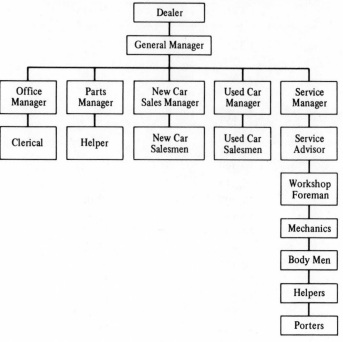

PRICING STRATEGY

30.
The Children's Library
Experimenting with Price Changes

The Children's Library is a medium-sized publisher of books for pre-school-age children. The books are composed primarily of color illustrations, but include some narrative which parents can read along with children to add to their understanding and enjoyment.

For many years, these books have been sold for twenty-nine cents in book, drug, department, and toy stores all over the country. During this time, total sales volume has been increasing in a very sluggish manner; likewise, the company profit picture has been relatively stable over the years with only slight improvement each year.

To increase its share of the market for children's books, the company reduced its price per book from twenty-nine cents to nineteen cents last year. Much to management's surprise, the company's sales volume and market share declined sharply. Moreover, major competitors did not follow suit and drop their prices. As a result, their sales volume and share of the market rose substantially.

Not knowing what to make of this unusual market behavior, management immediately restored book prices to the original level of twenty-nine cents. Subsequently, the company's sales volume rose to around previous levels, and so did its market share. Hoping to make additional gains in sales and market share, the firm raised its price per book to thirty-nine cents the following year. However, management was again disappointed as sales volume and market share once again declined.

QUESTIONS

1. What explanation can you give for the unexpected response of the market to changes in book prices?
2. What price would you set for the children's books? Why?

31.

Jackson's Department Store

Pricing an Unprofitable Item

Jackson's Department Store, an independent store located in the downtown section of a city with a population of over 200,000 has sales in excess of $25 million. Throughout the years, it has been noted for selling quality merchandise at reasonable prices. In the 1960s, competition from nearby shopping centers had grown intense and Jackson's annual sales began to decline. In self-defense, management opened a second store in one of the outlying shopping centers. With the opening of the new unit, sales of the downtown store dropped 15 percent. As a result of declining sales, the five-story store building has some unused space. Currently, the fourth floor and part of the fifth are used only for storage.

The trading area served by Jackson's has undergone considerable deterioration during the past ten years as many of its higher income families moved to the suburbs. The families which replaced them frequently had lower incomes. However, in 1965 the city launched a renovation program, and several attractive high-rise apartments were constructed within Jackson's trading area. Furthermore, the urban renewal program spread into the downtown shopping district itself. Store fronts and buildings all along the main street were refurbished. More importantly, a number of old buildings on nearby back streets were demolished and the space converted into spacious parking lots. Moreover, two new multilevel parking garages were under construction. With the addition of the new parking facilities, the downtown businessmen felt that their worst problem would be alleviated. They were hopeful that the declining sales trend would be arrested and, perhaps, even reversed.

By the start of the 1970s, Jackson's was faced with a serious pricing problem. Competition from the many discount houses and discount department stores in and around the metropolitan area became intense and represented a challenge to the store's position in the market. To meet this threat, Jackson's, reacting in the same way as many other stores, adopted a policy of meeting the low prices charged by discounters on popular items. As a result of this policy, automatic toasters, a favorite "loss leader" for discounters, became an unprofitable item for the store. This led the store's merchandise executives to question whether some change should be made in its toaster operations. Several popular lines of leading nationally advertised brands of toasters were sold by Jackson's. The toasters were stocked in the housewares department on the third floor.

Promotional efforts were limited to local newspaper advertising which, in every case, was paid for by the manufacturer of the brand being featured. Generally, one or two advertisements were run each week. Suppliers usually suggested the use of an appeal based on the toaster's construction and performance, but price was always featured prominently. Competitors' prices were determined from daily reports issued by Jackson's Comparative Shopping Office, which was charged with the responsibility of shopping in competitors' stores and recording the prices of many items, including toasters. Store prices were adjusted daily to meet changes in competitors' prices.

Sales floor stocks of goods were replenished twice a week and the toaster section was frequently low on stock. Based on the average monthly inventory, Jackson's toaster stock was turned over fifty-two times last year. This high rate reflects the hand-to-mouth, weekly purchasing of the toaster line. In addition, during "loss-leader" promotions of competitors, when the stock on the sales floor was once exhausted, it was not replenished until the promotion had ended.

No precise expense figures were kept for the toaster line, but it was obvious to store management that the realized gross margin was inadequate to produce a profit. To assist the merchandise manager in determining the proper course with regard to the toaster line, one of the buyers for the housewares department was requested to submit a report on his toaster operation. After a careful study of sales, margins, and expenses, the buyer submitted the statement contained in Exhibit 1 to his superiors.

After reviewing the buyer's report, the store's merchandise executives and the buyer held a conference to discuss the toaster situation. While some of the executives attending the meeting favored discontinuing toasters completely, there were others who disagreed. This latter group argued that toasters attracted a considerable amount of traffic to the store. With sales of $50,000 a year, toasters enjoyed one of the highest volume-to-space ratios in the entire store.

Moreover, these same executives also pointed out that Jackson's was a full-line department store and to discontinue an item as popular as toasters might impair this image. On the other hand, Jackson's average gross margin on toasters was extremely low, and the department was losing money.

QUESTIONS

1. Assume the decision reached was to discontinue the toaster line and that the freed space would not be used due to the store's surplus of space. What effect would this action have on total store profits?
2. Since the attractiveness of the surrounding trading area and the downtown itself was being improved, might it be possible for Jackson's to drop its discount policy and trade up both its merchandise and prices?
3. If you were one of the executives at the meeting, what recommendations would you make to the group?

EXHIBIT 1

Comparison of Electric Toasters and Housewares Products*

| | Toasters | | Typical Housewares Products |
	Dollars	Percent	Percent
Sales	$50,000	100.0	100.0
Cost of goods sold	46,500	93.0	61.8
Gross margin	$ 3,500	7.0	38.2
Newspaper cost	0	0.0	1.1
Salespeople's salaries	1,040	2.1	4.9
Delivery expense	500	1.0	2.0
Fixed expenses charged to dept.	8,460	16.9	25.0
Total expense	$10,000	20.0	33.0
Net profit or (loss)	(6,500)	(13.0)	5.2 (profit)

*Annual figures

32.
Farm-Fresh Foods, Inc.
Pricing in Response to Cost Increases

Farm-Fresh Foods, Inc., is a profitable fresh vegetables processor serving primarily the Eastern market with its line of frozen vegetables, including corn, peas, green beans, turnip greens, green peas, and other similar items. The company has a reputation for high quality products which are marketed under the Farm-Fresh family brand. Recently, it enhanced its already strong market position by developing its own plastic "cooking pouch" to compete with similar recent package innovations in the industry. This cooking pouch enables housewives to cook the vegetables in their own natural juices and in fresh butter without having to add water as with conventional preparation methods.

Unlike other brands of frozen vegetables, Farm-Fresh has been noted over the years for its reasonable prices. However, recent increases in costs associated with frozen green beans have prompted management to consider a price increase for this product. Within the last year, labor costs have increased nearly 10 percent while material costs have risen by almost 5 percent. Manufacturing costs for the green bean product are allocated on the following basis: labor, 50 percent of cost; materials, 35 percent of cost; and overhead, 15 percent of cost. The present price charged to wholesalers is twenty-five cents per package of frozen green beans, and 40 percent of this price represents Farm-Fresh Foods' markup.

QUESTIONS

1. Using present pricing methods, what price should Farm-Fresh Foods charge for its green bean product?
2. Would it be advisable to hold to the 40 percent margin if a price increase would result in a loss of customers? (To answer this question, use marginal analysis to indicate the circumstances under which it

would be best for Farm-Fresh Foods to reduce price, raise price, or maintain the present price.)

3. If the price calculated above (Question #1) would result in a 10 percent decrease in the next year's quantity sold over last year's 1,200,000 packages, what can be said about the elasticity of the firm's demand for its green bean product? Assuming other costs and expenses remain constant, how would the calculated price increase affect total profit? Why?

4. At the new price determined above, what quantity of green beans would have to be sold in order for the company to break even?

33.

Price Agreements

A Problem of Definition

Officers of a dozen leading manufacturers of certain types of equipment used in road construction meet for lunch twice a year. These are informal luncheon meetings which are not related to convention activities or formal meetings of the association. No secretary is present to keep minutes of meetings. While no formal agreements are made, the group does talk over prices. Those manufacturers who would like to set higher prices try to convince their more conservative-minded competitors to follow suit. If the latter will not, the former group suggests somewhat lower prices until, finally, compromises are reached.

When the men leave the room, each one knows what the others are going to charge for their products during the coming season. These informal agreements do not mean that prices will be absolutely the same. Differences in design, reputation for quality, and demand for the products of the different firms account for certain differentials in price. For instance, on one piece of equipment, company A has a price 5 percent higher than company B, the largest producer; while company C, a small new producer, usually sets its prices from 5 to 8 percent higher than company B.

QUESTIONS

1. Do these informal meetings violate the law?
2. Are price agreements made at these informal luncheon meetings?
3. Are such meetings in the interest of or opposed to the interest of the public?
4. What should be the government's attitude toward such agreements?

34.

Tasty Turkey Company

Choosing the Best Price for Soybean Turkey

The Tasty Turkey Company is trying to determine the best price to charge for a new turkey product, Soybean Turkey. The company is trying to decide between three prices: thirty cents, thirty-five cents, and forty-seven cents per pound. The company is extremely worried about its main competitor, who is now marketing Seaweed Turkey. This competitor may react with a strong promotion program or may not react at all to the price the company sets.

The Tasty Turkey Company does not have the funds to match the large promotional budget that its competitor may expend. The marketing manager feels strongly that the competitor will react to the marketing of Soybean Turkey with a large promotional expenditure. He is 70 percent sure of a competitive reaction. If the competitor does react with major promotion expenditures, profits are expected to be $1,800 at the lowest price for Tasty Turkey's new product. Profits will be $7,000 at the thirty-five cents per pound price with a competitive reaction, and a loss of $1,500 will be sustained if the forty-seven cents per pound price is chosen.

On the other hand, if the competitor does not react, profits will be $9,000 at the higher price, $2,500 at the middle price, and $2,000 at the lower price.

The marketing manager decides to use the expected monetary value criterion to calculate the optimum price to charge for Soybean Turkey (see Exhibit 1). This criterion is a methodology to decision-making under risk and uncertainty and includes six steps to the decision-making process:

1. Define the *problem* and state *objectives*.
2. List major decision *alternatives*.
3. Identify key *uncertainties* (events).
4. Gather relevant *data*.
5. Estimate the *value* of alternative outcomes.
6. Choose the *best* alternative as defined by the objectives.

QUESTIONS

1. Relate the six steps in the decision-making process to the problem facing the Tasty Turkey Company.
2. The expected monetary value for each major decision alternative is equal to the sum of the probabilities of occurrence of each event multiplied by the profit realized from the combination of the event and the decision alternative. For instance, in Exhibit 1, the expected monetary value of the first act is $1,860 (.70 x $1,800 + .30 x $2,000). Compute the expected monetary value of the other two acts. What action do you recommend for the Tasty Turkey Company in its pricing problem?
3. What other considerations may enter into this pricing decision?

EXHIBIT 1
Expected Monetary Value for Three Alternatives

					Alternatives			
		Act 1		*Act 2*		*Act 3*		
Event	*Probabilities of Event*	30¢ Price	*Expected Value*	35¢ Price	*Expected Value*	47¢ Price	*Expected Value*	
Competitive reaction	.70	$1,800	$1,260	$7,000		-$1,500		
No competitive reaction	.30	$2,000	$ 600	$2,500		$9,000		

35.

Tucker Company

Calculating the Most Profitable Stocking Level

The Tucker Company markets machine levelers, which are purchased at a cost of $600 per unit. Pete Bennett was attempting to determine how many levelers the company should order per three-month period. Quantity demanded per quarter ranged from fourteen to eighteen units. The company's policy has been to order fourteen levelers and have customers wait for future shipments if demand exceeds supply.

Bennett recently has received a number of customer complaints for failure to have the product in stock. He has examined past company records to determine customer demand for previous quarters over a five-year period. The orders received for each of the previous five years and their frequency of occurrence are shown below. The mean quantity demanded was 15.75 units.

Quantity Demanded	Percent Occurrence
14	20
15	20
16	35
17	15
18	10
	100%

The company's cost of placing an order was computed to be $100. Handling cost was $40 per unit and included crating and customer preparation expenses.

Bennett believes a charge should be made in the cost calculations for being out of stock when customer demand exceeds supply, that is, a stockout penalty. The penalty is assigned because of loss of customer goodwill and customer refusal to wait for future shipments. An underage cost of $55 per unit when demand is greater than supply was assigned by Bennett. This included $10 clerical cost for back orders plus $45 lost sales charge. The $45 is approximately one-half of the profit earned per unit.

Bennett also realized that it was company policy to dispose of any overage (units in excess of demand) by reducing the selling price. Selling price per unit was $900 with the overage or salvage price most likely being $700.

The normal industry carrying charge of 25 percent of the cost of the average quantity on hand was assigned to the levelers on a quarterly basis. This figure represents the costs of the storage facility, insurance, taxes, transportation, depreciation, and interest. Sales of the levelers per quarter have previously been evenly spread over the months with little seasonal variation.

Profit Functions

Bennett decided to compute the expected profit or outcome of stocking 14, 15, 16, and 17 units per quarter by incorporating the demand information which he had gathered and the cost data he had tabulated. He was planning to recommend that the company stock the number of levelers with the highest expected profit value.

Total profit for stocking a specific quantity, given one of the five demand levels, is equal to total revenue (TR) minus total cost (TC). When a demand level (Di) equals or is greater than the quantity stocked (Qj), profit is equal to:

$$Pr\,(Qj/Di) = PQj - [CQj + HQj + \tfrac{1}{2}\,(.25\,CQj) + U\,(Di - Qj) + 0]$$

In the equation, Pr (Qj/Di) is the profit from stocking Qj given that Di quantity is demanded; PQj is total revenue which is the price multiplied by the quantity sold, where P = $900.

CQj is the cost of the goods bought where C is the cost per unit, $600; HQj is the handling cost where H is the handling cost per unit, $40; $\tfrac{1}{2}$ (.25 CQj) is the carrying cost where .25 represents the percentage of inventory to be charged to inventory carrying costs and $\tfrac{1}{2}$ is the average stock on hand over the quarter; U (Di − Qj) is the underage charge where U is equal to $55. In the case when demand is equal to supply, U (Di − Qj) is zero because Di − Qj = 0. When demand is greater than supply an underage charge is made for every unfilled unit order; and 0 is the ordering cost and is equal to $100.

When demand is less than the quantity stocked (Di < Qj), the profit function is:

$$Pr\,(Qj/Di = PDi + S\,(Qj - Di) - [CQj + HDi + \tfrac{1}{2}\,(.25\,CQj) + 0]$$

The gross profit of stocking 14 units when 14 units are demanded is calculated as follows:

Pr (14/14) = $900 (14) − [$600 (14 + $40 (14)) + $\frac{1}{2}$ (.25 ($600) (14))
$$+ \$55 (14 - 14) + \$100]$$
Pr (14/14) = $2,490.

The gross profit of stocking 15 units when 14 units are demanded is calculated:

Pr (15/14) = $900 (14) + $700 (15 − 14) − [$600 (15) + $40 (14) +
$$\tfrac{1}{2} (.25 (\$600) (15)) + \$100]$$
Pr (15/14) = $2,515.

Exhibit 1 shows the profit outcome for stocking a given amount of levelers and experiencing a particular quantity demand. Expected profit value (EPV) for each stocking level is found by multiplying the probability of occurrence of a particular demand level by the profit outcome of a specific stocking level and summing these values for each stock level. The highest expected profit value among the stocking levels is the highest average profit that could be expected of stocking levelers on a repeated basis at that given stocking amount. Probability of demand is assumed to be equal to the past observed proportion of occurrence of various demand levels.

QUESTIONS

1. The expected profit value of stocking 14 levelers is calculated in Exhibit 1 to be $2,313.75. What are the expected profit values of stocking 15, 16, and 17 levelers?
2. What recommendation should Bennett make as to the number of levelers to be stocked?
3. What alternative means of calculating the ideal stocking level would be available?
4. What factors might change and, therefore, upset the profit functions developed by Bennett?

EXHIBIT 1
Calculating the Expected Profit Value of the Four Stocking Levels

		Stocking Levels							
Demand	Probability of Demand	14	EPV	15	EPV	16	EPV	17	EPV
14	.20	$2,490	$498	$2,515					
15	.20	2,335	467						
16	.35	2,280	798						
17	.15	2,225	333.75						
18	.10	2,170	217						
			$2,313.75						

36.

The Caustic Consultant (A)

Pricing in Response to Competition

John Lee, a marketing consultant, was developing a reputation for being laconic, terse, and sound in his judgment. Small businesses appreciated both his wisdom and his brevity.

One Tuesday morning, he responded to a phone call from the worried president of the Burr Rods Manufacturing Company, located eighty miles east of Lee's home. Lee drove to the factory where welding rods were made, met the president, Frederick Thatcher, and listened carefully. Thatcher was worried over Japanese entry into the welding rod market.

Thatcher stated, "You're an expert on pricing, I'm told, and I want to know if I should cut my price."

Lee asked for more data and an inspection of the product line. Grudgingly, Thatcher led him to the warehouse, showed him different sized welding rods, rod holders, and related equipment. Thatcher again asked for a price decision—should he cut the price by 5 percent to meet the Japanese price, or by 10 percent to drive out the competition?

Lee said nothing for a minute, then asked to see catalogs. He leafed through two, slowly. His next question was about other competitors. Thatcher replied that Westinghouse had stopped making rods and now bought from him and that a small firm in Cleveland was also closing down.

Lee asked for market share estimates. Thatcher initially indicated that the data were not important and then reluctantly admitted that Burr Rods accounted for about 96 percent of the rod sales in its field and 80 percent of the sales of rod holders.

Lee next dug into channels and found that mill supply houses in this country carried Burr Rods, but the overseas houses did not. Thatcher didn't want into foreign markets, nor did he want foreigners in American markets.

Lee spoke levelly to Thatcher, who wrote down Lee's comments.

143

QUESTIONS

1. How would you have approached the pricing problem? What data would you want?
2. Are the Japanese a threat? What does Thatcher need to know about them to answer the question?
3. How would you characterize the market for welding rods? Is price a major determinant of demand in this market?
4. What would you, consulting on a retainer basis, want to research on the customer end? What information would you seek from the middle-men? What specific questions would you ask?
5. What do you think Lee's comments to Thatcher were?

37.

Triangle Electric Corporation
Pricing of New Industrial Products

The market for heavy duty industrial circuit breakers and fuse boxes is shared by several major electrical equipment manufacturers, one of which is Triangle Electric.

Triangle manufactures many types of fuse boxes and circuit breakers which vary in size and ampere load capacity and is presently concerned with establishing a price for each of its three new small industrial circuit breakers, Models T-100, T-200 and T-300.

The following table gives cost and other relevant data for each of these three models:

Model	Variable Production Cost/unit	Forecasted Sales (units)	Separate Items Per Unit
T-100	$ 5	6,000	1
T-200	10	7,500	2
T-300	12	12,000	3

Other Expenses Associated with Forecasted Sales

Sales salaries	$20,000
Sales commission	5% of gross sales
Order and billing costs	500
Advertising	5,000
Packaging	9,400

The models vary in the number of items in each "unit." For instance, model T-100 is a single item that comprises the entire circuit breaker unit; model T-200 consists of two separate pieces, each packaged independently; model T-300 is made up of three separate pieces, each requiring packaging. Each piece requires approximately the same amount of packaging material.

Salesmen are paid a salary plus 5 percent commission on gross sales. Each salesman specializes in selling only these three circuit breakers to small electrical and hardware wholesalers.

Company advertising, which appears in a trade journal, stresses no particular product; instead, the theme essentially revolves around educating industrial buyers as to what the company represents and what general type of products sells.

QUESTIONS

1. What price should be set on each model if the firm desires to break even?
2. If the firm desires to make a $50,000 total profit on sales of all models combined, what price should be established?
3. What price should be established if the firm desires to maximize profits?

38.

National Salt and Mineral Company
Using Demand-oriented Methods of Pricing

National Salt and Mineral Company is one of several processors of table salt and other related commercial and industrial chemicals. Most of its products, such as potassium, sodium and ammonium nitrates, and chlorides are sold to industrial users of "chemically pure" ingredients.

Although it is a major competitor in industrial circles, National is the smallest of the three firms which process and package most of the table salt consumed in the United States. The consumer market is dominated by a single, large firm which has successfully built a brand name that has become almost a generic term for table salt. Neither National nor the other competitor share quite the reputation and brand image created over the years by the industry leader. Although National is not a major force in the salt market, it enjoys a sizable annual sales volume.

Despite the fact that table salt is generally considered to be a homogeneous product, there are noticeable price differentials which exist among competing brands. At retail, the leader's brand sells for about fourteen cents per box, while the other competitor's brand sells for twelve cents. National's brand has typically sold for about eight cents per box.

For many years, National has relied on cost-oriented pricing methods to determine the selling price for its table salt. Typically, National uses its own "cost-plus" formula to compute selling price. Recently, however, the company became interested in bringing consumer demand into its pricing decisions. As a result, the firm is experimenting in the market with small price variations under "controlled" conditions in an effort to learn more about consumer demand for table salt. Data from these pricing experiments have been summarized through statistical regression techniques into an estimated demand function: $P = \$0.200 - \$0.00000005 \, (Q)$, where P denotes price and Q represents quantity. Based on this demand function, National should sell two million boxes at a price of ten cents, and 2.4 million at eight cents.

Variable costs per unit remain relatively constant at three cents per

box, while fixed costs total approximately $30,000. During its entire sale
history, the company has never sold more than three million boxes of salt
nor less than one million in a year.

QUESTIONS

1. Describe the competitive environment in which National competes for
   sales of table salt.
2. What explanation can you give for the price differentials associated
   with what is generally considered to be a homogeneous product?
3. What price should National establish in order to maximize profits?
4. What price would you establish for National's table salt? Why?

39.

Texize Chemicals, Inc. (D)

A Pricing Policy Decision

While traveling in Europe, a Texize Company executive became aware of a unique product being marketed in most West European countries. The product was a stain remover which was different from any commercial preparation used in the United States. It worked quite well to remove various common stains from different kinds of materials and on both natural and synthetic fibers.

Upon his return to the United States, the executive inquired into the feasibility of marketing this unique product in the United States. From his investigation, he learned that the exclusive production and distribution rights for the territorial United States and Canada were available. Before acquiring these rights, however, the company decided to undertake extensive research into the market for stain removers.

The results of the research indicated that the market for stain and spot removers was quite small, but as yet undeveloped. There was only one major competitor, a product which used a liquid naptha formula as its major ingredient. The only other competition was in the form of various "home-made" stain removing concoctions. Both the liquid naptha stain remover and the "home remedies" required subsequent dry cleaning of the fabric to completely remove the cleaning agents and any decomposed stain residue. Unlike other removers, the Texize product—tentatively named K2r—because of its unique chemical formula, requires no subsequent dry cleaning. Applied as a paste from a small tube, K2r is rubbed thoroughly into the stained area and allowed to dry. The white powdery spot that emerges can be briskly brushed away with a stiff clothing brush, carrying all cleaning agents and stain residues with it.

Typically, stain removers have been distributed primarily through grocery stores, with limited distribution in variety stores and hardware stores. Inventory turnover for this kind of product is customarily low but is compensated for by a relatively good margin earned by retailers. Consequently, Texize management feels that there would be no insurmountable problem in making K2r attractive to the retail grocery trade. Moreover, unlike present commercial stain removers which take up the grocers' limited and costly shelf space, K2r would be packaged so as to utilize wire dispensing racks which would take up very little shelf space.

Because of wide differences in the European and American markets, Texize could not use the U.S. equivalent of K2r's European price. Instead, Texize decided to conduct price experiments at the same time K2r was being test-marketed for consumer acceptance. The results of the pricing experiments indicated that demand for K2r was highly inelastic over the price range of seventy-five cents to ninety-nine cents. Consumers were just as willing to purchase the spot remover at nearly $1.00 as they were at seventy-five cents. At prices below seventy-five cents, quantity demanded dropped off somewhat.

Other market tests indicated that K2r would be widely accepted by various segments of the consuming public. The product would not create its market by pirating a significant volume of its customers from competitors. Instead, all indications were that K2r would actually expand the stain removing market by converting users of "home remedies" and by attracting others who formerly used the services of professional dry cleaning institutions for such purposes.

Although experiments indicated a highly inelastic demand, Texize management did not want to price K2r too high and present unusually high profit opportunities which might attract other competitors into a small volume market. Nor did Texize want to price K2r too low because pricing experiments indicated that quantity demanded would decline sharply.

QUESTIONS

1. Would you advise Texize to follow a penetration or a skimming policy in making its price decision? Justify your choice.
2. The pricing experiments indicated that consumers would tend not to buy K2r if price was dropped below seventy-five cents, that is, quantity demanded and price are directly related (as opposed to the usual inverse relationship). What does this information reveal to Texize management?
3. Recommend and justify a specific retail selling price for K2r.

40.

The American Heating and Manufacturing Company
Establishing Pricing Policies

The American Heating and Manufacturing Company is the producer of a specialty-type of space heating system. It is a young, growing corporation which has been in existence for a relatively short time and has met with good product demand response. As a result, American is experiencing many of the normal growing pains common to such companies. The company, which is incorporated in the State of Tennessee, has been selling on a nationwide basis since its inception and, as such, encounters many questions regarding marketing policy. At the present time, American Heating is concerned with two primary marketing problems which are considered very important to the future of the firm. The first concerns some specific pricing policies and the second pertains to the question of private branding of the company's heaters.

Background

The firm had its beginning in the 1960s when its founder and president, R.O. Victor, recognizing the opportunity for production of a space heating system which would involve a low initial investment, simple controls, dependability, clean heat, and require no floor or wall space, began to manufacture an electric duct heater. Victor previously had had experience in the heating and air conditioning fields and, therefore, was acquainted with production methods, distribution channels, and market characteristics. Since each item has to be designed for the customer's particular requirements, a great deal of engineering know-how regarding mechanical and electrical design, as well as control systems, is necessary. Victor provided this expertise.

The first orders for the product were filled, and the product delivered six months after the founding of the firm. Orders then increased substantially, forcing an early shift in production facilities from a small shop to a larger building. A year later, the company moved for a second time into a still larger plant. There was little doubt that such a move was necessary, and it resulted in the solution of many growth problems—including reduction of a lengthening lead time in filling orders. Keeping pace with demand and expanding facilities required the hiring of additional employees periodically, a task which was accomplished with some difficulty in an area with a relatively tight labor market.

All indications pointed toward steadily increasing sales of the current product line, and the possibility of expanding the line in the future certainly existed. However, at the present time, the firm has a backlog of orders, and no thoughts of additional product introductions are entertained.

The Product and the Industry

The electric duct heater is made for installation into forced air ducts for space heating. The product is of heavy-gauge corrosion-protected steel construction. Most of the heaters are installed by cutting a hole in the duct and sliding the heater in place. Control terminals are easily accessible and protected by a heavy-gauge steel cover. Features include safety protection and the advantage of being "made to order" (depending on the customer's requirements of size, wattage, volts, phase, and number of steps) In addition to these standard features are numerous optional ones (contactors, transformers, etc.) and remote accessories (control thermostats and auxiliary controls). The pricing structure is based on this breakdown of product features.

The product is reputed to be of good quality and is sold emphasizing this quality aspect. The heater compares very favorably to competing products in this regard. In addition, the product has obtained a listing from Underwriter's Laboratories (UL), a fact which has contributed to the product's quality image.

Victor estimates that there are approximately twelve competing firms—although there are often significant differences in the quality of products and in product features. Some of the firms are large manufacturers of heating and air conditioning equipment who sell space heaters as a small part of their total product line (e.g., General Electric). Others are companies comparable in size and with similar marketing problems. The firms compete in what is considered to be a growing electric heating market.

Selling to the Electric Heating Market

The American Heating and Manufacturing Company employs approximately fifty manufacturer's representatives (agents) scattered throughout the country. Most of these representatives do not take title to the product, but some (as explained below) do act as distributors. The agent middlemen operate on a long-term agreement in a limited territory in accordance with terms dictated by the manufacturer. Ordinarily these representatives act for several organizations producing noncompeting products. Nearly all selling effort is carried out through these representatives who contact contractors and other potential customers. Occasionally, sales are made directly by American to the customer, but the representative receives credit for all sales made in his territory.

Nearly all sales of American products are commercial and industrial. The heaters are being used most often in schools, office buildings, stores, shopping centers, and so forth, as opposed to private housing. In the past year, sales of duct heaters have been made for these and several other commercial heating system requirements.

The principal customers of American's representatives are contractors. In the past, they have been primarily "mechanical" contractors, but increasing interest has been shown by "electrical" contractors—and some sales have been made to this latter group.

Of great importance to American are "repeat" sales which are obtained when engineers "specify" that a certain heater (e.g., American duct heater or equal) be used on a project. The normal procedure in the idustry is for the architect on a job to call in mechanical (or electrical) engineers as "consultants" for the electrical or heating work. The contractors bid on a contract to perform the construction work, but the specifications of the architect and the engineers have to be followed. Thus, by providing a satisfactory heater on one job, the company can generate many repeat, specified sales on other projects.

It is important for American to convince engineers of the merits of the heater—for it is this group which can specify that a specific heating system (or its equal) be used for the job. The contractor's concern with a product is threefold: (1) that the product will provide satisfactory performance, (2) that the life of the product will be long enough to avoid customer dissatisfaction, and (3) that his cost will be the lowest possible. The manufacturer's representatives stress such product attributes in meetings with contractors.

Commissions paid to representatives amount to 20 percent on sales to contractors and 15 percent on sales to original equipment manufacturers (OEM's) according to American's price scheme. These margins are comparable to those given by other manufacturers and are believed to be competitive.

Promotion

With respect to advertising and other promotional activities, American has not found it necessary to devote considerable time or expense. The firm's original promotion effort was directed toward contractors and other potential customers who American felt would have an interest in the heaters. It consisted of a cover letter emphasizing the money-saving features of the heaters and offering assistance with any electrical heater problems. In addition, the company's bulletins describing the products, their features and dimensions, method of installation, and ordering procedures were furnished along with pricing and discount schedules. Since that time, no extensive advertising has been undertaken other than mailings announcing the obtaining of the UL listing one year after distribution had begun. However, similar promotional literature is available for representatives and is sent out to all interested customers on request.

Victor feels that further advertising is unnecessary at this time. He and his assistant have devoted considerable effort toward seeking out qualified, aggressive representatives throughout the country to perform the sales and marketing activity. American's representatives are considered to be qualified in the marketing fields for which they carry products. Some advertising of heating equipment by other firms appears in publications of the heating and air conditioning industries, but American has not followed their example.

Pricing Considerations

One of the firm's most important problems pertains to pricing policies. The firm uses pre-established, standard pricing—as per the base price list which is made available to representatives and potential customers. Although it is somewhat difficult to "police" the representatives regarding their pricing practices, Victor feels that, through the use of the standard price list, some degree of control is exercised.

American's policy is, upon receiving a request for a price list from a potential customer, to mail the data immediately if he is not in the same city as or nearby to the representative in that territory. If the customer is in the same locality, a letter is sent to him explaining that a representative will soon call on him, and the representative is subsequently notified of the action.

Prices for products had been established by Victor when the company was formed—based upon his knowledge of market conditions, costs to some degree, and his experience in the field. An examination of competing firms and products had shown his prices to be comparable. The "made-to-order" nature of the products prohibits any direct comparison, but Victor estimates that his standard price schedule (based on size of unit in square inches and power usage) is competitive. (Exhibits 1 and 2 are examples of American's pricing structure). He has ascertained that some other heaters are generally priced below and some above the American heaters. Those which are lower-priced are usually not equal in quality to American's. The firm has had success in competitive bidding, probably attesting to the quality and reasonable price structure. Victor is satisfied with the price structure and is not considering a general price increase.

A primary question of concern is with respect to general pricing policy. Victor has been under increasing pressure from representatives who desire more control over prices quoted to customers. The representatives want to be able to quote higher prices in situations which present the opportunity for more profit for them. They point out that they are allowed more pricing latitude with other lines which they also handle.

Presently, American is attempting to maintain pricing control. The home office sells to contractors through the representatives (who most often do not take title to the heaters) and is responsible for directly billing the customers in about 90 percent of the transactions. However, American has relinquished some degree of control in allowing the remaining 10 percent of its representatives to do their own billing. That is, the representatives for the company purchase the heaters from American and then resell them to customers. Thus, American bills the representatives for the gross selling price less discounts and commissions and the agents, in turn, bill the customers. In such cases, American specifies that the *basic price list* still be adhered to, and that the representative report the name and address of the final customer. There is no evidence that different prices are being charged to different customers by representatives—although Victor recognizes that such a possibility exists and that checking on it will be difficult.

Victor wonders whether or not the present policies are the best possible under the circumstances. He feels that he has, at least, several pricing policy alternatives: (1) continue to employ the standard price list, send it to those who request it, and bill customers from the home office; (2) discontinue circulation of the price and discount lists to customers; instead, allow the representatives to quote the price or discount which appears feasible and receive the same percentage commission; (3) allow pricing freedom and arrange some percentage sharing of any "overages" obtained through a higher price—or make a similar compensation arrangement; (4) allow more representatives to purchase from American and then do their own billing. Victor feels that there could probably be other alternatives as well.

Both Victor and his assistant have expressed concern over the ethics involved in allowing price differentials to be quoted by the representatives, even though such practices are rather common and may not directly violate any laws. He also wonders about the possible application of the Robinson-Patman Act to his firm (See Exhibit 3). Although he can foresee greater immediate profits on a short-term basis if higher prices are obtained, he wishes to weigh carefully all current and future effects on his business before relinquishing control over his pricing policies to his representatives.

The Question of Private Branding

The question has recently arisen as to the advisability of private (distributor) branding American's products. Several larger companies which produce and market related product lines have recently approached Victor with the intention of entering into private branding agreements. They propose that private branding will greatly increase the market coverage with respect to American's heaters, will make possible the utilization of established sales organizations, and enhance American's profits. Most of these companies do not presently produce electric heaters but have some experience with related products in the heating and air conditioning industries.

Victor is uncertain as to the advisability of adopting such a policy at his company's stage of development and wishes to consider all the possible far-reaching effects of such action.

Overview

Victor and his assistant feel that they are being realistic in their estimation of future sales potential and the attendant problems of growth, but they wish to be prepared for as many future contingencies as possible, especially with respect to problems of marketing. They feel that it is all-important to balance the present situation of the firm with the requirements of the future before taking action, but they find this task difficult in many respects including relations with representatives, pricing problems, and private branding. They are certain that a continuing and thorough analysis of such questions is necessary—based upon the considerations of marketing policy which are relevant to the American Heating and Manufacturing Company.

QUESTIONS

1. What action should the company take regarding its pricing policies?
2. What are the arguments for and against American maintaining tight control over their representatives' pricing activities?
3. Should the firm enter into any private branding agreements with other firms?
4. Is the Robinson-Patman Act applicable to the pricing situation facing American? Why?

EXHIBIT 1
Pricing Schedule*

Instructions for Pricing Heaters:

1. Multiply the duct height by the duct width (in inches). Determine the required power usage. Refer to the base price list below for the appropriate base price.
2. Add the list prices obtained in similar fashion as above for optional or remote equipment (Note: these list prices are not shown in this exhibit).
3. Apply the appropriate discount as shown in the discount schedules. (See Exhibit 2).

Base Price List

Power Usage (KW)	\(Height \times Width (square inches)\)					
	10-100	101-400	401-1600	1601-3600	3601-6400	6401-22500
0.0-5.0	$ 60	$ 78	$ 88	$130	$162	
5.1-10.0	75	88	113	159	185	
10.1-20.0	120	136	160	192	265	$ 330
20.1-30.0	180	210	263	308	400	444
30.1-40.0	222	253	300	345	451	475
40.1-60.0	270	292	354	404	500	530
60.1-90.0		385	420	555	643	697
90.1-120.0			700	738	797	900
120.1-150.0			870	911	960	1010
150.1 plus			----- Inquire at factory -----			

F.O.B. Factory   Terms: net 30

*Schedule is available on request and is the basis for all price quotations.

EXHIBIT 2

Following are the discount schedules used for resale or for sale directly to original equipment manufacturers or distributors. They are applied as per step 3 of instructions for pricing heaters (See Exhibit 1).

Resale Discount Schedule*

Combined Heater List Price	Discount
$0-149	22%
$150-$599	28%
$600-$1499	32%
$1500-$6000	36%
Over $6000	Consult factory

*Additional quantity discounts for identical heaters are sometimes given.

O.E.M. or Qualified Distributor Discount Schedule*

Combined Heater List Price	Discount
$0-$149	30%
$150-$599	35%
$600-$1499	40%
$1500-$6000	42%
Over $6000	Consult factory

*Additional quantity discounts for identical heaters are sometimes given.

EXHIBIT 3

R.O. Victor, due to his concern over his pricing policies and the question of private branding, took note of several provisions of the Robinson-Patman Act which appear to be relevant:

THE ROBINSON-PATMAN ACT

Sec. 2. (a) That it shall be unlawful for any person engaged in commerce, in the course of such commerce, either directly or indirectly, to discriminate in price between different purchasers of commodities of like grade and quality, where either or any of the purchases involved in such discrimination are in commerce, where such commodities are sold for use, consumption, or resale within the United States or any Territory thereof or the District of Columbia or any insular possession or other place under the jurisdiction of the United States, and where the effect of such discrimination may be substantially to lessen competition or tend to create a monopoly in any line of commerce, or to injure, destroy, or prevent competition with any person who either grants or knowingly receives the benefit of such discrimination, or with customers of either of them.

(b) Upon proof being made, at any hearing on a complaint under this section, that there has been discrimination in price or services or facilities furnished, the burden of rebutting the prima-facie case thus made by showing justification shall be upon the person charged with a violation of this section . . .

(d) That it shall be unlawful for any person engaged in commerce to pay or contract for the payment of anything of value to or for the benefit of a customer of such person in the course of such commerce as compensation or in consideration for any services or facilities furnished by or through such customer in connection with the processing, handling, sale, or offering for sale of any products or commodities manufactured, sold, or offered for sale, by such person, unless such payment or consideration is available on proportionally equal terms to all other customers competing in the distribution of such products or commodities.

(e) That it shall be unlawful for any person to discriminate in favor of one purchaser against another purchaser or purchasers of a commodity bought for resale, with or without processing, by contracting to furnish or furnishing, or by contributing to the furnishing of, any services or facilities connected with the processing, handling, sale, or offering for sale of such commodity so purchased upon terms not accorded to all purchasers on proportionally equal terms.

THE PROMOTION
AND SELLING EFFORT

41.

Elite Beauty Products

Advertising to a Specialized Market

Elite, Inc. manufactures beauty aids for exclusive use by Negroes. Products such as King's Elite hair dressing for men and Queen's Elite hair conditioner for women already have been introduced to the Negro market with a "fair" degree of success.

The advertising campaign which introduced these products used a $200,000 budget for the eight-week introductory period. Television spot announcements were used in Chicago, Detroit, New York, Philadelphia, Los Angeles, and Washington, D.C. Research showed that 30 percent of all Negroes in America lived in these areas, and that 2,000,000 Negro TV homes were located in these six markets. Television was employed because it was thought that nearly all Negroes living in these areas could be reached through this medium.

Recently, Elite has developed two more products exclusively for Negroes: Prince Elite deodorant and Princess Elite lipstick. Since only a "fair" degree of success was obtained through previous media strategy, company executives are trying to develop a media plan which will yield better results.

QUESTIONS

1. What mistakes, if any, were made in media strategy in introducing the original two products?
2. Should any factors other than the number of Negro households influence basic media strategy?
3. What basic media strategy should be developed for introducing the two new products?

42.

Schwartz and Sons, Inc.

Choosing An Advertising Target

Schwartz and Sons, a Milwaukee brewer, distributes Schwartz beer in five Midwestern states. In the past, it has aimed its advertising at the heavy beer drinker with such copy themes as "Multiple bottles multiply your pleasure." Lately, research has shown that the heavy beer drinker is declining in importance as a primary advertising target.

Schwartz executives face the problem of identifying a new target group at which to direct their advertising and promotion efforts. Three possible target groups have been suggested: (1) the young, college group which has a heavy beer consumption rate per capita and is still forming its beer drinking habits, (2) the blue-collar working man who "drinks a few brews" to relax after a hard working day, and (3) the middle-aged, white-collar worker who likes to give frequent parties for his friends and associates.

Schwartz plans to spend $1,500,000 on advertising for the coming year. In the past, most of the advertising dollars have been spent in sponsoring a heavy regional sports television schedule which featured National Football League games on CBS-TV and National League baseball games on NBC-TV. Competitive beer manufacturers have also been spending most of their advertising dollars on televised sports events.

Schwartz is trying to secure a competitive advantage by concentrating on a specifically identified, high-consumption, beer-drinking group rather than by directing its advertising to beer drinkers in general.

QUESTIONS

1. What advantages can Schwartz beer obtain by concentrating its efforts on a specifically defined advertising target?

2. Is any one of the three suggested target groups identified clearly enough to serve as an advertising target?
3. Which one of the three suggested target groups would you select as the most promising on the basis of what you presently know about the beer industry?
4. How should Schwartz proceed in pinpointing its advertising target?

43.

Masters, Inc.

Using Pre-recorded Promotional Messages

In promoting its disposable line of bedspreads, pillow cases, operating gowns and patient clothing, Masters, Inc., a Columbus, Ohio, manufacturer, is experimenting with a cassette tape to pre-sell hospital administrators prior to salesmen's calls. The tape is in a cartridge which can be played on any cassette-type tape recorder. Most hospital administrators have such a recorder.

The market for disposable hospital products seems to be growing. Cost studies indicate that it costs less to use disposables than to launder ordinary fabrics after each use. An added incentive for some hospitals is that the disposables can help fuel hospital furnaces equipped to burn coal.

A recent tape to promote Masters' disposable products attempted to capitalize on the good name of a famous actor who personally recorded the sales message. This tape was mailed to 500 hospital administrators and a complete sampling of all products mentioned in the recording was timed to arrive approximately the same day as the tape. The entire cost of the promotion was $8,000.

QUESTIONS

1. Do you think this is an effective way to promote disposable items to hospitals? Why?
2. Will Masters' salesmen like the new promotion method?
3. Do you believe pre-selling by mechanical devices is a coming thing in salesmanship?

44.

Great Western Insurance Company
Selling Capitalism

For over thirty years, the Great Western Insurance Company of San Francisco has identified itself with strong anti-communism and has promoted the benefits of the capitalistic system. It has taken strong stands against government intervention in business and the evils of welfare statism in a unique promotion program designed to sell capitalism to persons in the western part of the United States.

Great Western is a medium-sized insurance company with over $800 million of life insurance in force. It specializes in selling all types of life insurance to persons in California, Oregon, and Washington. Management believes that by making the truth about our capitalistic system available to the citizenry at large "The system will be better known and understood and the creeping cancer of socialism will be halted."

The promotion program of Great Western consists of five distinct phases:

1. Each year, Great Western mails over three million pieces of literature to its 100,000 policyholders. Copies of such works as the Declaration of Independence and the booklet, "Capitalism—The Truth About Our Economic System," have been mailed free to all policy holders. Another million copies of this literature are distributed free to elementary, junior, and senior high schools.

2. Each month, Great Western mails two short essays on basic economic principles prepared by well-known economists to all its policy holders.

3. Great Western maintains a Speaker's Bureau which lists fifty prominent economists Great Western will pay to speak to any groups which request them. At each speech, some Great Western literature is distributed, and the speaker suggests that those who wish to help with Great Western's crusade purchase their life insurance from Great Western agents.

4. On the college level, Great Western sponsors a "Freedom Seminar"

which runs for a full year. The 100 participating liberal arts students meet every Saturday for two hours and are paid $8 a week for attending.

5. Advertisements in major West Coast media are placed by Great Western. These advertisements explain the profit-oriented capitalistic system and compare it with other economic systems throughout the world.

Great Western spends $450,000 a year on this five-step promotion program. Its literature is often quoted in the editorial columns of newspapers and is widely used as teaching aids in primary and secondary schools. As nearly as can be determined, Great Western's program brings in 30 percent of its new policyholders, and various government officials have commented favorably upon the uniqueness of Great Western's approach to promotion.

QUESTIONS

1. Is Great Western spending its promotion dollars efficiently by promoting capitalism?
2. Is another type of promotion program needed to supplement Great Western's present efforts?
3. Evaluate each phase of Great Western's promotion program as to possible strengths and weaknesses.
4. What factors would dictate whether another company might successfully use Great Western's approach to promotion?

45.

Bunyon Paper Company
Changing the Corporate Image

A recent attitude survey indicates that Bunyon Paper Company is regarded as "old-fashioned, stodgy, conservative, and out-of-touch with the times." Bunyon has manufactured fine paper products since 1878 and presently produces paper and paper products which are sold to industrial and institutional markets.

Bunyon executives wish to discard the present image and replace it with the look of "a progressive, modern, profit-oriented corporation." The company has grown and become progressively more profitable through the years but is being overlooked because few people know that Bunyon supplies special papers for special purposes. For example, Bunyon makes a grease-proof paper which keeps people neat when they're eating french fries, fried chicken, or pizza.

In an effort to establish the new corporate image, Bunyon executives plan an advertising campaign in *Business Week* and *The Wall Street Journal*. This campaign will feature the many modern paper products manufactured by Bunyon and utilize headlines like "We didn't put the grease in french fries," and "Soaked records don't mean lost profits" (which tells of the ability of special Bunyon paper to be submerged in water and still not stretch or tear).

QUESTIONS

1. Will the planned advertising campaign have a noticeable effect upon Bunyon's image?
2. What other basic steps does Bunyon need to take to change its corporate image?
3. How can Bunyon determine whether or not its corporate image is changing? Will any such changes be rapid or slow?

46.

Jordan Electric, Inc.

Controlling Salesmen's Time Mathematically

Jordan Electric, an industrial manufacturer of switches, relays, and other electrical apparatus for industrial users, is trying to determine whether its salesmen are spending too much or too little time on individual accounts. Sales management would like to put itself in a position where they could help salesmen apportion their selling time to accounts on a rational basis.

Jordan's sales analysis department developed a mathematical formula based upon three factors: customer sales, customer sales potential, and selling time spent with each customer. By using multiple regression analysis, a relationship between selling time, customer potential, and market share was established. Then, these factors were weighted to mathematically pinpoint the time a salesman should spend on an account based upon the share of business he is now getting from a customer and the potential sales.

The formula developed from the estimates made by Jordan's seventy salesmen is as follows:

$$.97 + .0050\,(P) + .14\,(MS) = T$$

In the formula, .97 is a constant—the amount of fixed time to be spent on any account regardless of size, P is the account's potential size in thousands of dollars, MS is anticipated market share in percentage, and T is the percentage of a salesman's total time which should be spent with a specific account.

To obtain computer input, each salesman was asked to estimate sales potential for each of his customers and how much time he spent on each account. This information was fed into a computer and the multiple regression technique applied to the data.

An example will illustrate the use of the formula. On an account with a sales potential of $500,000 and with an expected market share of 30 percent, the calculations would be as follows:

Fixed time	.97%
.0050 × $500	2.50
.14 × 30	4.20
Percent of man's total time to be spent on the account	7.67%

All of Jordan's salesmen are paid on a commission basis. To give more impact to the salesman's judgment, a ± 20 percent leeway in selling time spent on a particular account is allowed. In the above example, the salesman could spend from 6.14 percent to 9.20 percent of his total selling time on the account.

QUESTIONS

1. Has Jordan Electric discovered an accurate way to allocate its salesmen's time?
2. Could another company use the same formula to allocate the time of its salesmen?
3. What uses can Jordan sales management make of this approach to allocating sales time?
4. Under what conditions would the Jordan formula work best? When would it be of little value?

47.

Kitchen-Master, Inc.

Compensation of Salesmen

Kitchen-Master, a Los Angeles corporation, makes a complete line of detergents for kitchen use in restaurants, hospitals, and other institutions. Its best selling product is Dish-Kleen, an automatic dishwasher compound, but it also makes Pot-Kleen for pots and pans, Sparkle-Kleen for removing sulfide buildups and other stains from silverware, and Liqui-Kleen, an all-purpose liquid detergent for general use.

Kitchen-Master's 500 salesmen traditionally have been paid a basic salary of $500 per month and a 15 percent commission on the dollar value of products sold. They have the use of an automobile and presently are paid expenses. The sales of Dish-Kleen amount to 90 percent of the sales of all four products. Therefore, Kitchen-Master's sales manager wished to encourage the sale of the other three products. He decided to do so by rewarding salesmen for putting forth more effort in selling Pot-Kleen, Sparkle-Kleen, and Liqui-Kleen.

Basically, the salesman's new compensation plan would work as follows: (1) Salesmen would still receive $500 per month salary providing they reach a management-determined sales volume quota for their respective territories. (2) The commission feature would be retained but salesmen would receive 5 percent commission on the sales of Dish-Kleen and 20 percent on the sales of the other three products. (3) A yearly bonus of 10 percent of dollar sales would be paid each salesman providing he significantly increases the sales of each product over the previous year's sales. (4) As before, an automobile would be provided and expenses would be paid.

Kitchen-Master's sales manager believes the new compensation plan will put more sales emphasis upon Pot-Kleen, Sparkle-Kleen, and Liqui-Kleen while retaining the present high sales volume of Dish-Kleen. In addition, the yearly bonus would get each salesman to put forth a maximum effort to sell every product in the line.

QUESTIONS

1. Evaluate the new compensation plan from both the viewpoint of the salesman and sales management.
2. What important guidelines must management consider in developing a compensation plan for salesmen?

48.

Telrad Corporation

Determining Why a Salesman Doesn't Sell

Telrad Corporation, a manufacturer of radio and television tubes and parts, hired Ralph Baldwin, a star salesman of Calco, Inc., another manufacturer producing essentially the same products. After selling the Telrad line for six months, Baldwin's performance is under evaluation by his district sales manager.

Baldwin has not made his sales volume quota and seems unable to sell Telrad's customers enough products to warrant retaining him as a salesman. He has been selling essentially the same products in the territory he previously worked for Calco. The only apparent difference is that he is now calling on wholesalers and retail dealers rather than manufacturers.

Mr. Baldwin was hired on a straight commission basis and put immediately into the field to capitalize on his sales ability. His sales influence on customers is revealed by the following conversations between the district manager and two accounts on which Mr. Baldwin calls regularly.

The buyer for a wholesaler had this to report. "Mr. Baldwin never gets to the root of a problem. He keeps talking about using your products in production lines and completely ignores the fact that most of our business is with retail dealers and small repair shops."

A retail dealer appraised Mr. Baldwin in these words. "He doesn't seem to know my needs. He's a walking encyclopedia on how tubes and things are made, but he knows almost nothing of selling radio and TV tubes to the 'do-it-yourselfer.' In fact, the last time he was here, he didn't even know about your special promotion offer. How can I do business with him?"

The district sales manager called Baldwin into the office to discuss his progress with Telrad. Over a cup of coffee, Baldwin said: "I know I haven't done well with Telrad. The big reason I came with you is that I thought I'd make more money on straight commission than I was making on a salary-bonus plan. But, I'm not able to make anywhere near as much as I did with Calco. I guess I'm just better equipped to sell Calco's products."

QUESTIONS

1. How can Baldwin be a star salesman for Calco and do so poorly selling the same general line of products for Telrad?
2. Was Telrad wise to put Baldwin on a straight commission compensation plan?
3. Should Baldwin have been put right into the field or should he have received some sales training from Telrad?
4. What should the Telrad sales manager recommend now?

49.

The Caustic Consultant (B)

Analysis of an Advertising Problem

John Lee, marketing consultant, was notified by phone by an upstate advertising agency, Davenport's, of the need for a meeting. Lee had the reputation of being accurate, expensive, and blunt. Marion Flaberty, an account executive for Davenport's, insisted on seeing Lee despite the latter's heavy schedule and protests.

Lee asked Flaberty to drop in the following Saturday morning at 8 A.M. Flaberty had to rise at four o'clock to drive down to Lee's office for the session. Lee was waiting impatiently when Flaberty arrived at 8:05 A.M.

"Sit down, Mr. Flaberty," offered Lee. "What's your story?"

"I have a problem, Mr. Lee. It's to figure out an advertising campaign for my major client, the Northern Plastics and Ceramics Corporation."

"Flaberty, what's so different about your client? Is it insolvent?"

"No, Mr. Lee, just the opposite. The ceramics division has sold everything it makes and is working three shifts to supply a Swedish development in long-range power transmission which requires a complete reinsulation of high tension wires. The company's backlog is growing rapidly. The forecast sees no letup for two years."

"Flaberty, you're wasting time for both of us," said Lee. "You have no problem. I'll drop you a note when I send you my bill. Good day, Mr. Flaberty." Lee got up and walked out. Flaberty looked at his watch. It was 8.07 A.M.

QUESTIONS

1. Was Lee correct in his judgment that Flaberty had no problem?
2. If Flaberty didn't have a problem, what did he have? Who had the problem?

3. The consulting bill arrived—the fee was $100. A small note was attached. Was the fee reasonable? What would you, as Lee, have put in the note?
4. How would René Descartes have analyzed the situation?

50.

Acme Tool and Die Manufacturing Company

Sales Force Management During Unfavorable Economic Conditions

Acme Tool and Die Manufacturing Company, which has its headquarters in the industrial Northeast, is a large manufacturer of end mills, drill bits, dies, and other related industrial tools. Its major distribution channel is a network of small and medium-sized industrial tool distributors located in major industrial cities throughout the United States.

Acme does some advertising in prominent trade publications in order to keep the company name before industrial distributors and other buyers. For its main promotional effort, however, Acme relies on its personal selling force. These men call on various industrial distributors in their territories, taking orders and working with industrial distributors' salesmen and their clients. Creating new distributorships is also a responsibility of the company's salesmen because, when one distributor in an area fails to move Acme's industrial tools, another one is appointed to take his place. Moreover, with a growing demand for tools, new distributors are constantly needed to service new customers.

Over the past several months, the growth of the economy has been somewhat sluggish, and sales by major industrial firms have been declining. Most recently, many production workers have been laid off because of insufficient demand and stockpiling of inventories.

Acme management has noticed the beginnings of its own sales decline and has initiated its own measures in anticipation of an even more unfavorable sales picture. The effect of the economic recession also is being felt by many salesmen who are beginning to experience cancelled orders by local distributors. Some distributors are beginning to return much of their inventory stock to the company for refund or credit.

Alarmed by these continuing occurrences, management, through the company sales manager, asked that drastic measures be taken to reverse the company's unfavorable sales trend. Responsibility for achieving results was assigned to the sales manager. He immediately called a sales meeting at which he made the point quite clear that any sales person who did not meet his yearly sales quota would be subject to termination. Moreover, as an economy measure, the sales manager informed all sales personnel that all selling and traveling expenses had to be cut. Sales personnel who had been with the company for many years and would be approaching retirement in about ten years had no choice but to respond to the sales manager's edict.

Company sales personnel began to use "hard push" or "pressure" selling tactics in an effort to make their quotas. It was very difficult to make much headway, however, especially since management clamped down on entertainment and traveling expenses. Customer resistance and ill will began to build up because customers resented the salesmen's attempts to overstock them, and the mounting resentment made it increasingly difficult to make a sale at all.

With no sales being generated and selling expenses mounting, the company sales manager announced a further tightening of travel expense. As a result of the further cut-backs, many salesmen began to travel only two days a week and stayed close to home so they would not have to incur motel expenses and could, at the same time, keep automobile expenses down. Further expense-reducing measures on the part of the salesmen included a reduction of automobile maintenance costs. Salesmen intentionally neglected periodic dealer inspections and engine tune-ups. The automobiles, which were owned by the company, were now running twice as many miles between oil changes. Many salesmen had not had their automobiles washed since the economy measures were announced.

After several months had passed and the industrial distributors' inventories had been depleted to low levels, company sales figures began to show signs of a leveling off in its sales slump, and tool distributors began again to order merchandise from the company. All was not the same, however. Salesmen reported that there had been significant penetration of the market by competing tool manufacturers during the economic slump. Acme lost several good, long-time customers which had been sole distributors of Acme tools. As one salesman put it, "While we were cutting costs and alienating our customers with the 'hard-sell,' our competitors were continuing to consistently call on our distributors and managed to win some of them over."

QUESTIONS

1. What were the *major* problems confronting Acme during this period of economic decline?
2. How would you evaluate the sales manager's approach to these problems?
3. Under these same circumstances, what approach would you have taken to solve these problems? Explain.

51.

Foto-Print, Inc.

Appraisal of the Total Promotion Program

The reproduction of written records by "xerography" was first developed by Chester Carlson in a kitchen on Long Island, New York. The name for the process comes from the Greek term "xerographis," which means "to write dry." From the original primitive process has grown the dry copying industry with a government and business market of $200 billion per year. Corporations in the industry include the Xerox Corporation, 3M, and Eastman Kodak. Although these larger firms dominate the industry, many smaller corporations are engaged in tapping the industry's vast sales potential.

Foto-Print, Inc., manufactures "desk top" dry copying machines which range in price from $800 to $2,700. The company produced its first machine in 1959 and presently has sales of $30 million spread over five models—FC-101, FC-102, FC-103, FC-104, and FC-105. These machines range from small machines which produce one copy at a time to large machines which produce multiple copies. All can be housed on top of a standard-sized office desk.

To promote the sales of its dry copying machines, Foto-Print has been spending 10 percent of the previous year's net sales. Net sales and the total promotion budgets for recent years are as shown in Exhibit 1.

Foto-Print has been using a promotion mix consisting of personal selling, sales promotion, advertising, and publicity. Fifty percent of the total promotion budget is spent on personal selling, 35 percent on advertising, 10 percent on sales promotion, and 5 percent on publicity. This is the average way promotion dollars are allocated to promotion tools by the leading companies in the industry.

Personal Selling

Foto-Print has a sales force of 380 men scattered throughout twenty-five sales offices in leading metropolitan areas. A typical large branch office, such as the one in New York City, employs about fifty people. Beside employees who handle customer service and supply, each large branch office has a branch sales manager and three district sales managers, each of whom directs an average of eight sales representatives, two sales trainees, and three systems specialists.

Sales representatives are paid an average salary of $14,000 per year plus expenses and a $3,500 branch group bonus. In order for a sales representative to get his bonus, every sales representative in that branch office must reach his sales volume quota. It is felt that such a bonus plan promotes team spirit among the salesmen.

Sales trainees are college graduates and start on a straight salary of $9,000 per year plus expenses. Foto-Print prefers to hire trainees who have had some sales experience although it does not necessarily have to be in the business-machines industry. Criteria for hiring sales trainees are personality, I.Q., emotional stability, and desire to succeed. Sales trainees are recruited exclusively from college campuses, and business administration majors have the best chance of being hired. Each applicant is interviewed by at least five people and is given an intelligence test and personality test. The applicant's credit rating and personal references are also checked by mail.

The new trainee is indoctrinated at the branch sales office where he receives a thirty-day product and sales knowledge training course. At the same time, he is given sales skill training under the supervision of the district manager or an experienced salesman. Most of his sales skill training consists of making calls on Foto-Print's customers to learn about Foto-Print's products and their applications. The skill training continues for another sixty days past the initial thirty-day training period. At the end of this time, the trainee is assigned a sales territory.

Sales Promotion

Foto-Print's customers are mainly office managers, purchasing agents, and secretaries. To reach and demonstrate equipment to these three groups, the company has annual exhibits in 600 business and trade shows. When a new product is introduced, twenty-five, one-day seminars are conducted for customers and prospects at the branch sales offices. Sales brochures, instruction booklets, and so forth, are also prepared and distributed to customers and prospects. Other sales promotion devices are not considered to be of much value in selling copying machines.

Advertising

Foto-Print spends most of its advertising budget in business publications such as *Business Week, Business Automation, Forbes, Nation's Business*

The Office, Administrative Management, Modern Office Procedures, and *Today's Secretary.*

The objective of Foto-Print's advertising is to sell its copying machines. Management believes that keeping its name in front of its prospect groups will eventually lead to a brand franchise and increased sales and profits. The advertising budget is split about equally among the five machines in the line.

Pilton, Rossen and Young, Inc. is the advertising agency retained by Foto-Print. This agency prepares all advertisements and writes the sales promotion literature. No particular advertising campaign themes are used as the advertising agency believes that selling the industrial and business markets is largely a matter of "reason why" advertising. Each advertisement is created separately and made to stand on its "own two feet." Advertisements are not tested since both Foto-Print and the agency believe the money that might be used for advertising tests is better spent on trade publication space for the product line.

Publicity

The publicity program at Foto-Print varies somewhat from year to year. When a new machine is introduced, the "new products" editors of the leading business publications receive a two-day trip to New York with expenses assumed by Foto-Print. At this gathering, the new machine is shown and demonstrated, and related literature is also distributed.

Other business publications and newspapers receive publicity releases with photographs of the new machine and explanatory literature. As a result of these efforts, Foto-Print receives much publicity on the new product in the "New Products" columns of business magazines and newspapers.

Company executives and branch managers are encouraged to join business groups, clubs, and so forth, to become officers of these groups, and to make speeches when appropriate. Any expenses involved are charged to the publicity budget.

A clipping service is retained to keep track of magazine and newspaper lineage generated by the publicity program. As nearly as the company can determine, each dollar spent for publicity returns $15 worth of space in magazines and newspapers.

QUESTIONS

1. Does Foto-Print's method of determining and allocating its promotion budget agree with correct marketing practices?
2. Evaluate Foto-Print's salesman compensation plan.

3. Does Foto-Print have well-planned recruiting, selection, and trainin[g] programs for salesmen?
4. Evaluate Foto-Print's sales promotion, advertising, and publicity pro[-] grams.

EXHIBIT 1
Net Sales and Total Promotion Budgets
of Foto-Print, Inc. (1960-1970)

Year	Net Sales	Total Promotion Budge[t]
1960	$ 5,050,725	$ 481,237
1961	7,480,869	505,072
1962	10,270,452	748,086
1963	15,390,243	1,027,045
1964	17,873,487	1,539,024
1965	18,954,729	1,787,348
1966	19,805,274	1,895,472
1967	21,481,576	1,980,527
1968	25,711,015	2,148,157
1969	27,403,819	2,571,101
1970	30,000,000*	2,740,381

*Forecasted

52.
Lakeland Laboratories
Promotion of Pharmaceuticals

Overview of Operation

Lakeland Laboratories is one of the top five drug manufacturers in the United States with sales of over $90 million. It is one of a dozen leading firms which are engaged in laboratory research for developing new drug compounds and products. The pharmaceutical industry is composed of over 500 firms, most of which are small or medium-sized. The smaller firms do not engage in new product research and development. Instead, they manufacture widely accepted drugs on which patents have expired. Since drugs are life-preserving, in most instances, patents on them are not renewable.

Lakeland's research and manufacturing complex, located in Philadelphia, contains over fifty buildings. Some manufacturing is also done in facilities near Oklahoma City and Los Angeles. Lakeland Laboratories has two major divisions: the pharmaceutical division which markets more than sixty prescription drugs through wholesalers and retailers and the fine chemicals division which manufactures vitamins sold mostly in bulk to food and drug manufacturers.

The pharmaceutical division has an enviable reputation, having pioneered in the development of a number of important new drug products. For instance, Lakeland was a leader in developing tranquilizers, sleep-inducing agents, and pain-relieving drugs.

Distribution and Storage

Physical distribution is accomplished through four regionally located distribution centers in Atlanta, Denver, Philadelphia, and St. Louis. These four centers store and deliver drugs to wholesalers, retail pharmacies, hospitals, and other institutional buyers. In the storage of drugs, temperature control is important since many compounds are sensitive to heat, light, and moisture change. Many items have to be refrigerated and it is often necessary to store drugs in vaults to protect against theft.

Promotion

A study of the organization chart, shown in Exhibit 1, reveals the great emphasis management places on the personal selling function. Reporting to the general sales manager are the heads of four separate departments with specialized sales or sales-related functions.

Since Lakeland is an ethical drug manufacturer, advertising plays a secondary role in its promotional efforts. Lakeland does not advertise through such mass media as television, radio, and newspapers. Ethical drug advertising is restricted largely to the medical journals read by doctors and other medical personnel. In addition, sales literature is prepared and sent to doctors through the mail or is delivered to the doctor's office by the visiting sales representative. The advertising department also furnishes the services of a product advertising manager to the promotional planning team that is set up by Lakeland for each product.

Sales Organization and Planning

Six regional sales managers head the field sales organization. Each of these regional managers has up to nine division sales managers reporting to him. The division sales managers, together with the six regional sales managers, supervise the activities of 500 Lakeland salesmen. Typical activities of field sales management include recruiting and selecting salesmen, supervising their field training, and compensating and motivating them. Through the collection and analysis of daily and weekly reports submitted by the salesmen, these sales managers control the sales activities in the field.

The sales planning department is staffed by twelve product sales managers. Each of these product sales managers is responsible for planning the promotion of certain Lakeland products. Each serves on a team which also includes a product advertising manager, a product research man, and a product marketing manager. These four men are responsible for developing the advertising and sales plan for their products in each of the company's forty divisions. Together they determine the type of advertising literature that is to be distributed to doctors and pharmacists. They plan the amount of time salesmen should spend calling on doctors, druggists, and institutional staff members. For established products, more time might be allocated for detail work in drug stores. On the other hand, when a product is being introduced for the first time, doctors are the prime targets. Since the sales interview must be brief, the planning team has to decide which product benefits are to be stressed, what sales literature should be left at the doctor's office, and which literature should be sent him through the mail.

The Sales Effort

Because of the many tasks the pharmaceutical salesman performs, frequently he is referred to as a "detail man." Nevertheless, he is the most important force in the promotional mix. Lakeland has 500 sales specialists. Each man calls on the doctors in his territory. Physicians are so busy today that they frequently do not read the advertisements in the medical journals and the literature they receive by mail. It is the responsibility of the detail man to get the message to the doctor.

Unlike most other types of salesmen, the drug salesman cannot close the sale in the doctor's office and write up the order. He can ask the doctor to prescribe the new medicine on a trial basis. Moreover, he has a scant five or ten minutes in which to talk about the benefits of his product. In the past, salesmen often left free samples in the doctor's office, but this practice is on the decline today.

A salesman's calls on druggists, wholesalers, and hospitals must be fitted around the doctor's schedules. A typical call upon a druggist might include a brief chat with the pharmacist behind the counter. After explaining the benefits of a new drug, the salesman might then check the inventory in the druggist's refrigerator, remove outdated biologicals, resupply the stock if necessary, and then depart.

To help evaluate the effectiveness of the sales force, Lakeland subscribes to the services of a research firm that calls on drug stores and "audits" the filled prescriptions. In this manner, an actual count of brand market share is obtained for each territory.

One regional sales coordinator is assigned to each of the six regional sales managers by Lakeland. The coordinator works on special problems associated with selling drugs to large institutional customers such as hospitals. By working closely with managers, he is able to determine the needs of the specific institutions. Since institutions purchase in large quantities, the work of the regional sales coordinator is very important.

Sales Career Development Department

This department is responsible for the development and implementation of a variety of training programs. One of the most important of these is the training of young men who have been recruited for the sales force. The recruits are brought to Philadelphia for a six-week program of intensive study of products and communication techniques. Special seminars for sales managers also are conducted.

Another important activity of the sales career development department is the certification program for senior salesmen. In this program, candidates study, take written examinations, participate in seminars, and plan and develop a written project. Successful completion of this comprehensive program leads to a sizable salary increase and a promotion.

QUESTIONS

1. Is the team approach to the planning of the promotion of each product a workable system? What are the advantages and the disadvantages of such a system?
2. From the standpoint of marketing economy, would it be wise for Lakeland and other leading pharmaceutical firms to switch to the use of mass advertising media and thereby reduce the cost of detail selling?
3. If the practice of giving free samples to doctors is discontinued by the drug firms, what should be the role of the sales representatives?
4. Evaluate the organization of Lakeland's promotional activities. What are the strengths? Are there any weaknesses?

EXHIBIT 1

Organization of Lakeland Laboratories–Pharmaceutical Division

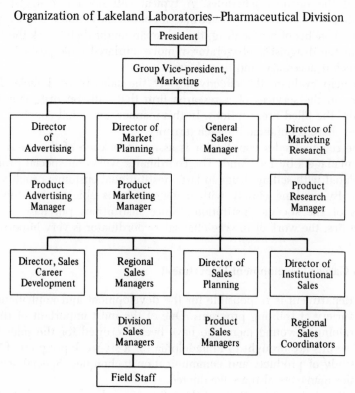

53.

Components, Inc.

Measuring Salesman Performance

Components, Inc. manufactures and sells a line of electrical equipment products directly to industrial buyers. The company has been undergoing substantial changes in such important facets of the business as product line expansion and diversification, promotion policies, and organization of the marketing department. Company executives are particularly concerned about the ability of the field sales force to adapt to the changes which will affect their activities.

In recent months, sales have been somewhat disappointing. It appears that the sales force is not operating as efficiently as was expected. The firm's vice-president has suggested that the general sales manager begin to accompany some of the field salesmen on their sales trips in order to determine the effect the recent company changes have had on the sales effort and to analyze the performance of the salesmen.

The sales manager, in conferring with the vice-president, expressed his desire to experiment with a new technique which he had devised for measuring the performance of the company's salesmen. He pointed out that any personal observation which he, as general sales manager, could make may not be as satisfactory as a less direct method. He went on to discuss some of the special characteristics of the selling job which dictate against the common observation method.

First, the creative nature of some selling jobs may attract an individual who is an individualist by nature and who works alone by choice. He may prefer to work in his own way, on his own schedule, and by himself. Company prescribed routine may even bore him; indeed, routine may frustrate his senses and lower his efficiency. However, a self-imposed, highly routinized work week may be acceptable when rigidly self-enforced. Thus, effective performance may be achieved when sales force routine considers different personality traits.

Second, each selling situation, each customer, each prospect, and even each day may have unique characteristics to which the salesman must respond. These factors require adjustments in sales approach and in time allocation which ultimately result in wide variations in the returns on selling expense and in the use of job standards.

Third, sales operations are performed away from supervisors. Thus, an observer must make obvious and bias-producing efforts to collect pertinent data. Observation may result in a salesman operating abnormally to coincide with some preconceived notion of the desires of management or of job standards. An observer of a nonroutine function such as selling has little chance of detecting and measuring abnormal behavior.

Fourth, since observers must allocate an amount of time equivalent to the study period for each salesman, a relatively large expenditure of observation time must be made. Consequently, the company must either use a team of observers large enough to finish the project within a reasonable period of time or, since the firm is not endowed with unlimited research staff resources, extend the study over a relatively long time period.

Fifth, customers may even react to observation in a way which can bias results. For example, a customer may act abnormally in an effort to be a "good friend" by helping the salesman.

As an alternative to the suggested personal observation, the sales manager requested that he be allowed to experiment with a time and duty study to answer the vice-president's questions about the sales force. After some further discussion, the permission was granted. The study was a week-long census of all regular salesmen in a selected region who were on duty during the whole study week and who were present for an intensive explanatory sales meeting prior to the study week. The most unique aspect of the study was that, unlike other known time and duty analyses, this study was self-administered: each salesman kept his own time-activities records.

During the preliminary study design period, the elements of a salesman's job were analyzed in conversations with all regional and district management personnel who had any connection with the salesmen or who had any knowledge of their activities. Also, the sales manager spent one week traveling with and observing three salesmen. Through these discussions and observations, sufficient job description information was obtained to design a preprinted activities form. Specifically, the form was designed to collect data which could identify activities, define the time spent on each, and determine the location of the activity, that is, in the field, in the office, at home, or in transit.

The company scheduled a two-hour sales meeting for a formal introduction to the study. The manager of the region involved emphasized the strong interest which company management has in the results of the study and requested complete cooperation by each salesman. The general sales manager then reemphasized and explained the need for cooperation. The help of each salesman was enlisted by carefully reviewing the objectives of the study and by showing how the aggregate data could be used to form a profile of the sales force. The preprinted questionnaire and accompanying procedures were presented and were discussed in detail. Essential to the success of the study was a promise of anonymity; the sales manager guaranteed that the individual activities which would be listed on personally mailed daily forms would be analyzed by an outside research group and only summary data would be divulged to company management.

The salesmen professed keen interest in the project. Only one man expressed an adverse reaction on being called upon to participate. Also, in only one case was the daily activity report filled out in such a manner as to indicate that the salesman had filled out the questionnaire after several calls, or at the end of the day, rather than as he progressed. The data which were generated contained no evidence of confusion or misunderstanding in regard to the allocation of time to the various listed activities.

Follow-up discussions with 25 percent of the salesmen verified the high degree of interest and cooperation of the respondents and the clarity and understanding of procedures. When the study was over and the data analyzed, company management was able to make decisions which resulted in the reallocation of sales force responsibilities and in a more effective sales organization. The vice-president was well satisfied with the study results and considered applying the theory to other problem areas.

QUESTIONS

1. Analyze and contrast the do-it-yourself method with the personal observation method.
2. Specifically, compare the two methods as to the following: preliminary project design planning; tabulation and evaluation of data; timing problems and time requirements; potential disruption of sales activities; cost; and validity, sample size, and bias.
3. Would the performance analysis procedure, in which the salesman keeps his own records, be effective for all types of sales jobs? Explain.

54.

Orange Growers' Association
Cooperative Promotion of Oranges

Background

Recognizing the need to help themselves, the orange growers of Florida, Texas, Arizona, and California banded together into an association with the purpose of extensively promoting oranges and orange products. This Association attempts to increase the domestic demand for oranges and orange products by promoting them as a product class (primary demand) rather than promoting specific branded orange products (selective demand). The Orange Growers' Association provides the overall promotion program for its grower-members and leaves the promotion of brands to the individual producers. The Association's promotion efforts go toward establishing oranges as the "best" citrus for the American public to consume.

Prior to the establishment of the Orange Growers' Association in 1946, chaotic conditions prevailed in the orange-producing sections of the country. These conditions were due to: (1) unorganized marketing activities of orange growers; (2) the selling of oranges of substandard quality; and (3) oversupplies of oranges which led to depressed prices.

United States producers of oranges were an independent group, not inclined toward cooperative effort and very resentful of outside interference in their business affairs. After several particularly bad years, which resulted in the bankruptcy of numerous growers, efforts were made toward cooperative marketing of the orange crop.

The lack of grade inspection requirements and standards on oranges undermined dealer and consumer confidence in the quality of oranges grown in the United States. Much "green" (immature) fruit and freeze-damaged fruit was shipped to market with almost complete disregard for its effects on future market conditions. The reaction of dealers and consumers to this poor-quality fruit was so bad that it led one leading orange grower to remark that "Customers who used to swear by our fruit are now swearing at us."

The rapidly growing volume of oranges to be marketed in the face of a rather apathetic demand by consumers was another serious problem that faced growers. Increased plantings of orange trees in prior years had led to oversupplies of oranges which resulted in depressed prices. These depressed prices tended to remain since the average life of an orange tree is eighty years.

Orange growers realized that so long as they sold their fruit as individuals, they would be at the mercy of speculators and commission buyers. This realization led to the formation of the Orange Growers' Association shortly after World War II.

The main objective of this organization is to market its members' oranges at the best possible prices. It controls shipments, not production, and it has the power to decide on what fruit is to be shipped immediately to market, what is to be temporarily withheld, and what is to be permanently withheld from the market. Oranges that are permanently withheld are sent to byproducts plants to make pectin and essential orange oils.

The Association set up a grading system for oranges which is utilized when its 30,000 grower-members, who make up 80 percent of all U.S. orange growers, market their oranges through Association packing houses. Each grower is credited with the exact grades and sizes he delivers and is paid accordingly upon marketing or processing of the fruit.

To stimulate the sale of oranges, the Association carries on extensive advertising and publicity activities. Promotion budgets are counted in millions of dollars and are financed by assessments on each box of oranges handled by the Association. Presently, the assessment is eight cents per standard carton.

Advertising Objectives

For each of the last five years, the advertising objectives of the Association were as shown in Exhibit 1.

These objectives were used to guide the Association's advertising efforts. The 1970 advertising budget was $6,000,000. Lambert-King, Inc., the Association's advertising agency since 1963, used these objectives to guide its creative advertising efforts.

Advertising Copy Themes

The Association has used various consumer copy themes in the advertising of oranges. Since 1966, the copy themes were as shown in Exhibit 2.

The basic copy theme for the year is repeated in each advertisement regardless of the media in which the advertisement appears. The Association believes a new fresh copy theme is needed for each year, and the same theme is not repeated two years in a row.

Basic Media Strategy

The Association identifies its market for oranges as the United States consuming population. The basic media strategy is to select media which will expose the largest part of the U.S. consuming public to the Association's advertising. Some of the other basic media strategies are: (1) to utilize media which offer the maximum opportunity for the exploitation of new copy; broadcast time and printed space must be sufficient to permit a complete and detailed delivery of the copy story; (2) whenever possible, the budget should be concentrated in one advertising medium so that the Association can appear to be a "big" advertiser in that medium; and (3) continuity and flexibility in media are a necessity.

From these statements concerning media strategy, it can be seen that continuity, flexibility, and "bigness" have been basic Association considerations in media selection. The way the Association has spent advertising dollars by media class is shown in Exhibit 3.

Advertising Agency Selection

Although the Association has stated no general policy in regard to the selection of advertising agencies, it has a basic philosophy on this subject. Whenever the Association feels a change in advertising agencies might be desirable, various agencies are invited to make speculative presentations at public hearings. In 1970, seven advertising agencies were invited to make speculative presentations for the Association account.

The Association has stated its position as: "Periodically, the Association should look at some new ideas and copy strategy. The field of marketing is constantly changing, and our orange crop is getting steadily larger."

Advertising agencies have been changed on occasion based on speculative presentations. A list of Association advertising agencies and the years they represented the Association are as shown in Exhibit 4.

Publicity Program

The Orange Growers' Association has conducted a consumer publicity program since 1946 to "secure consistent, frequent, and favorable stories in the nation's food press." Since its inception, the Association's publicity program has tried to secure as much "free" space and time as possible and insure that news about oranges and orange products is placed in the print and broadcast media where "advertising cannot be purchased or sensibly afforded."

Yancy, Warwick, Young, Inc., of New York City has been the Association's publicity agency since 1946 and has conducted a varied publicity program. A home economics department is maintained by the agency, and the test kitchen of this department develops new ideas, uses, and recipes for oranges and orange products. Recipes developed and tested there are sent to the food editors of newspapers, magazines, radio stations, and television stations throughout the United States.

Publicity releases, stories, color and black-and-white photographs, electrotypes, mats, and so forth, are released to printed media and national press syndicates. Radio and television scripts are prepared and sent to stations for broadcasting purposes. Short films have been produced for television and are utilized by television stations in their daily programming.

The Orange Growers' Association is represented by its publicity agency at important media and professional conventions such as the Newspaper Food Editors' Conference, American Home Economics Association, American Dietetic Association, and American Medical Association. Meetings of the National 4-H Club and other youth groups are attended and literature is distributed.

Luncheons for food editors, tours for food editors through the orange-producing regions of the U.S., traveling home economists, and consumer contests round out a full publicity program. The success of many of these activities is difficult to measure except in an indirect way, that is, through such measures as total circulation of print media, the number of programs on radio and television, and the dollar value of space and time utilized for Association publicity messages.

Exhibit 5 shows the circulation of Association newspaper food page publicity by season. This exhibit indicates that Association publicity messages were seen by an increasing number of persons over the past ten years.

Conclusion

The Orange Growers' Association is not completely satisfied with its promotion program. Overproduction of oranges and the accompanying depressed prices are still problems. Consumers seem unwilling to greatly increase their consumption of oranges and orange products despite the promotional expenditures of the Association. Unless some way is soon found to market the bulk of the orange crop at profitable prices, grower membership in the Association is expected to decline.

QUESTIONS

1. Should the Orange Growers' Association change its copy theme every year as is the present practice? Why?

2. Is the Association's market for oranges the entire U.S. consuming public? Is this assumption helpful in advertising oranges? Why?
3. Do you agree with the basic media strategies underlying the selection
   of media for Association advertising? Explain.
4. Are speculative presentations made by advertising agencies a rational
   way for the Association to select an advertising agency? Why?
5. What improvements can the Association make in its advertising program? In its publicity program?

EXHIBIT 1

Orange Growers' Association Consumer
Advertising Objectives (1966-1970)

Year	Consumer Advertising Objective
1966	To increase consumption of oranges in the United States.
1967	To dispose of the Association's orange crop at price levels profitable to members.
1968	To build in the consumer's mind the need and desire for oranges.
1969	To increase the demand for oranges by increasing per capita consumption.
1970	To obtain greater use of oranges by present consumers.

EXHIBIT 2

Orange Consumer Advertising Copy Themes
Used by the Orange Growers' Association (1966-1970)

Year	Copy Theme
1966	"For that glow of health, eat oranges."
1967	"Good health can be closer than you think when you eat oranges."
1968	"Make sure your family has plenty of oranges—they're loaded with vitamin C."
1969	"Three reasons for squeezing fresh oranges are extra juice, extra vitamin C, and extra flavor."
1970	"Oranges are a powerhouse of vitamin C."

EXHIBIT 3
Allocation of Orange Growers' Association
Advertising Expenditures by Media Class (1966-1970)

Year	Newspapers	Magazines	Radio	Television	Outdoor
1966	26.3%	13.5%	7.0%	52.6%	0.3%
1967	20.1	18.2	5.5	55.8	0.4
1968	10.1	18.7	2.5	68.77	———
1969	23.0	35.0	———	42.2	———
1970	36.7	54.0	———	9.3	———

EXHIBIT 4
Orange Growers' Association
Advertising Agencies Employed (1946-1970)

Advertising Agency	Period of Employment
Ryan and Associates	1946-1947
Lambert-King, Inc.	1947-1955
Blackston-Singleton-Wilton, Inc.	1955-1958
Narstel Advertising, Inc.	1958-1963
Lambert-King, Inc.	1963 to present

EXHIBIT 5
Circulation of Orange Growers' Association
Newspaper Food Page Publicity (1961-1970)

Year	Circulation
1961	571,400,177
1962	660,835,242
1963	711,627,086
1964	740,672,019
1965	775,826,003
1966	802,497,521
1967	835,411,014
1968	870,003,979
1969	905,982,115
1970	932,223,055

III.
MARKETING
IN SPECIALIZED AREAS

MARKETING
OF CONSUMER SERVICES

55.
Home Rentals, Inc.
An Opportunity to Capitalize on a New Life-style

William Smith, who had been looking for a small business investment opportunity, was impressed with an Associated Press story in his hometown newspaper. It stated that an estimated 41.5 million Americans moved in 1968. The gist of the article was as follows: mobility is a dominant life-style in a nation founded by immigrants, expanded by pioneers pushing West, and revolutionized by the move to the big city and industry. America is a nation in which more than three million hotel and motel rooms, night after night, await the traveler. America is also a nation in which only 15 percent of the population is content to remain in the same county for a lifetime; where the typical American family stays in the same house only 6½ years.

As he mulled over these statistics, Smith began to wonder what effect mobility was having on family shopping behavior and on retailing in general. Suddenly, he remembered that the neighbor across the street was going to be transferred to Atlanta, Georgia, in the near future. Jim Jones worked for General Electric and every three or four years was promoted to the managership of a larger branch office. Smith phoned Jones and asked him what effect the knowledge that he and his family would move every few years had on their purchasing habits. Jones replied without a moment's hesitation that many of his household possessions were scratched and damaged as a result of moves about the country. For this reason his family was turning more and more to renting.

"My wife and I recently gave a buffet supper party for thirty-four people and, while we have all the equipment to handle a party of that size, I rented everything. Since my wife works, catering and renting have become the only way to handle anything larger than dinner for eight."

"Our young son and his bride have just rented their first apartment in an Atlanta suburb and, along with the apartment itself, they rented everything that goes into it—bed, chairs, tables, couch, appliances, kitchen utensils, linens, decorations, etc." "It's great," he wrote us recently. "We

197

won't be stationed here long, so why burden ourselves with possessions we'll have to pack up and ship somewhere else?"

"As the advantages of renting become apparent, it should be possible to rent any kind of merchandise for the family and home," Jones added. "For example," he continued, "in the near future more and more families will probably turn to renting the second and third car instead of buying them. This may be due to the fact that rental charges can be reduced with increased patronage. On the other hand, the cost of car repair and maintenance to the individual owner will probably continue to rise."

This conversation gave Smith an idea. Why not open a local rental branch for a national franchising organization? Not only has the American family become more mobile, but it also has more leisure time. The increased leisure time has challenged many individuals to develop their handicraft skills through a variety of hobbies requiring special tools and supplies. Simultaneously, the demand for family activities such as camping and travel has created new needs for specialized equipment which is used but once or twice a year, but which can be used on a rental basis more economically than if it were purchased.

William Smith was quite familiar with the survival statistics on new small businesses. According to Dun and Bradstreet data and information published by the Small Business Administration, a large percentage of small stores and other types of small businesses fail during the first or second year due to undercapitalization and the lack of experience in such specialized activities as buying, promotion, and the general management of the business. On the other hand, Smith knew that franchised motels, restaurants, and other types of small service enterprises are springing up all around the city—many of them on arterial highways. To the best of his knowledge, none of these had failed.

Enthused with his idea, Smith called the Atlanta office of Home Rentals, Inc. and talked to Dale Lambert, the regional Marketing Director, who agreed to send him the company literature on their line of rental merchandise.

The literature contained much of the information Smith needed to make a decision. The brochure indicated that he could start with a capital investment ranging from $10,000 to $25,000, depending on the size of operation desired. He would also need from $8,000 to $15,000 cash to cover payroll and other operating expenses. If an agreement was reached and a contract signed, location experts would come into Smith's city and together they would select the site. A good location is the single most important factor in the success of a rental business. The quality and quantity of homes, income level of owners in surrounding residential areas, display frontage and parking facilities for store customers, the relative location of arterial trafficways, size of store, storage and maintenance facilities related to rent, pass-by traffic and location of other businesses, lease terms —all were factors which had to be examined in site determination.

The brochure indicated that, once the site is agreed upon, a franchisee is given exclusive rights to a surrounding territory which is large enough to profitably support his business and provide a base for continued growth. With the site and the quality of the market determined, experts from the home office are then able to decide on the new unit's inventory which must be on hand for profitable rental on the day the new franchisee opens his doors. Providing inventory is a critical step in getting the business off on the right foot. The vast experience of Home Rentals management and its continuing analysis of what sells best in rental centers around the country is of great importance. Inventory selections are based on the items best suited to maximize profits for each kind of community.

Smith felt that the brochure's statement with regard to financing a new venture was quite accurate. It indicated that often a qualified individual, in his desire to own a business, commits all of his personal funds to the enterprise. He then has no adequate resources to tide him over the starting-up period. A Home Rentals franchisee does not have to commit all of his resources. If he qualifies, Home Rentals helps to finance his start. As he grows and develops his credit standing, additional dollars are available for expansion purposes.

Two weeks before a "grand opening" of a Home Rentals store, the franchisee is brought to the Home Rentals Training School for one week of intensive on-the-job preparation. Because this week of schooling is an absolute necessity to the successful operation of a Home Rentals Store, the company pays all costs of training, travel to and from the training center, and accommodations for the week.

When the trainee leaves the training center, he has learned store operation, inventory control, use of rental contracts, maintenance control procedures, telephone selling, and the planning and use of advertising and publicity materials. Furthermore, regional supervisors and other counselors will periodically visit the rental center and continue to give whatever help is needed for as long as the business is in operation.

Smith was very impressed with the expertise, the financial resources, and the thoroughness with which the central headquarters planned every step in the organization and opening of a new Home Rentals unit. He thought that he now understood why so few franchise operations in retailing failed, and he planned to spend more time in studying other franchising opportunities before making a final decision.

QUESTIONS

1. What are three advantages to the consumer of renting merchandise?
2. What other factors besides consumer mobility have contributed to the rapid growth of Home Rentals and other similar franchised stores that offer merchandise for rent?

3. What other small business opportunities should Smith examine before making a final choice?
4. Does the company literature tell the entire franchise story?
5. Are there any potential pitfalls to operating such a franchise?

56.

Ralston's Barber Shop
Revitalizing a Service Business

George Ralston is the owner and operator of his own barber shop about six blocks from the downtown area of a medium-sized city. He has just recently purchased the business (Happy's Barber Shop) from a friend, "Happy" Riley, who had experienced some business problems for several years and whose health had failed recently.

Ralston, who is forty years old, has been a barber for nearly three years. He has been working in a large shop in a suburban shopping center about three miles from his new shop since his graduation from a mid-western barber college. Ralston decided to be a barber after many years of hopping from one construction laborer job to another. His ultimate objective was to own his own barber shop. His wife encouraged this thinking strongly. Therefore, when his friend Riley indicated an interest in selling his business, Ralston borrowed some money from an out-of-town friend and bought the shop.

The shop is located in a neighborhood which, years before, had been quiet and completely residential. In recent years, the downtown area has expanded and several small businesses have sprung up in the area. Two large apartment buildings have also been built nearby. The overall character of the neighborhood is becoming commercial, although residential housing is still predominant. A junior high school is four blocks away, but very few students are customers.

Before buying the shop, Ralston talked extensively with Riley, who told him that most of the shop's clientele had remained the same for several years. Many of the customers lived in the neighborhood when Riley opened the shop nearly twenty years ago and appeared to be satisfied with the service. As the neighborhood changed, new customers were occasionally attracted, but most did not become steady customers. Riley volunteered to recommend to his customers that they continue to patronize the shop.

Most of the business was of the "walk-in" type, although Riley was willing to take appointments as well. If someone called to make an appointment, he was accommodated. If there were walk-in customers waiting, they were informed that the customer with the appointment would move in ahead of them. Generally, this policy caused little difficulty because Riley worked rapidly when several customers were waiting. Very rarely did any customers complain that the fast haircut was not of the usual quality.

The shop has two barber chairs; however, except for a six-month period five years ago, Riley had been the only barber since the volume of business had not justified hiring another barber. The shop is small, but clean. On some days, business was very slow and Riley busied himself keeping the shop in good order. His desire to keep the shop neat and clean led him to decide against stocking a large quantity of hair oils, conditioners, and other supplies. He turned over very few of the items on a regular basis and made no effort to promote them. In fact, Riley had never advertised his shop except through the Yellow Pages.

The shop has no strong competitors in the immediate area although there is one large shop and several small ones in the nearby downtown area. Riley felt that the changing neighborhood provided even more potential customers than were available before.

There is parking space for three cars in front of the shop. A customer can usually park on the street (metered parking), within a block or two, at most times during the day, however, on Saturday, it is more difficult for customers to find parking spaces. Two years ago, Riley had been approached by the proprietor of the drug store two doors away who offered to rent him parking space for his customers in the drug store's rather large lot. Riley had decided against paying for the space because most of his customers walked to the shop.

The price of a haircut in the shop has been $1.25 for several years. A year ago, Riley unwillingly raised his price to $1.50. Although some of his customers kidded him about the increase, Riley knew of no customers who had decided to go elsewhere. When he heard that a downtown barber was charging $2.50 for haircuts, Riley was surprised. Riley felt that the other barber was probably trying to discourage customers who were not interested in having their hair styled. Ninety-five percent of Riley's business was haircuts; very few customers asked for shampoos, shaves, or massages.

In the last few years, the shop has served a declining number of customers. However, operation costs have continued to increase. For example, property taxes, cost of supplies, and laundry service costs are higher. When combined with higher overall living costs, the result was a serious financial problem for Riley. Therefore, he was happy to sell the shop when health problems added to the difficulties.

When Ralston became aware of the problems, he knew that he was faced with making several important decisions. He felt that there was still great potential for the shop. Although the character of the neighborhood is changing, the shop's proximity to downtown and to other commercial establishments could be looked upon as an opportunity. Although he has only about $300 available to put into the business and knows that he must soon begin to generate income, he feels that he has a solid enough base upon which to build a successful operation.

QUESTIONS

1. What were the major problems which Ralston had to overcome?
2. Why was the volume of customers decreasing?
3. What steps should Ralston take in the short run to revitalize the business? In the long run?
4. What effect has the recent trend toward men's hair styling had on the business and how can Ralston adapt his own operations to the change?

57.

Shaw Nursery and Landscape Company
Solving Customer Service Problems

Background

Shaw Nursery and Landscape Company is one of the leading landscaping firms in the Greater Miami area. Its president, Joseph C. Shaw, founded the company shortly after his discharge from the Marine Corps at the end of World War II. With the help of his father, who was skilled in the budding, inarching and grafting techniques needed for the propagation of fruit trees and tropical shrubs, Shaw developed a retail nursery along a well-traveled highway.

At the same time, he enrolled in a four-year program in business administration at the University of Miami. To help him in his business, he took botany and landscape design courses as electives. Since his afternoons were free, he organized a small crew of men who could perform all kinds of landscaping services. His men cut lawns, planted fruit and shade trees, sprigged yards, and designed gardens.

Following his graduation in 1950, he decided to go into landscaping work full time. Miami was undergoing a construction boom, and the demand for landscaping services was growing. Consequently, he hired a second crew of men and placed one of the experienced landscapers in charge of it. Shaw was able to supervise the work of the first crew himself. Since he could see the potential for a larger company, he bought a sizable tract of land along another arterial highway and opened a second nursery. It was a wholesale nursery in which large quantities of certain shade, fruit, and other staple plants needed on his landscaping assignments could be grown economically in large quantities.

Both nurseries thrived, homeowners often stopped along the highway to make their own selection of plants. Shaw's busiest day was Sunday and he had to hire extra men to accommodate the many customers.

Expansion Strategies

As his business expanded, Shaw decided to discontinue the lawn maintenance part of his landscaping services. Since many of his regular lawn customers were loyal customers who had helped him get his start while he was still attending the University, he was careful in selecting a person to take over their accounts. He finally turned them over to a friend who was studying business administration and who, like himself, wanted to get a start in nursery and landscaping.

To expand his business further, Shaw concentrated on large contracts. He subscribed to the *Dodge Construction Reports* and other services which kept him advised of the progress of large construction projects in the Greater Miami area. Large private companies, new hotels on nearby Miami Beach, and numerous public buildings needed to have their grounds landscaped. To help him submit bids on the various landscaping opportunities, Shaw hired two salesmen with formal training in landscape architecture and design from the University of Florida. He also hired one man whose practical knowledge of plants and landscaping had been obtained through years of experience. These salesmen drew up landscaping plans and submitted bids to the principal contractors in charge of construction.

Shaw paid his salesmen a small salary plus a 10 percent commission on all business brought in by them. After some experimentation, he decided on this method of compensation because it rewarded the men for productivity and kept his selling expenses at a fixed percentage of sales. The men were pleased with this arrangement since it gave them opportunities to use their design skills.

As the salesmen became more productive, Shaw's landscaping work increased, and he was able to add new foremen and crews of workers. In the 1960s, his payroll expanded to over sixty employees, and he hired the services of an accountant to keep records. The accountant had previous experience as a business manager with a competitor and very quickly developed as the second man in command. Whenever Shaw went on a business trip, he left him in charge.

One of the most difficult management problems faced by Shaw was scheduling the daily work for the crews. Service requests came in from all parts of Miami, and the assignments had to be organized and divided among the crews in such a way as to minimize travel time between jobs. A crew could often finish a small job in two or three hours and would then have to be transported to the next assignment. For this reason, Shaw preferred the larger contracts. Some of the projects would keep one or two crews busy for a week or longer. With travel time reduced, these jobs were usually more profitable.

Promotion of the Service

Quite early in his landscaping career, Shaw learned that the best advertising for his services was word-of-mouth recommendations of satisfied customers. Roadside nursery signs and prominent telephone directory advertisements were the only promotional methods used. Shaw had tried the Welcome Wagon service as a method of attracting customers. Welcome Wagon hostesses visit newcomers to the city and present them with gifts from cooperating businessmen. Shaw gave away free plants, and some of the families later visited his nursery to purchase additional shrubs and trees. However, after two years of experimentation, Shaw dropped this form of promotion. The business this promotion brought in was mostly small orders, and he found that his own salesmen were able to attract the larger accounts.

At an early stage in his business growth, Shaw discovered that indirect methods of promotion through public relations work constituted the best advertising for his services. He became very active in the Chamber of Commerce and other civic organizations and also built goodwill through numerous donations to worthy causes. For example, when the Catholic Church constructed a new building, he contributed plants and donated the services of one of his crews for the landscaping work. The church was just two blocks away from his retail nursery, and the work on the grounds served as an effective testimonial to the quality of his work. Shaw had two children who attended the local schools, and he contributed generously to various school activities. For instance, one public relations gesture was to give orchids to all the girls who attended the Senior prom at the school which his daughter attended.

Shaw was also very active in the work of the various local, state, and regional nursery and landscape associations. He worked tirelessly on committee assignments. As a result of these activities, he was asked to landscape the grounds of the Florida pavilion at the 1964–65 World's Fair in New York City. Later, he submitted articles on various aspects of this special landscaping work to the trade and professional journals which served the nursery and landscaping industries.

Service Problems

At the start of the 1970s, Shaw was well-established in his business, but had a number of service problems that needed solution. The overall problem faced by Shaw was that of soaring costs. Since 1967, there had been rapid inflation, and the price of labor, materials, and equipment kept rising. To offset these increases, he was looking for ways to reduce his operating expenses. There were three areas in which Shaw felt that costs could be reduced substantially.

1. *Credit and collections.* Before his salesmen bid on a job and agreed to a price, they first checked the credit standing of the potential customer through local credit sources. If the credit rating was good, a down payment on the contract was obtained and the landscaping work began. On large contracts, it was customary to ask for a second payment when the work was half completed. Upon the completion of the contract, the customer was billed for the balance.

An examination of accounts receivable revealed that a number of the larger accounts were past-due. Whenever a customer was delinquent, it was the responsibility of a salesman to call him and to send the necessary collection letters. Accounts which were more than six months past-due were turned over to the company lawyer who usually was able to collect by threatening the customer with a lawsuit. For his services, the lawyer retained 50 percent of the amount collected.

Shaw asked his entire sales and managerial staff to study this credit and collection problem. He thought that if the salesmen could take certain precautionary measures and if the company instituted other changes in the collection procedure, it was possible to substantially decrease these costs.

2. *Adjustment of complaints.* A second service problem which increased landscaping costs appreciably was the adjustment of customer complaints. Like all reputable firms, Shaw Landscape guaranteed its work. Crews were supervised by experienced foremen who were skilled in setting out plants and shrubs. If fertilized, planted, and watered properly, the shrubs easily survived transplantation from the nursery. However, many of the transplanted trees and shrubs had to be watered daily for several weeks to insure survival. It was the responsibility of the homeowner to keep up the daily watering. Sometimes, a customer forgot to water his new plants for several days and, if the plants died, it was natural for him to blame Shaw Landscape for poor planting. Certain control measures had to be instituted to minimize these losses. Even when he was not at fault, there was a strong temptation for Shaw to replace the dead plants and shrubs. He was apprehensive of the ill will an unsatisfied customer could generate through complaints to friends and neighbors.

3. *Small order problems.* Shaw realized that his operating costs were much higher than they should be due to the large number of small accounts. He asked the accountant to study this problem. Shaw thought it might be more profitable to lose 10 to 15 percent of his sales by not accepting any customer contracts for less than $100 and concentrating on larger contracts. However, salesmen were anxious to accept as many small orders as possible since several of these orders would add substantially to their commission earnings.

QUESTIONS

1. What procedures and policies might Shaw adopt to reduce his credit and collection expenses?
2. What control measures might be instituted to reduce the losses incurred from the adjustment of customer complaints?
3. If you were the accountant, what recommendation would you make with regard to the small order problem?
4. Evaluate the promotional program used by Shaw Landscape. Do you think that other methods of advertising should be tried?

58.

Allstate Insurance Company

Innovating in the Marketing of Insurance

Allstate Insurance Company of Skokie, Illinois, is a subsidiary of Sears, Roebuck & Co. It has grown from a small, virtually unknown company to a giant in the automobile insurance industry by utilizing unique methods of marketing automobile insurance.

Allstate has had more success than the automobile insurance industry as a whole in meeting the twin problems of soaring accident claims and rapidly increasing automobile liability insurance rates. In its early years, Allstate offered automobile insurance only through the Sears, Roebuck catalog. In 1933, it started installing agent-manned booths in big city retail stores of the Sears chain. Later, Allstate reduced its premium rates by rejecting the traditional American agency insurance system in which the agent is an independent broker-salesman who normally handles the policies of more than one insurance company at a time and generally receives a 20 percent commission on both new policies and renewals.

Allstate hires its own insurance salesmen, and these salesmen receive 15 percent commission on new business and 6.5 percent on renewals. Since Allstate does much of the paperwork and servicing of policies, Allstate agents earn as much per year as independent agents. Allstate benefits in yet another way by having its own sales force. It avoids "agency leverage," a practice whereby an independent insurance agent is able to persuade a represented insurance company to take poor automobile liability insurance risks by threatening to reduce the amount of profitable business allotted to the company. Allstate receives no such pressure from its exclusive employee-agents.

Allstate made a statistical study of the correlation between the number of miles a driver drives during a given period and that driver's chance of having an accident during that period. From this study, Allstate developed a risk system of rating drivers according to whether they used their cars for driving to work or for pleasure only and whether they drove over or under 7,500 miles a year. The lowest risk drivers were offered a 30 percent discount from bureau rates. Ultimately, Allstate expanded its risk classification to include thirty-two factors such as age, sex, and marital status. The policy of classifying on the basis of risk has brought Allstate a "bonanza of business" from low-risk drivers who do not want to pay for "carrying" the poor risks.

Allstate is known for settling meritorious automobile insurance claims quickly and even maintains a "drive-in claim service" in many areas for handling minor accident claims. However, the company maintains a "hard line" against apparently fraudulent or greatly exaggerated claims and does not hesitate to fight these in court.

To help improve the nation's driving habits, Allstate has given over $500,000 in grants to colleges and universities to help train high school teachers as driver-training instructors. It has also distributed millions of copies of accident prevention booklets to school and community organizations, and its agents give thousands of talks each year on driver safety.

QUESTIONS

1. Evaluate the innovations in automobile insurance marketing Allstate has brought to the insurance industry from a social standpoint. From a long-run profit viewpoint.
2. Can other insurance companies copy Allstate's "new" ways of doing business? Why?
3. What unique advantages does Allstate have over other companies in the marketing of automobile insurance?

59.

Patrone's Cleaners and Laundry

Serving a College Student Market

Background

Patrone's is a sole proprietorship owned and operated by Anthony C. Patrone in Columbia, South Carolina, which encompasses a Standard Metropolitan Statistical Area of over 300,000 people. Columbia is the capital of South Carolina, and the University of South Carolina, with its student body of over 13,000, is located only three blocks from the major complex of state offices.

Patrone's cleaning plant is located one block from the State capitol and three blocks from the University of South Carolina campus. A branch pickup office is maintained directly across the street from the major complex of men's residence halls. Patrone's customers are mainly University students with minor amounts of business coming from state employees and local apartment dwellers.

In addition to individual consumers, Patrone's does substantial commercial work for hotels, motels, schools, and hospitals. This commercial business is essential to the survival of Patrone's because it provides income during the summer months when many University students are not attending school.

Patrone's annual gross sales average about $100,000 per year with 65 percent of this coming from consumers and 35 percent from commercial accounts. Total net profit ranges from $10,000 to $12,000 per year.

Management Policy

Mr. Patrone operates his own business and is a firm believer in dynamic, personal management. Plant workers are supervised personally by Patrone and are responsible directly to him. Through personal supervision, Patrone believes he can do a better job than a hired manager who would have no personal interest in the business. Besides, customers want to be able to see the owner and have personal contact with him.

Pricing and Service Policies

Patrone's prices are about 10 to 15 percent lower than the competition on consumer business as is shown in Exhibit 1. All commercial work is obtained by "bidding," and Patrone has been quite successful in getting his share of this business.

In order to offer lower prices than the competition, Patrone's does not provide many special customer services. In selling to the student market Patrone's makes essentially a price appeal and does not offer services such as car drop-offs, pickup and delivery, and storage facilities. However Patrone's does offer its customers charge accounts, quantity discounts, and monogramming services. A comparison of Patrone's customer services with major competitors' is shown in Exhibit 2.

Promotion

Patrone's does no promotion of any kind but prefers to depend upon its low prices and convenient location for business. Competitors use news papers, radio, and point-of-purchase advertising.

New Plant Location

Because the present plant location is being taken over by the State to build state office buildings, Patrone's will have to move shortly. Plans have been made to move the plant to South Main Street, about two blocks west of the University of South Carolina campus. This move will cost Patrone's the business of state employees and apartment dwellers living close to the old location. However, the new plant will be one-quarter of a block from a new, 100-room motel, the Sheraton Motor Hotel.

The new plant will be built underneath a building which presently houses the Big Bird Restaurant, a barber shop, a pool hall, and a sandwich operation. The land lends itself to this type of construction, and $50,000 worth of new equipment will be installed.

Market Research

Because of the impending move to the new location, Mr. Patrone was concerned about the effects of the move on his college patrons. Therefore he contracted with a team of four marketing seniors from the University to determine what college business, if any, he will lose because of the move and whether or not he ought to increase his prices to reflect the new image made possible by the new plant and its facilities.

The students took a simple random sample of students living in residence halls on campus and conducted 252 personal interviews. A breakdown of the interviewees by class standing at the University is shown in Exhibit 3. Other information uncovered by the research team is in subsequent exhibits.

QUESTIONS

1. What factors make marketing a service such as dry cleaning different from marketing a product?
2. What is Patrone's pricing policy? Should it be maintained at the new plant location?
3. Should Patrone's do any advertising or promotion? Suggest some possibilities.
4. What information of value to Patrone's can you get from the survey conducted? Does this survey indicate any necessary changes in Patrone's present way of doing business?

EXHIBIT 1
Patrone's Cleaners and Laundry Prices
Compared with Local Competition

Article	Patrone's	LaBelle	Dixie	Masters	Sunshine	Robinson
Shirts	$0.27	$0.28	$0.27	$0.30	$0.30	$0.30
Blouses	.27	.60	———	.40	.40	.50
Slacks	.55	.60	.60	.70	.70	.70
Dresses	1.10	1.20	1.20	1.35	1.35	1.35
Overcoats	1.20	———	———	1.50	1.35	1.35
Sweaters	.55	.60	.60	.70	.70	.70
Sheets and towels	.18	.15	———	.13	.15	.13
Suits	1.10	1.20	1.20	1.35	1.39	1.35
Skirts	.55	———	———	.70	.70	.70

EXHIBIT 2
Patrone's Customer Services
Compared with Major Competitors

Cleaners	Offers Charge Accounts		Offers Quantity Discounts		Offers Free Minor Repairs		Offers Mono-gramming	
	Yes	No	Yes	No	Yes	No	Yes	No
Patrone's	X		X			X	X	
Dixie	X			X		X		X
LaBelle		X	X			X	X	
Masters	X			X	X			X
Robinson	X		X			X		X
Sunshine	X			X		X		X

EXHIBIT 3
Class Standing of Interviewees at the
University of South Carolina

Class Standing	Number	Percent
Freshman	106	42.0
Sophomore	56	22.3
Junior	38	15.0
Senior	50	19.9
Graduate student	2	.8

EXHIBIT 4
Dry Cleaners Patronized by Interviewees

Dry Cleaner	Number of Respondents	Percentage
Sunshine	56	22.2
Dixie	40	15.9
Martinizing	18	7.1
Patrone's	17	6.8
LaBelle	9	3.5
Masters	7	2.8
Arnold Palmer	5	2.0
Forest Drive	2	.8
Other cleaners (local)	14	5.6
No local cleaner	84	33.3

EXHIBIT 5
Length of Time Present Dry Cleaner Patronized by Interviewees

Time Period	Number of Respondents	Percentage
0 up to 6 months	89	35.3
6 up to 12 months	57	22.7
12 up to 24 months	53	21.0
24 months or over	53	21.0

EXHIBIT 6
Reasons for Patronizing Present Dry Cleaner

Reason	Number of Respondents	Percentage
Close location	95	37.7
Speed in cleaning clothes	59	23.4
Low price	50	19.8
Good cleaning job	30	11.9
Extra services	10	4.0
Other	8	3.2

60.

Oasis Inn

Serving the Traveler

Background

Jack Livingston is reviewing the construction plans for a 150-unit motel he has decided to build on the outskirts of Orlando, Florida, on family-owned property. The motel is to be situated along Route 4, a four-lane superhighway that is heavily traveled throughout the year. It serves as the connecting link between Interstate 95 and Sunshine Parkway, the two principal arteries used by tourists and businessmen traveling from north Florida to south Florida and back. Livingston's family owns a two-and-one-half acre lot adjacent to Route 4 in the suburbs of Orlando.

Livingston believes the land is ideally suited for a motel development. The property is two miles away from downtown Orlando and three miles distant from the City airport. Within two blocks of the planned motel site are two modern service stations and an attractive restaurant.

Livingston had given serious thought to alternate uses of his strategically located property during the four years he attended the University of Florida, where he studied business administration. One of his marketing professors had called his attention to the rapid growth of tourism in Florida and suggested that he look into the profit opportunities offered by various tourist-serving businesses. Livingston acted on this advice and wrote to several associations which represent the travel industry. He was particularly impressed with the growth statistics sent him by representatives of the motel industry. Gradually, he became completely convinced that a motel offers the best investment opportunity for his property.

Livingston knew that the heavy traffic along Route 4 would get even heavier in the next decade. Orlando, a rapidly growing city, was attracting much new industry. Moreover, the Disneyland recreational complex, which is currently under construction, will draw hundreds of thousands of additional visitors to the area. The availability of this nationally known recreational facility will add substantially to Orlando's attractiveness as a convention city. Groups of all kinds can hold business sessions in comfortable meeting rooms while their families enjoy themselves at Disneyland and other recreational centers in the area.

Immediately upon his graduation from college, Livingston accepted a position with the Holiday Inn chain to gain the needed experience in motel operation. He worked as a service manager for one year and carefully studied all aspects of motel management.

Livingston has ample funds at his disposal for the development of a high quality motel. He wants to make Oasis Inn—the name he had tentatively selected for it—as attractive to tourists as are the Holiday Inns. The 150 units will be furnished with single and twin beds, desks, chairs, luggage racks, and have comfortably appointed bathrooms. The rooms will have wall-to-wall carpeting, air conditioning, and color television.

Since construction will begin within two weeks, Livingston wants to finalize as many decisions as possible. He is particularly concerned with the service facilities. The success of his enterprise will be determined, to a large extent, by the general attractiveness to travelers of the entire package of services. From his experience with the Holiday Inn system, he knew customers want not only a place to rest but also ready conveniences and quick service. In his preliminary planning, he listed eight potential services from which he could choose for his motel. Now he is faced with the task of deciding which of these services should be included in the final plans. A discussion of each of them follows.

Eating Facilities

Tired motorists want convenient eating and refreshment facilities such as candy machines, soft-drink and ice dispensers, and a place, such as a coffee shop or restaurant, in which they can get warm meals. Travelers who are in a hurry are satisfied with the availability of a coffee shop. However, other tourists want to spend several days at motels, especially those who come to enjoy Disneyland or to attend a convention. These visitors want to relax and enjoy fine food in a casual atmosphere.

Within two blocks of the planned Oasis Inn, there is an excellent restaurant that serves steaks and sea food specialties. Furthermore, there are a number of good eating places in downtown Orlando which are but two miles away from Livingston's motel. One of his alternatives is not to build a large restaurant, but to print small brochures which list the better eating establishments in the Orlando area as a service to his customers. The brochures can be placed in the rooms and in other conspicuous places. If Livingston chooses this course, he may be able to settle for a coffee shop which serves refreshments, sandwiches, and other light snacks.

Swimming Pool

Such a facility is a must to Livingston. Travelers of all ages like to relax at the poolside. Livingston thinks that a 40′ × 25′ pool with plenty of surrounding space for lounge chairs and other pool furniture will be sufficient.

Golf Putting Green

Since he has sufficient space, Livingston is considering developing a sizable putting green adjacent to the swimming pool. With this arrangement, the youngsters can swim while adults can either lounge at the poolside or practice putting. Livingston knows golf is growing in popularity and that many travelers carry golfing equipment in the trunk of their automobiles. Many of these travelers welcome an opportunity to sharpen their putting game. Although the Holiday Inns do not offer a golfing facility to their customers, Livingston noticed that many of the other new motels in Florida are adding such attractions when space permits. The cost of installing and maintaining a green will be minimal. Livingston's blueprint calls for the development of a large three-hole green so that several golfers can use the facility at the same time.

Conference Rooms

If he is to cater to businessmen who do business in the city and to those who prefer lodging outside of the city, Livingston feels he will need at least one large meeting room which can be used for banquets and other activities. By using partitions, the room can be divided into smaller seminar and conference rooms. Motels near airports are proving to be ideal places for conventions and other business meetings. For instance, salesmen of companies with national or regional distribution can fly into Orlando and hold conventions at the Oasis Inn, which will be close to the airport and away from the congestion, distractions, and noise which are typically a part of the downtown hotel and motel environment.

Courtesy Bus

Since he is only three miles away from the airport, Livingston wonders whether he should cater to air travelers by offering a courtesy bus service. He would either have to maintain his own bus or contract with a private company to furnish prompt to-and-from airport transportation. To use this free service, an incoming traveler will call Oasis Inn and ask for transportation just as he might call a private company for taxi service.

Cocktail Lounge

Livingston knows that a favorite place for relaxation among adult travelers is the cocktail lounge. Some motels provide a small room with tables around the bar. Others offer more elaborate facilities with space for such entertainment as piano playing. Still others provide an even larger room with space for a band and dancing. Livingston is uncertain as to the type of facility he should provide.

Coffee Host

This service is offered by a number of high-quality establishments such as the Howard Johnson's Motor Lodges and Holiday Inn motels. The service involves placing coffee-making equipment in each room. It allows the traveler the "luxury" of getting himself started in the morning with a quick cup of coffee.

A more common practice is to offer room delivery. With this service, a guest can phone the motel kitchen and order coffee and other breakfast items to be delivered to his room. Livingston wrote the leading motel association for its recommendations as to the type of coffee service motel guests preferred. The reply from the association secretary indicated that there was no survey information available on this question.

Individual Kennels

From his recent experience with the Holiday Inn system, Livingston knows that its motels offer a unique service to travelers with animals. Most travelers like to keep their dogs and other pets with them in their motel rooms. However, some tourists, when presented with the opportunity, prefer to place their animals in a kennel behind the motel where the animals cannot disturb motel guests. Livingston's property is large enough to accommodate individual kennels. The construction costs will be minimal.

The availability of this service could be advertised in the service pamphlet placed in each room. While few travelers have the need for this facility, it might help to build the image of Oasis Inn as a quality-service motel.

QUESTIONS

1. Which of the eight services described in the case should be included in Livingston's plans for Oasis Inn? Which ones, if any, are inappropriate? Explain your answer.

2. Plans for which of the eight services should be finalized before the construction of the motel begins? Which ones can be deferred until after completion of Oasis Inn?
3. What additional services, not mentioned in the case, do you think should be included in the offering of a quality motel such as Oasis Inn?

THE LEGAL, SOCIAL, AND ETHICAL ENVIRONMENT

61.

Consumer Protection

The $100 Million Refund by Drug Firms

In the summer of 1969, consumers across the country filed to get portions of a $100 million fund which was set up by five drug firms for customers who used certain wonder drugs between 1954 and 1966. This money-back program was a result of a price-rigging case pressed by the federal government and involving five leading pharmaceutical companies. The mailing deadline for the claims was August 1, 1969. On July 1, 1969, the drug companies' notice to claimants about the refund program appeared in about 1,500 newspapers throughout the country. Several thousand claims were received daily until August 1 by the law firm handling the refunds.

The $100 million fund was set up by Chas. Pfizer & Co., American Cyanamid, Bristol-Myers, E. R. Squibb, and Upjohn Co. American Cyanamid, Bristol-Myers, and Pfizer were convicted of the price-rigging charge on December 29, 1967. Upjohn and Squibb were not defendants but were named as co-conspirators in the Justice Department suit.

Over thirty drug products marketed under different names, all containing tetracycline, were involved in the refund program. The federal government charged that tetracycline, regarded as one of the most effective antibiotics, was produced for as little as 1.6 cents a capsule, but retailed for 51 cents each. Claimants stated they spent an average of 50 to 85 cents per capsule, with some paying as much as a dollar.

The government suit stated that $1.7 billion of the drugs were sold over a thirteen-year period. The convictions opened the door to a number of civil law suits, all for triple damages.

The problem had begun for the drug firms on July 28, 1958, when the Federal Trade Commission issued a complaint against the five firms as defendants and co-conspirators, charging them with unfair methods of competition and acts and practices in commerce in violation of Section 5 of the Federal Trade Commission Act. The complaint alleged that Pfizer unilaterally attempted to monopolize the tetracycline industry by fraud and misrepresentation, caused a patent on tetracycline to be issued by the United States Patent Office, and issued invalid licenses under the patent.

The complaint further alleged that all defendants by conspiracy fixed the prices of tetracycline, chlortetracycline and oxtetracycline; foreclosed and prevented competition in tetracycline and chlortetracycline by licenses and cross-licenses; attempted to and did monopolize tetracycline. In addition, Pfizer and Cyanamid withheld material information from the Patent Office. Pfizer issued, and Cyanamid, Bristol, Squibb, and Upjohn accepted licenses under the tetracycline patent with knowledge of such withholding and misrepresentation, and independently thereof, with knowledge that the invention was unpatentable.

At various times from January 5, 1959 to February 4, 1960, hearings were held before a hearing examiner. On October 30, 1961, the examiner submitted an initial decision in which he found that the charges had not been sustained by the evidence and ordered the complaint dismissed.

An administrative appeal was made and on August 8, 1963, the Federal Trade Commission issued an opinion voiding the initial decision and made known its own findings of facts and conclusions of law. The Commission found that Pfizer and Cyanamid did make certain misrepresentations and withheld other information in connection with Pfizer's application for a patent on tetracycline, which prevented the patent examiner from making an accurate appraisal of the patentability of tetracycline. The Commission further found that the conspiracy charge before the Patent Office involving Pfizer and Cyanamid was "not proven," and that Bristol, Squibb, and Upjohn did not engage in any unfair methods of competition before the Patent Office. However, the Federal Trade Commission did find that the five drug firms were guilty of engaging in a conspiracy to fix, maintain, and stabilize the price of tetracycline.

The drug firms took the matter to court and the case dragged on for several years. Finally, in December 1967, the Justice Department was able to convict Cyanamid, Bristol, and Pfizer on the price-rigging charge. While this conviction was still being appealed through higher courts at this writing, the five pharmaceutical companies decided to set up the $100 million fund, and on July 1, 1969, they ran advertisements throughout the country in 1,500 newspapers to notify the general public of the refund program.

QUESTIONS

1. While the cost of producing tetracycline was only 1.6 cents, what heavy expenditures may not be included in this figure?
2. Do you think that advertisements in 1,500 newspapers are sufficient

notice to the thousands of customers who had purchased the drug during the 1954–1966 period?

3. What other potential or real dangers associated with the manufacture and marketing of drugs ought to be regulated to protect the consumer?

62.

Line Profusion Confuses Consumers
An Example of Packaging Differences

Over the past five years, product lines in many packaged, household consumer goods have broadened at an extraordinary pace. There are now, however, indications that this trend toward stretching the depth and breadth of product lines at the manufacturing level is at its peak and that a reverse trend toward line shrinkage may have begun. Several of the causes are:

1. Increasing costs at the manufacturing level due to shorter production runs and larger inventories;
2. Increasing wholesaler-retailer resistance due to a decrease in turnover;
3. Increasing shopper confusion with consequent irritation and resentment.

With reference to the third point, California's Consumer Counsel recently decided to conduct a shopping test to determine the degree of confusion consumers experience while shopping in a supermarket. A recent DuPont Company supermarket study had determined that the typical shopper, on an average visit, bought 13.7 items. Therefore, a list of fourteen items was drawn up for the consumer Counsel's experiment. The list included packaged products, common staple foods, and household necessities. For the investigation, a typical supermarket in the Sacramento area was chosen. Along with the items chosen for the survey, the store offered a total of 246 possible package choices. Five housewives were selected to participate in the test. Although picked at random, they were not "average" shoppers. Each had some college training as well as considerable family shopping experience.

The five cooperating housewives were given the simple instructions to make their selections solely on the basis of the packages with the largest quantity at the lowest cost. Each of the women was given $10 and set loose in the supermarket to purchase the fourteen items. Although allowed as much time as needed, they were clocked from the time they entered the store until they reached the checkout counter.

The DuPont survey had estimated an average shopping time of twenty-seven minutes. But only one of the women came in under this time at twenty-five minutes. The other four took thirty-five, forty, fifty-five, and sixty minutes.

How did they fare? To understate the results, badly! All five did succeed in picking the lowest-priced package of one item, cheddar cheese. But this was the only one. For two of the products, all five shoppers were fooled.

With the passage of *The Fair Packaging and Labeling Act* in the summer of 1966, Congress has made the Commerce Department responsible for working with various consumer groups in different industries to determine whether the package sizes used by the firms of each industry have proliferated to the point at which consumers have trouble making comparisons and value judgments.

This law provides for approaching proliferation problems through a voluntary cooperative operation. The Department of Commerce and its National Bureau of Standards are working on the development of voluntary standards suitable for each industry group. The law gives manufacturers in an industry the choice of setting their own standards or availing themselves of NBS assistance. If progress is not made within a reasonable period of time, the Commerce Department must then report to Congress what legislative action should be taken.

QUESTIONS

1. Why were the five women shoppers in California's Consumer Counsel's experiment often unable to pick the largest quantity at the lowest cost?
2. Cite as many cases as you can where industry groups are voluntarily trying to reduce the number of product lines and package sizes used by firms within their industry in order to comply with the spirit of *The Fair Packaging and Labeling Act*.
3. Would it be desirable to have a federal law which would force manufacturers to reduce the number of package sizes offered to consumers?

63.

Advertising and Its Effect on Competition
Protecting the Consumer and the Small Businessman

In the mid-1960s, interest in consumer welfare began to grow, and the "consumer movement" became a driving force. Attendant with this emphasis was a critical evaluation of the marketing function and its influence on the consumer. Coming under particularly close scrutiny were promotional and advertising methods.

Advertising attracted the interest of government officials as well as consumer groups. In 1966, Donald F. Turner, Head of the Antitrust Division of the United States Department of Justice, precipitated considerable discussion with a now-famous address expressing his views on advertising. While admitting the economic benefits which advertising provides to society, Turner maintained that "advertising has significantly adverse effects on competition in consumer goods markets." [1] The point was made that, in some consumer goods industries, there was a "significant correlation between the proportion of industry sales devoted to advertising and the average profit rates which were earned." [2] The implication, of course, is that high advertising outlays by certain firms give them an economic advantage which is difficult to overcome by companies which cannot match the expenditures.

According to Turner, there may be several ways in which advertising expenditures promote industrial concentration. One of the most significant ways is that extensive advertising creates barriers to the entry of new firms into markets. Turner explained the viewpoint in this manner:

> In a competitive industry we normally expect to find firms entering and leaving the market during any given period of time. Although the exit of firms will continue, entry will be made more difficult as a result of the barriers created through extensive advertising. To the extent that

[1] Donald F. Turner, "Advertising and Competition," address delivered at the Briefing Conference on Federal Controls of Advertising and Promotion, Washington, D.C., June 2, 1966.
[2] *Ibid.*

consumers are unable to evaluate the relative merits of competing products, the established products may have a considerable advantage and it is this advantage that advertising messages tend to accentuate.

A further significant factor is the existence of economies of scale in advertising and other forms of promotion. To the extent that larger firms can provide more messages per dollar than their smaller rivals, they will have a strong competitive advantage, and this will be so even if smaller firms spend proportionally as much. Economies of this sort lead directly to the expansion of larger firms relative to their smaller rivals and thereby to more concentrated market structures.[3]

The situations described by Turner are of obvious significance to marketing, particularly in light of increased government and consumer activity in recent years. The Turner speeches prompted a series of responses from marketers, economists, and various academicians. The issues have yet to be resolved, but their importance cannot be denied.

QUESTIONS

1. What types of studies could be undertaken to test the validity of the arguments proposed by Donald Turner? What factors need to be known before the issues can be resolved?
2. It is implied in the "barriers to entry" claim against advertising that new firms, particularly small ones, cannot compete effectively against the larger firms which are able to commit large sums of money to advertising and other promotional methods. What chance does the smaller businessman have of being competitive and how may he do it?

[3] *Ibid.*

64.

General Motors Corporation and Competition

A Response to the Critics of Bigness

It is recognized that the automobile industry plays a substantial role in sustaining the steady growth of the American economy. The automobile is one of the most visible signs of the country's affluence. Thus, the operations and the condition of the industry and of the companies making it up are of interest to businessmen, government officials, and consumers alike. When it was asserted that competition in the automobile industry had been replaced by planning and regulation of the market by its firms, the industry reacted.

For many years (since the late 1940s), General Motors Corporation has sold over 40 percent of the annual total of new American autos purchased in this country. In several of these years, the General Motors market share was over 50 percent. Thus, when the questions of market control and decreasing competitive rivalry in the industry arose, General Motors prepared a statement which was given to two subcommittees of the United States Senate in defense of industry competition. The following passages, taken from the nearly 100-page statement, summarize the company's position.

Each year millions of car owners shift from one make of car to another. No customer can be regarded as a captive, and each firm must constantly compete to retain, as much as possible, the loyalty of its present customers and to win over new customers. Thus, statistics as to annual sales shares constitute a composite of innumerable choices reflecting many shifts in patronage, and indicate no power to control any portion of the market.

The intense competition among auto firms has resulted in substantial shifts in sales shares in postwar years. General Motors' share has varied from 38 percent in 1946 (when steel allocations were in effect), up to 51 percent in 1954, down to 43 percent in 1959, up to its high of 52 percent in 1962, and down to 48 percent for the first eight months of 1968. Ford has shifted from under 19 percent in 1948, up to about 31 percent in 1954, and down to 24 percent in 1968. Chrysler, which had exceeded Ford in the 1936–49 period, had almost 26 percent in 1946, fell to under 10 percent in 1962 and rose to over 16 percent in 1968. American Motors, presently accounting for about 3 percent, reached almost 7 percent when it came out with its successful compact car. Striking evidence of the free play of competition in the American market has been the postwar entry of the foreign cars which now command about 10 percent of the market.

An examination of various aspects of market behavior of auto firms gives further evidence of shifts in customer preference and the absence of market control. Thus, there have been wide regional differences in demand for the products of the individual firms. There have been variations in acceptance of each manufacturer's offerings within closely related product categories such as domestic compact, intermediate, and specialty cars. And a product may be highly successful in one year, as was Buick in 1955 with over 10 percent of new car sales, and may later miss the market badly, as it did in 1959 when its share declined to 4 percent.

If further evidence is needed of the vitality of competition and its control of the automobile market, it is to be found in the several forms in which competition exists, particularly in the areas of product, price, and marketing competition.

The automobile industry has been characterized by product competition producing a steady stream of product innovations—some dramatic, some less so—but all contributing in the aggregate to producing automobiles of greater value, safety, and reliability. All are the result of competition within the industry. The important fact is that all auto manufacturers have contributed to product development through innovation spurred by competition, as each has striven to produce cars with greater mass appeal and thus to increase sales and profits.

The other principal competitive areas in the industry are pricing and marketing. General Motors' 1969 model price announcements illustrate the forces of competition. While substantial labor and material increases applied to the production of all General Motors 1969 cars, price changes varied from a decrease of $1 to an increase of $144, reflecting the disciplines of market forces. During the last decade, when the Consumer Price Index rose over 20 percent, the Index of New Car Prices actually declined slightly as a result of competitive forces. Although car prices are announced at the beginning of each model year, how much profit—if any—may be earned will not be known until the end of each year, and will depend upon how well the company performs against competition—in the factory and in the showroom.

Price competition has been both long-term and short-term; long-term, as the manufacturer has sought to develop improved models and new product types which would provide customers with better values than competitors and, at the same time, reduce cost through improved technology and thereby improve his competitive position; short-term, as reflected throughout the model year in various incentive plans, dealer bonuses, and product promotion allowances. These programs, conducted periodically by all auto manufacturers, are a continuing series of intensely competitive actions and reactions throughout the model year, and are responsive to the forces of the marketplace.

The fact that the number of U.S. automobile manufacturers is small is of no relevance to the intensity of competition among them. Each year since 1921, except for a few years in the mid-1920s, the three largest producers have accounted for 75 percent or more of total U.S. new car output. Neither the quality nor the quantity of competition in the auto industry can be measured by counting number of sellers or by market shares. The small number of domestic competitors does not mean that General Motors can in any way control market supply and increase prices above competitive levels, the prime requisites for monopoly power.

The fact that General Motors has a larger market share than others is no basis for concern about the vitality of competition. The several large and extremely capable domestic and overseas competitors have the potential and ability to win the larger share away from General Motors at any time they develop superior products or do a better job of selling and servicing those products.

In the automobile industry, the customer exercises a free choice and shifts from one manufacturer to another as he pleases. Thus the superior product, as determined by the consumer, captures the greater share of the market because there is no other means by which the manufacturer can "control" the customer's choice. General Motors has gained a large share of the business because—and only because—the consumer more often has regarded its product as the best.

QUESTIONS

1. Discuss the validity of the General Motors Corporation's defense of competition in the automobile industry.
2. Does the extensive statement by General Motors indicate a "consumer orientation," an awareness of the legal and social environment within which the firm must operate, or both? Discuss as best you can based upon the statement and on your understanding of the automobile industry.

65.

Promotion Ethics

Six Short Problems

1. You have worked for a large advertising agency for ten years on two of its most important accounts. Lately, you have been unhappy with your agency and confide in the advertising managers of both accounts that you are thinking of quitting and setting up your own advertising agency. Both advertising managers say they will transfer their accounts to your new agency when you open your doors. Do you take them up on their offer?

2. As advertising manager of a frozen food company, you have learned that a major competitor is conducting a Sales-Results test in an effort to select the best of two advertising campaigns to release on a national level. More than $50,000 has been spent so far, and you know that by changing your advertising at random in the test cities, you can foul up the test results until they are of little value. It won't cost you over $500 to make the necessary changes. Should you do so?

3. You have accepted a new job as assistant sales manager of a major competitor of your old company. You received a handsome salary increase and have moved your family 1,000 miles to the new location. On your first day at work, the sales manager asks you for all sorts of confidential information about your former employer. Should you tell him anything?

4. You have been after the $4,000,000 advertising account of a major appliance manufacturer. You invite the advertising manager to visit your agency, and you show him some past work done for a small, regional manufacturer. The advertising manager asks to see the small account's current advertisements. They are finished but have not yet been shown to the client. Should you let him see them?

5. The D. P. South advertising agency is considering two candidates for an account executive position. Mr. Fry is white while Mr. Amos is black. Mr. Amos is definitely the better qualified, but two of the

231

agency's accounts indicate they will not work with him while other accounts have not commented. Which man should be hired?

6. Your company sends you and a brand manager to a national Garden Supply Show. The brand manager becomes inebriated and talks too much about your company's unannounced entry into the pet supply business. On the trip home, the brand manager asks you not to say anything about his "talking spree" to your marketing manager. What do you do?

66.

Automobile Liability Insurance

A Problem of Serving the Public

Increases in bodily injury and property damage claims have put nearly all the big automobile insurance companies in the red on liability insurance despite increases in premium rates. Of the four kinds of automobile insurance, only "collision" and "fire, theft, and comprehensive" are profitable. Profits from these two forms of automobile insurance often go to offset losses on the two liability coverages, "bodily injury" and "property damage."

The automobile insurance industry's worst losses are on bodily injury claims in which the damages to people are often intangible and the costs of "personal repairs" are very hard to determine. "Whiplash" injuries to the neck and spine caused by rear-end collisions are difficult to dispute, and jury trials usually result in substantial awards being given the injured parties.

Automobile insurance companies have a tendency to settle emotionally appealing claims out of court. They are trapped between efforts to keep losses down and the fear of getting a "hard-nosed" reputation on personal injury claims.

Juries are usually composed of local people who think that insurance companies are so rich they can afford to pay almost any claim. Lawyers, specializing in bodily injury claims, have developed the art of "parting an insurance company from its money" to a high degree and even have their own National Association of Claimants' Compensation Attorneys, which publishes its own journal.

Lawyers often handle bodily injury claims on a "contingency fee" basis by which the injured party pays little or nothing unless his lawyers can collect. If damages are awarded, lawyers' fees often are one-third to one-half of the award.

Repeated efforts to change the contingency fee system by law have been unrewarding since many state legislators are lawyers. In California

233

alone, it is estimated that 70 percent of the State's lawyers receive most of their income from the contingency fee system.

In an effort to reduce losses on liability insurance, insurance companies use a plan whereby accident-prone drivers are put into an "assigned risk" group. The companies doing business in a state accept high-risk drivers in direct proportion to each company's share of the total automobile insurance business in that state. For example, a company which has 10 percent of the automobile insurance business in a state takes about 10 percent of the "assigned risk" drivers. Even though drivers in the assigned risk group have to pay higher rates, insurance companies continue to lose money on them.

In the automobile liability insurance business, total claims keep rising and liability insurance premiums rise with them. However, even when insurance companies are able to get a liability insurance rate increase from state commissions, it takes about two years for the increase to be fully reflected in increased income, and by that time, the rising frequency and cost of claims has eaten into the temporary underwriting profit margin.

Repeated liability insurance rate increases have failed to make liability insurance profitable to handle, and insurance companies have been drastically restricting the risks they will accept. Some insurance companies are refusing to renew the policies of drivers with heavy claim records. Fierce competition for preferred risk drivers has developed. Every company tries to get a "representative book of business," or its share of the preferred risks.

Many drivers resent the rising costs of automobile insurance and are pressuring state legislatures for more state control of automobile insurance. State control over automobile insurance would be increased by a plan in which accident liability insurance claims would be put on a fixed award basis similar to workman's compensation for death or injury on the job. Each state would set the official premium rates for automobile liability insurance and draw up fixed compensation schedules for claimants.

QUESTIONS

1. Do you agree with the plan whereby each state would set official premium rates for automobile liability insurance and draw up fixed compensation schedules for claimants? Why or why not?
2. What can automobile insurance companies do to make the liability insurance portion of their businesses profitable?
3. Should companies, such as the automobile insurance companies, be forced to accept business which they know will result in losses? Why or why not?

67.

Quality Brands, Inc.

Conforming to the Fair Packaging and Labeling Act of 1966

Quality Brands, Inc., Toledo, Ohio, is planning to put "Jumbo," its new pancake mix, on the national market. Jumbo is a ready-mix pancake product with flour, sugar, leavening, milk solids, salt, and artificial color as its main ingredients. It will be packaged in a two-pound (32 oz.) size. A meeting of the production manager, Mr. Keller, the sales manager, Mr. Rockton, and the advertising manager, Mr. Gray, is taking place to discuss the packaging and labeling of the new product.

Keller stated: "As I see it, our basic problem is to put 'Jumbo' in a package which can be easily processed by our present packaging machinery and protect the contents until it is sold to housewives."

Gray responded: "That is part of the problem. The other part is to design a package label with some real sales punch—one that can pull customers away from established products such as 'Aunt Jemima' and 'Hungry Jack.' "

Rockton offered his opinion: "Like Gray says, we need a label with some real sales impact—one that will shout 'take me home!' to the housewife as she passes the display."

During a three-hour discussion, the three executives arrived at the following decisions regarding the packaging and labeling of Jumbo:

1. The front panel label illustration will be a four-color photograph of an oversized pancake held in the trunk of the line drawing of an appealing baby elephant. The background color will be canary yellow to give the package "visibility" on supermarket shelves.

2. Copy on the front, or display side of the package, will read "Jumbo—a king-sized pancake mix for king-sized appetites."

3. On the back of the package will be easy-to-follow directions on how to prepare eight, fifteen, and thirty Jumbo pancakes. At the bottom will be listed the ingredients, weight in ounces, and the illustration of a hungry man "wolfing down" a Jumbo pancake.

4. The two side panels will have promotional copy designed for consumers. The top and bottom panels will have "Jumbo Pancake Mix" with a price spot for the retailer to stamp in the price.

A package artist is to be given these decisions to guide him in designing an attractive, attention-getting package label for the pancake mix.

QUESTIONS

1. Do any of the decisions reached by the three executives violate the federal law, the Fair Packaging and Labeling Act of 1966? What provisions are being violated?
2. Can use of the brand name "Jumbo" bring about any legal difficulties when used on a package? Explain.
3. If any laws are violated, what federal agency assumes jurisdiction?

68.

I. B. Lowe Company

Taking Advantage of Slum Dwellers

The I. B. Lowe Company sells eyeglasses to slum dwellers in Washington, D.C. Despite television and newspaper advertisements which offer discount eyeglasses for "$6.50 and up," this retailer uses high pressure sales tactics to get prospective customers to order eyeglasses which cost substantially more than the advertised price. Very few eyeglasses are sold for $6.50. The majority of customers pay about $40.

Sales on credit are made, utilizing an installment sales contract. The contract is misleading in the way it states the loan amount and the average annual interest rate, which is 87 percent. "Easy credit" claims in the company's advertising are backed up by a forceful collection department which files suits against 40 percent of the credit customers, most of whom are Negroes.

QUESTIONS

1. Is I. B. Lowe violating any laws? Which ones?
2. What legal body has primary jurisdiction over the company's methods of selling eyeglasses?

69.

Bonner Appliance Store

Bait and Switch Advertising

The Bonner Appliance store of Phoenix, Arizona, runs local newspaper advertisements which offer twenty-three-inch color television sets in console models for $399 each, about $200 below prices charged by competitive retailers. However, when customers inquire about the advertised sets, they are shown one set which is so badly out of adjustment that the picture quality is extremely poor. Then, salesmen are quick to show customers a much higher-priced model which is properly adjusted and has good picture quality. Of course, salesmen try to trade customers up to the higher-priced set and will not sell the lower-priced one under any circumstances.

QUESTIONS

1. Are any violations of existing laws taking place? Who would have jurisdiction over possible violations?
2. To what agencies can the consumer complain if he is victimized by these questionable business practices?

70.

Chapin-Forswald, Inc.

Questionable Selling Practices

This company manufactures and sells direct to consumers the Dust-Master vacuum cleaner through its 1,000-man national sales force. Personal selling practices of the company are: (1) salesmen tell prospects that a selling contest is going on and that the prospects have won a prize when, in fact, both statements are untrue; (2) salesmen sell used machines as new ones; and (3) salesmen often pose as demonstrators to gain admittance to prospects' homes.

QUESTIONS

1. Are Chapin-Forswald salesmen guilty of violating any laws?
2. What effects do such selling practices have upon consumers? Upon salesmanship in general?

71.

Gaywear, Inc.

Mailing of Unordered Neckties

Gaywear, Inc., of New York, N.Y., manufactures and distributes necktie
to consumers by mail over the Eastern half of the United States. Eacl
month, 15,000 unordered ties are mailed to persons whose names are on a
mailing list which Gaywear maintains. Each person on the list is sent a
tie along with a letter asking for $1.98 payment for the item. If no money
is received within three weeks, Gaywear starts sending a series of threat
ening and misleading letters which try to frighten the consumers into
paying for the ties.

QUESTIONS

1. Is Gaywear, Inc. violating any existing laws? Which ones?
2. Do persons who receive the unordered ties have to pay for them?

72.

Hartwell Company
Labeling Dangerous Products

Two home dishwasher detergents of the Hartwell Company contain sodium metasilicate, a chemical compound which can cause severe eye irritation and is poisonous if swallowed. However, no mention of this is made on the packages of the products or in product advertising. The products are presently being sold nationally through supermarkets.

QUESTIONS

1. What law is the Hartwell Company violating? Who enforces this law?
2. What are the provisions of the law which apply to this case?
3. What action can be taken to stop distribution of the two products?

73.

Cigarette Industry
Resolving a Social and Economic Problem

Background

In 1969, the Federal Communications Commission ruled that all advertising of cigarettes on radio and television be eliminated as of January 1 1971. The action was expected to have a significant effect on advertising practices and on the relationship between advertising and government The issues involved were complex, and a substantial amount of controversy existed prior to and after the decision was made. The significance of the debate and of subsequent actions can be better understood by reviewing the events which took place prior to 1970.

In 1964, *Smoking and Health,* a Public Health Service report, condemned the use of cigarettes, but not cigars or pipes. The action initiated a bitter controversy over the effects of cigarette smoking on an individual's health. The Federal Government, through its various agencies, took the position that a relationship existed between cigarette smoking and lung cancer, heart disease, emphysema, and numerous other diseases. The cigarette industry, which is by far the major purchaser of the nation's tobacco crop, maintained that there was no conclusive proof of a positive relationship between cigarette smoking and poor health.

Opposition to Cigarette Smoking

Among the anticigarette forces, the Department of Health, Education and Welfare, the Public Health Service, the Federal Trade Commission, and the Federal Communications Commission took the lead in making the public aware of the dangers of cigarette smoking. Studies which were undertaken by HEW officials indicated that cigarette smoking was associated with an increase in overall mortality and morbidity. Public Health Service reports suggested that cigarette smoking was the main cause of

50,000 deaths which occurred annually from lung cancer and 25,000 deaths from emphysema and chronic bronchitis. According to this source, one-third of all deaths of men between the ages of 35 and 60 were related to cigarette smoking.

Few scientists doubted that a direct relationship existed between smoking and lung cancer. One cancer expert explained that although improved medicine, public health, and living standards added four years to the expected life span of white males from 1919 to 1965, about 3.4 of those years were erased by cigarette smoking.

The advertising of cigarettes was the special target of the Federal Trade Commission and the Federal Communications Commission. The FTC repeatedly made its position clear on cigarette advertising. In the words of the Commission "Cigarette advertising continues to depict smoking as an enjoyable activity while ignoring completely the health hazard." [1]

Cigarette advertising aimed at teenagers was particularly disturbing to the FTC. In its view "Teenagers are exposed to an endless barrage of subtle messages that cigarette smoking increases popularity, makes one more masculine or attractive to the opposite sex, enhances one's social poise, etc." [2] The Commission believed that such commercials were successful in persuading teenagers to smoke in spite of the known health hazard.

The FTC recommended a three-step program to combat cigarette smoking: (1) replacement of the warning on cigarette packages from "Caution: Cigarette smoking may be hazardous to your health," to "Cigarette smoking is dangerous to health and may cause death from cancer and other diseases"; (2) termination or drastic alteration of cigarette advertising on radio and television; and (3) conducting a vast educational campaign to negate the image of cigarette smoking as harmless and satisfying.

The Federal Communications Commission joined the FTC in its fight against cigarette smoking. The "Fairness Doctrine," which was originally developed to give opposing political candidates equal time on the air, was expanded to state that broadcasting stations carrying cigarette advertising must also carry a significant amount of time for the other view. A ratio of one antismoking commercial to every three cigarette commercials was established. This was in keeping with the FCC's view that stations which present cigarette advertising have the duty of informing their audiences that "however enjoyable, such smoking may be a hazard to the smoker's health." [3]

A broadcasting industry research organization reported that antismoking commercials on an annual basis numbered around 2,000 on network television and 3,150 on network radio in 1969. Some newspapers and magazines also carried antismoking advertisements. These anticigarette

---

[1] "It's War on Cigarette Advertising," *Broadcasting* (July 3, 1967), p. 9.
[2] "Can FTC Stunt Growth of Smokers?" *Business Week* (July 8, 1967), p. 34.
[3] "Fairness Applied to Cigarettes," *Broadcasting* (June 5, 1967), p. 9.

commercials received free air time, were expertly prepared, and were furnished by such private agencies as the American Cancer Society and the American Heart Association.

Cigarette Industry's Defense

The cigarette industry adopted the position that no published reports proved that cigarettes cause lung cancer or any other illnesses. The industry took the stand that cigarettes were a legitimate product and any prohibition of their advertising would be regarded as an unwarranted and punitive measure. Any specific measure to ban cigarette commercials from the broadcasting media would tread on the delicate ground of free speech and the First Amendment to the Constitution.

The broadcasting industry, faced with the loss of over $200 million in cigarette advertising revenue, joined cigarette manufacturers in opposing the banning of cigarette commercials from television and radio. The broadcast media believed that the loss of revenue from cigarette advertising would mean the difference between profit and loss for a number of broadcasters. Cigarette advertising, prior to 1971, accounted for approximately 7 percent of all national television revenue. Total expenditures on cigarette advertising from 1959 through 1967 are shown in Exhibit 1.

Cigarette Companies Diversify

The declining domestic consumption of cigarettes led cigarette manufacturers to diversify their product lines. Cigarette consumption from 1959 through 1968 is shown in Exhibit 2.

The domestic consumption of cigarettes declined sharply in 1968. This was the first year-to-year drop since 1964. Dr. Daniel Horn, director of the National Clearing House of Smoking and Health, said "There may be about 1.5 million fewer cigarette smokers now than there were a year ago although there are about 3 million more people in the United States." [4]

On a per capita basis, cigarette consumption in pounds turned downward in 1966. In 1967, the number of cigarettes consumed per capita also declined. In 1969, it was still too early to predict a declining future demand; however, indications of the development of such a trend were present. In light of these figures, cigarette manufacturers began to diversify.

By 1969, the American Tobacco Company owned Sunshine Biscuit and James B. Beam Distilling Company; Liggett and Myers had bought its way into the food and liquor fields; Philip Morris produced razors, blades, paper, packaging, textile chemicals, hospital products, and toiletries; R. J. Reynolds manufactured packaging and industrial corn products and op-

[4] "Cigarette Gains Go Up in Smoke," *Business Week* (December 21, 1968), p. 68.

erated a containerized freight and trucking system; and Lorillard intended for 40 to 50 percent of its sales to be of non-tobacco products within a short period of time. This movement away from complete dependence on cigarettes and tobacco indicated that the cigarette companies were taking no chances on the outcome of the cigarette controversy.

Economic Importance of Tobacco

Since colonial times, tobacco has been considered the "golden" leaf in the major tobacco-raising states of the United States. European demand for this "cash" crop contributed greatly to the early economic development of Virginia, Maryland, and North Carolina. In 1969, tobacco was still the mainstay of the agricultural sectors of many Southern states and contributed to the economic welfare of the entire nation.

The billions of dollars spent on cigarettes each year created jobs for many people and provided income with which to purchase the other products of our economy. In 1965, United States cigarette manufacturers employed 35,924 people and paid an annual payroll of $199 million. Exhibit 3 shows the growth in dollar sales of cigarettes for the period 1959 to 1968. During 1968, cigarette sales accounted for approximately 1.7 percent of total personal consumption expenditures in the United States.

The Federal Government also has benefited from high taxes on cigarettes throughout much of the history of cigarette manufacturing. As shown in Exhibit 4, cigarette taxes have provided a stable source of revenue. If the Federal Government were successful in reducing or eliminating the sale of cigarettes in the United States, it would have to find other sources of tax revenue.

The Importance of Tobacco to a Southern State: South Carolina

South Carolina is one of the nation's leading tobacco-producing states, and most of its tobacco crop is used in the manufacture of cigarettes. Tobacco is an important cash crop for over 12,000 commercial farmers in the Palmetto State. Any severe drop in tobacco sales or prices will have an adverse economic effect on the entire state. Over one-fifth of total cash receipts from all farm commodities in South Carolina is derived from tobacco, as shown in Exhibit 5. Loss of any substantial portion of the revenue from this crop would place many South Carolina farmers in serious financial condition. Among all crops, tobacco has one of the highest cash yields per acre. It would be difficult for the farmer to find another crop as suitable for South Carolina soil and having an equally high return per acre.

A decline in tobacco consumption would affect seriously not only tobacco growers but also approximately 9,000 seasonal tobacco laborers who have an annual payroll of almost $8 million. Others, such as warehouse workers, employees of business establishments servicing tobacco growers, advertising personnel, wholesalers, and retailers would not escape the financial "pinch."

Moreover, a decline in the demand for tobacco products would directly affect many public programs in South Carolina because the state also receives a considerable amount of revenue from taxes on tobacco products sold locally. Exhibit 6 presents the amount of tobacco tax revenue received by the state between fiscal 1959 and fiscal 1968. The loss of any great portion of these funds would certainly be detrimental to state programs. In all likelihood, it would mean increasing the burden of existing taxes or perhaps adding new levies.

QUESTIONS

1. Should cigarette advertising have been banned from radio and television?
2. Should cigarette advertising be banned from all media? What effect would such a ban have on the market share enjoyed by each brand?
3. Should consumers be protected against the promotion and/or sale of products which health authorities consider dangerous to health?
4. Since public health authorities were convinced that cigarette smoking contributed to lung cancer, emphysema and heart disease, why wasn't the sale of cigarettes made illegal?
5. What can cigarette manufacturers do to protect the sales of their cigarettes if the advertising of cigarettes is banned completely?
6. What can major tobacco-raising states like South Carolina do to counteract a shrinking demand for cigarette tobacco?
7. Evaluate the recent removal of cigarette advertising from radio and television in terms of its effects on cigarette manufacturers and cigarette consumption.

EXHIBIT 1
Expenditures on Cigarette Advertising, 1959-1967*
(in Millions of Dollars)

Year	Expenditures
1959	$138.2
1960	140.0
1961	141.9
1962	139.0
1963	174.6
1964	191.1
1965	188.7
1966	213.3
1967	265.2

Source: "Cost of Cigarette Advertising 1959-1967," *Advertising Age* (September 16, 1968), pp. 103-104.
*Totals are only for cigarette brands whose 1967 sales exceeded one billion cigarettes. Expenditures represent dollars spent in general magazines, newspapers, network TV, spot TV, and outdoor advertising (from 1959 through 1962). Radio advertising expenditures, costs of point-of-purchase materials, and nonmeasured media expenditures are excluded.

EXHIBIT 2
Domestic Consumption of Cigarettes in the
United States, 1959-1968

Year	Billions of Cigarettes	Per Capita Number of Cigarettes	Per Capita Pounds
1959	454	4,071	9.44
1960	470	4,171	9.64
1961	488	4,266	9.84
1962	494	4,265	9.69
1963	510	4,345	9.70
1964	497	4,194	9.21
1965	511	4,258	9.37
1966	522	4,287	9.08
1967	528	4,280	8.85
1968	523	4,186	8.65

Source: *Annual Reports on Tobacco Statistics*, Statistical Bulletins No.'s 356, 372, 397, 424, 435 (Washington, D.C.: United States Department of Agriculture, Consumer and Marketing Service), April, 1964, 1965, 1966, 1967, 1969.

EXHIBIT 3
Estimated Cigarette Sales in the United States, 1959-1968
(in Millions of Dollars)

Year	Sales
1959	$5,854
1960	6,244
1961	6,538
1962	6,675
1963	7,055
1964	7,024
1965	7,609
1966	7,997
1967	8,432
1968	8,910

Source: *Annual Report on Tobacco Statistics 1968*, Statistical Bulletin No. 435 (Washington, D.C.: United States Department of Agriculture, Consumer and Marketing Service), April, 1969, p. 35.

EXHIBIT 4
Federal Tax Receipts from Cigarettes
in the United States, 1959-1968
(in Millions of Dollars)

Fiscal Year	Cigarette Tax Receipts
1960	$1,864
1961	1,924
1962	1,957
1963	2,011
1964	1,977
1965	2,070
1966	2,006
1967	2,023
1968	2,066

Source: *Annual Report on Tobacco Statistics*, Statistical Bulletins No.'s 343, 372, 435 (Washington, D.C.: United States Department of Agriculture, Consumer and Marketing Service), April 1964, 1965, 1969.

EXHIBIT 5
Cash Receipts from Tobacco Compared with Total
Cash Receipts from All Farm Commodities, South Carolina, 1959-1968

Year	Tobacco Cash Receipts (in millions of dollars)	Tobacco Cash Receipts as a Percentage of Total Farm Commodity Receipts
1959	$ 90	24.9%
1960	91	24.7
1961	100	26.2
1962	116	29.5
1963	97	24.6
1964	94	23.0
1965	88	22.0
1966	88	22.4
1967	107	25.1
1968	81	21.5

Source: *Annual Reports on Tobacco Statistics*, Statistical Bulletins No.'s 308, 330, 356, 372, 397, 424, 435 (Washington, D.C.: United States Department of Agriculture, Consumer and Marketing Service), April, 1962, 1963, 1964, 1965, 1966, 1967, 1968.

EXHIBIT 6
Total State Tax Receipts and Tax Receipts from Tobacco
Products Sold in South Carolina, 1960-1968
(in Millions of Dollars)

Fiscal Year	Total State Tax Receipts	Tobacco Tax Receipts	Tobacco Tax Receipts as a Percentage of Total State Tax Receipts
1960	$214.1	$11.5	5.3%
1961	215.5	11.9	5.5
1962	221.3	12.1	5.4
1963	240.0	12.0	5.0
1964	253.6	12.4	4.9
1965	281.9	12.9	4.5
1966	329.0	13.3	4.0
1967	362.9	13.7	3.7
1968	377.2	13.7	3.6

Sources: *Annual Reports on Tobacco Statistics*, Statistical Bulletins No.'s 343, 371, 424, 435 (Washington, D.C.: United States Department of Agriculture, Consumer and Marketing Service), April, 1963, 1965, 1967, 1969. *Annual Reports of the South Carolina Tax Commission*, 1959-1968 (Columbia, S.C.: State Budget and Control Board).

IV.
COORDINATION OF
THE MARKETING EFFORT

74.

Worth Corporation

Changing the Corporate Structure

The Worth Corporation, in the period immediately following World War II, pursued a vigorous program of expansion through the acquisition of healthy domestic and foreign firms, through the construction of new plants in the United States and foreign countries, and through international affiliations. As a result of this rapid expansion, Worth's consolidated sales were approaching the $100 million mark in January 1970, and its worldwide operations were conducted through a network of thirty manufacturing plants in ten countries. These plants were grouped for management purposes into five domestic divisions, six international subsidiaries, and two international affiliates.

Worth products include a wide range of specialized materials. Frit was Worth's first product, and the company stands today as one of the world leaders in the manufacture of this material, which is the basic ingredient of all porcelain, enamel, and ceramic glaze finishes. Currently, Worth is a leading producer of plastic, glass, and porcelain colors used by manufacturers of refrigerators and other household appliances, automobiles, trucks, and electrical equipment. The company has also become an important manufacturer of chemical stabilizers which extend the life of plastics. It also produces fiber glass used in the reinforcement of plastics.

Worth's glass frit contains nutrients such as manganese and iron which are used in the fertilizer industry. When converted to granular form, these nutrients become an important fertilizer additive which dissolves slowly in the soil and provides efficient, controlled plant nutrition. Several years ago, Worth purchased a firm which makes containers that are highly resistant to intense heat. These containers are used to hold raw clay shapes as they are processed through kilns to become floor and wall tile, vitreous china, and artware.

While much of Worth's recent expansion has been gained through the acquisition of thriving plants, the corporation has always placed great emphasis on research and new product development. Currently, one of every five Worth salaried employees is engaged in a research or technical activity. By encouraging these specialists to improve their own capabilities, and by maintaining fruitful contact with scientists in the academic and professional communities, Worth has been able to gain a position of leadership in product improvement and new product development.

Many of its leading products were first developed in one of the company's twenty product development laboratories located in the United States and abroad. While these research laboratories are controlled by the local plant managers, they are given much freedom to do basic research. The technical center at the Centerfield, Iowa, headquarters is the principal research laboratory. It gives long-range support to the R & D activities of the widely dispersed product laboratories and, thereby, assists in the development of new products and processes. The research center in Centerfield encourages cooperative research and exchange of information between these product laboratories, giving Worth the ability to develop special products combining the know-how of all of the laboratories.

Since Worth produces industrial materials and products, direct selling is the principal method of promotion in the domestic market. Factory-trained sales engineers spend time in customers' plants, giving technical assistance and advice on their product needs. Coordinating and supervising the work of the sales engineers are four divisional sales managers located at regional headquarters. These divisional sales managers are also in charge of market research. While at times they make special studies, they rely heavily on the market information supplied them by the field sales engineers.

Domestically, Worth operates its plants on a decentralized basis. Control is achieved through the medium of sales and financial reports which have to be sent in periodically to the divisional managers. However, each of the fifteen domestic plants is treated as an autonomous profit center, and local plant managers are allowed to make their own marketing, production, and financial decisions as long as they operate profitably.

Central headquarters assists the divisional managers and the local plant manager in a number of ways. In addition to having a vice-president in charge of corporate research, Worth also maintains a manager of business planning and an advertising manager. The planning manager, through the collection and dissemination of all kinds of statistical information, encourages divisional and local plant managers to engage in both short- and long-range planning through such activities as sales forecasting, production scheduling, capital budgeting, and the estimation of expansion needs.

The manager of advertising is in charge of corporate publicity. Since Worth markets a wide range of products domestically and abroad, three independent advertising agencies are retained by the advertising manager to help with media selection, copywriting, and other details. Advertisements are placed in plastics, ceramics, enamels, agricultural, and other trade journals. Also, because of the diversity of products, general business periodicals such as *Fortune* and *Business Week* are used extensively.

The corporate advertising department is also in charge of trade shows. Display of new products at industry expositions in the United States and abroad is considered essential. Finally, the department, with the help of the three advertising agencies, is responsible for the distribution of novelty items and gifts to some 4,400 Worth customers.

As of January 1970, it was clear that the management organization of research, planning, and advertising at the Centerfield central headquarters was no longer adequate to serve the many needs of the far-flung Worth Corporation. The board of directors realized that an expansion of services and a complete reorganization of the corporate management structure was necessary if the company were to maintain its competitive efficiency. Moreover, top management was aware that a number of large industrial firms such as General Electric, which, like Worth, had also been heavily oriented traditionally toward engineering, were turning to a much greater emphasis on marketing at the corporate level.

The four divisional sales managers consult among themselves freely, but they have only the manager of business planning to turn to at the Centerfield headquarters. With regard to marketing research, the sales managers are left to their own resources. For information of a technical nature, they rely on the sales engineers in the field. However, they may retain the services of a marketing research agency in cases where special information is needed. Therefore, while the twenty product research department heads can turn to central headquarters for technical information, the four sales managers have no similar central agency to help them with the collection and dissemination of information.

Faced with the necessity of making radical changes in the corporate organization, the president retained the services of two outside marketing consultants and charged them with the task of developing a comprehensive reorganization plan which would give Worth's widely dispersed plants the marketing help they need.

QUESTIONS

1. If you were one of the consultants, what reorganization of the corporate management structure would you recommend?
2. Does a firm selling exclusively in the industrial market need to be as customer-oriented as one that sells to household consumers?
3. Is the organization for advertising on the corporate level adequate?

75.

E-P Electric Company

Competing in the Industrial Market

E-P Electric is a small manufacturer of electric and gasoline trucks and replacement parts. A sales volume of $8 million makes it one of the smaller firms in the electric and gasoline-powered lift truck industry. E-P is a specialty producer; it cannot compete directly with large mass producers such as Clark Equipment. Because of its inability to mass produce and compete on a price basis, E-P endeavors to make and sell a quality product and charge premium prices. While the firm retains a sales manager, it does not promote its line aggressively. For the most part, it waits for orders to come in from large customers such as General Motors.

E-P is represented in the national market by manufacturers' agents. Nearly fifty such agents send in orders to the firm's president. Many of these have been associated with E-P for twenty-five years or longer. Some of these men will retire soon, and the president is uncertain whether to replace them with other agents or with company-trained sales engineers. E-P also uses wholesalers to some extent, particularly in the distribution of parts. Since parts sales are highly profitable, close attention has to be given this segment of the business. Direct sales methods are used when selling to the government and, occasionally, when selling to a large customer.

The aluminum, steel, and automobile industries constitute the major targets for the company's marketing efforts. Firms in each of these industries contribute approximately one-third of the company's sales volume. E-P's sales vice-president and its factory engineers maintain close working relationships with the principal customers in each of these industries. The company attempts to engineer its products to meet the specifications of these major customers.

E-P's product line consists of large, medium-sized, and small lift-trucks. The large trucks are a specialty of the firm. E-P enjoys a dominant market position in large trucks, and sales in this category are the most profitable. A quality line is maintained in medium-sized and small trucks, but E-P experiences severe competition in these two product lines from companies which utilize mass production techniques. Small truck sales are the least profitable, and the company does not encourage this business.

Replacement part sales are highly profitable and the young Harvard-trained president is anxious to develop this end of the business further. However, the family-held company he has inherited is managed by men who have worked their way up the executive hierarchy, and many of them have served the company for thirty years and longer. These men are firmly set in their ways, and the president frequently finds it hard to sell them on new ideas.

The company does some advertising in the materials-handling publications. This promotion lends support to publicity in the trade journals. These journals publicize new products developed by E-P Electric through editorial comments. Management is seriously considering the merits of establishing an advertising department. Such a department would plan institutional and product advertising, conduct research studies, and set up a long-range program of corporate advertising in line with expansion plans.

The firm is in a tight position for cash, and top management is giving serious thought to making this privately held corporation a public one through the issue of stock. A stock issue would make it possible to obtain the cash needed for plant expansion and market development.

E-P's Research and Development Department has played an important role in the company's development. It was through the research activities of this department that the firm was able to achieve its dominant market position in large trucks. The R & D Department is headed by a sales engineer who supervises several laboratory assistants and technicians. Leading customers, such as General Motors, discuss their needs and factory problems with visiting E-P engineers. Ideas on product improvement and development are generated from these discussions.

An E-P marketing committee composed of leading company officers who are knowledgeable in the product area under consideration then meets to discuss the ideas further. They ultimately decide which product ideas are to be referred to the Research and Development Department for experimentation and the development of prototypes.

QUESTIONS

1. Does the firm need to establish an advertising department?
2. Should the president set up a management development program for top executives? If so, what types of training should be included in the program?
3. Should management replace retiring manufacturers' agents with new

agents, or should they set up a sales-training program and develop their own sales-engineers?

4. What other programs might the president initiate to improve the company's profit position?

5. Evaluate the company's procedure for carrying out product planning and development activities.

76.

Mason Plastics Company

Breaking into the Plastic Tile Market

Background and Organization

Two brothers, Douglas and Christopher Mason, recent graduates of the state university, decided to manufacture and sell plastic tile in 1969. Douglas Mason, age 27, who had majored in finance, had made enough contacts in the business community to obtain a loan of $25,000 and a line of credit for $75,000 more. He is to have the title of President as well as Comptroller. His younger brother, Christopher, age 25, had majored in production management. His title is to be Vice-president, Manufacturing. Christopher is familiar with most machine tools since he had partially completed an apprentice course as machinist. He had served in a machine shop each summer where machine tools and plastic molding were used. After working on both injection and compression molds, the younger Mason had suggested to his brother that they go into the plastics business, which was expanding rapidly. Two years of planning ended with the decision to enter the plastic tile field. They rented a small building near the railroad station in Columbia, South Carolina.

A secretary, Amy Smith, was hired to type, take phone calls, and keep the books. She had been working at the University and had a reputation for being honest, alert, and personable.

Two young men, Sam Whitford and Bobby Jo James, were hired away from the plastics plant where Christopher Mason worked. Both Sam and Bobby Jo had been friends of Chris and had often mentioned the hope of going into business for themselves. The lack of funds and managerial know-how had been barriers, but Christopher felt he could develop both men as the firm grew and eventually use them in management roles. Both were easy-going and could operate and maintain a variety of plastic mold machines. Sam was married, Bobby Jo was not.

After Bobby Jo and Christopher had inspected and tested three used machines, they purchased them from a Pittsburgh firm for a total of

$11,000 plus freight. New molds were obtained from Standard Molds; plastic resins and powder were obtained from both Dow Chemical and Monsanto. Dyes, lubricants, and other plant and office supplies and equipment were purchased, some on credit. These bills were to be paid within sixty days.

Both Douglas and Christopher recognized that the key problem area would be marketing. Since neither had any marketing experience and had taken only one course in marketing, they recognized their deficiencies early in the planning phase. They sought advice from Professor Mac Brown at the University, who offered them a prepared bibliography. Later, several of his research teams explored the market for tiles, the feasibility of such an enterprise, and made a forecast of future markets.

The Mason brothers discussed marketing problems on many evenings. They knew their decisions on components of the marketing mix would be complicated, but they felt confident that they could solve most of the problems.

Economic Environment

The sixties had been mainly boom years, although 1962 and 1967 were years of slower growth. The Nixon administration, in attempting to forestall inflation, had permitted a rising interest rate to dampen overexpansion in production, and brought about slowly increasing unemployment. The undeclared war in Viet Nam, the stalemate in Korea, and the hardening attitudes in the Middle East had channeled tax funds into defense and away from the war on housing. The Mason brothers recognized that money was very tight, but were willing to pay the high interest rate.

The Market and Competition

The plastic tile which the brothers planned to produce was designed for bathroom walls although it was useful for other rooms, too. The market was closely tied to the contracting market for homes. This market would, in the Mason's viewpoint, only limp along until interest rates dropped to below 7 percent. In the short run, survival in the market was the only problem. In the long run, the Masons knew, all the forecasts pointed to a housing boom. The sales volume they anticipated would necessitate operating their molds at least 70 percent of the time on two shifts of eight hours each, once the normal housing market returned. Demand elasticity paralleled that of the housing market as well as that of industrial development. In South Carolina, industry was coming into Beaufort and Orangeburg and expanding in the Charleston, Columbia, and Spartanburg-Greenville industrial complexes. The Mason brothers felt that the state of South Carolina offered an excellent long-run market. Later, they would expand to compete in the Southeastern region.

There was only one other plastic tile manufacturer in the Columbia area—the firm for whom Christopher had worked. In the ceramic tile field, there were no manufacturers, but there were several distributors. Although the Masons had not canvassed the other metropolitan areas in the state, they expected to find one or two ceramic and one nonceramic tile-maker in each area. They had scanned trade publications at the University library and were aware of special sources like the *Dodge Reports* of the McGraw-Hill Book Company.

Production and Marketing Considerations

The Masons offered Amy Smith an increase of $25.00 per month and an expectation of more when business became profitable. Both Sam and Bobby Jo were offered a $50.00 per month increase in wages and an option to become stockholders as the firm prospered. Both Masons believed in paying extra to get above average help, and this was a "must" for present operations and future development.

Until their product became well known, the Masons reasoned, their price should be identical to competitors' prices. Once a quality difference was established in the minds of the contractors and the distributors, the Masons would be able to raise prices to improve their financial picture. In the current tight market, however, they needed revenue to survive.

In addition to using modern machine tools to keep competitive, Christopher was introducing conceptual tools learned at the University. He felt that the most important was statistical quality control. With it, he could provide a better product to the customers and at the same time reduce scrap and cut material costs.

Channels of distribution were to be direct to contractors and indirect through wholesalers to retail outlets. Contractors and wholesalers would receive the same price. Retailers expected a 30 percent mark-up on sales to contractors and charged a 40 percent markup to do-it-yourself house owners.

Christopher planned to spend two half days a week contacting local distributors. Douglas would spend one day a week in Charleston, one day in the Spartanburg-Greenville area, and a third day in different parts of the state such as Aiken, Sumter, Camden, and Rock Hill. The forty-six counties were aligned so that he would visit each at least once a month.

Advertising would include the Yellow Pages in Columbia's directory, direct flyers to a list of the contractors and retailers in the metropolitan areas, and a small insert in a national trade journal.

Analysis of Early Sales Activity

The business opened its doors on January 15, 1970, with an accompanying feature story in the local paper. The Sunday edition of *The State* carried a feature story on the Masons' background and hopes. Sales, however, were meager the first two months, and the immediate prospects were dismal. People in the Carolinas were not building but were waiting for the mortgage money to loosen. The Masons were faced with the necessity of laying off, as of April first, the mold men and the secretary unless orders started coming in.

In late March, a telegram arrived. A Long Island builder had seen their trade advertisement and was interested. Could they provide him with a large volume of one size and a variety of six tints? The Masons knew their production capacity and wired back they could meet his needs if the written order was sent within the week. While price negotiations were in progress, Douglas Mason checked the credit rating of their potential buyer. John Dailey Builders, Inc. had a sound rating. The price was agreed on, approximating the contractor's price plus freight in. Terms were 2/10, net/thirty. Estimates of the shipment made by Christopher Mason resulted in a surprise—it would completely fill one box car. By working diligently on both shifts, the order was shipped two days ahead of schedule. New orders continued to trickle in slowly.

On the following Monday, a telegram from John Dailey was received. It stated that the tiles did not meet the quality specifications agreed on. The box car had been partially unloaded and had been shifted to their siding awaiting disposition instructions. In a subsequent telephone conversation, John Dailey offered to buy the tiles at 50 percent of their selling price.

QUESTIONS

1. What are the various marketing alternatives now available?
2. Describe the criteria most useful in evaluating these alternatives.
3. What stand should the Masons take in the price renegotiation issue now facing them regarding their shipment to John Dailey Builders? Explain.
4. With the future uncertain, how should the Masons structure their marketing program? Is their policy of meeting the local market price fundamentally sound?

77.

National Watch Company

Analyzing the Causes of a Sales Decline

Background

The National Watch Company was incorporated in 1930 by Mannie Simon to import, assemble, and sell wristwatches. After a lengthy period of persistent missionary sales work to jewelry and watch retailers, Simon and the company began to prosper. A significant portion of the credit for the success of the firm was attributable to Simon's personal sales ability, coupled with his strong desire to select capable employees and compensate them well. Employee loyalty to the firm was remarkable.

Over the years the company grew and by the late 1930s had become one of the half-dozen dominant companies in the industry, with a well-established reputation for quality timepieces. Company profits kept pace with sales growth. A consistent dividend policy was followed—dividends had been paid since 1935 and in 1950 a dividend pattern was established that paid approximately 75 percent of net earnings to stockholders. The market price of the stock was in good measure correlated to this payout.

During World War II, nearly all of the company's capacity was devoted to essential war production. Because very little output was available for civilian consumption during this period, expenditures for design and development of consumer products and for consumer advertising were sensibly limited to nominal amounts. After the war, production of ladies' and men's wristwatches was resumed, and re-entry into the consumer market was accomplished rapidly by producing the styles that comprised the line before the conversion to war production.

The existing sales force was then enlarged to pre-war size. This step was considered essential since all sales were traditionally made by company representatives directly to retail outlets. These outlets consisted principally of jewelry stores and some large department stores which had jewelry departments. Reacceptance of the National Watch line by the trade and by consumers was enthusiastic, and retail sales quickly supplanted the dwindling government contracts.

Problems of the Sixties

Sales and profits continued to grow slowly throughout the 1950s and early 1960s. During 1968, however, the company experienced a 10 percent decline in sales and suffered a slight net loss for the fiscal year. Because the economy was experiencing relatively strong growth and this was the first loss the company had sustained since the early Depression years, the senior executives of the firm were disturbed by the turn of events.

Mannie Simon, though nearing 70, was still quite alert and active in the firm, serving as president and chairman of the executive committee. The members of the committee, representing each functional area of the business, were seasoned executives who had been with the firm during the years of growth and development to its present position of prominence within the industry. Members of the executive committee owned or controlled 40 percent of the outstanding common stock and had always maintained effective voting control of the firm.

In early 1969, the committee held a series of meetings to establish the causes of the sales decline and to formulate possible corrective action. Following is a list of certain of the more important facts discovered and of the conclusions reached by the committee.

1. National lost market share during 1968, slipping from a 10 percent market share to 8 percent.
2. The quality of National's watches was as high as always and, thus, was not a problem.
3. The styles of National's watch line were considerably different from those being offered by some competitors. The company had been selling slight variations on basic styles developed in the late 1940s. Since these designs were relatively "young" in terms of exposure and the traditional life cycle for watches, it was felt by management that no significant changes were necessary at this time. They regarded the trend toward the purchase of very inexpensive, "mod-style" watches as a passing fad which was only a slight aberration from the life cycle.
4. Although dollar expenditures for advertising and sales promotion have not been relatively as large since 1963 as five close competitors', outlays have been maintained at the present level of $900,000 annually. It was decided to increase advertising expenditures by at least 10 percent during 1969.
5. Cash dividends are to be maintained at the previous year's level.
6. The decline in market share might logically be attributed to the sales department. Sales have been easy to make for the past several years,

and it was suggested that the salesmen may have become somewhat lazy. The executives agreed to institute increased supervision and control.

7. A one-year contract to produce private brand watches for a major catalog-retail store chain was signed. The contract is for two million dollars, and it is expected to cover only variable costs associated with the order. By accepting the order, the company can spread productive output more evenly over the whole year and keep its watchmakers fully employed.

8. Several members of the executive committee discussed selling a portion of their stock holdings in order to facilitate estate planning and/or to enjoy more fully the monetary rewards of their years of hard work. Several offers were received to purchase all of the stock held by the executive group, but no action was taken.

9. The executives decided to examine their distribution channels during 1969. National had been reluctant to sell its high quality watches in new outlets—especially in discount stores or "cut-rate" drug stores, as its competitors had done.

Evaluation of 1969

One year later—in early 1970—the company's executives sat down to evaluate the results of the action taken in 1969. After an examination of the records, several important facts became evident:

1. The company lost additional retail market share, declining from 8 percent of total market to 6.4 percent. Sales declined from $55.4 million to slightly less than $52 million.

2. Due to unexpected increases in material costs and wage rates, the contract to produce private label watches did not cover variable costs; the loss was $500,000. However, the customer is willing to negotiate another one-year contract on a different basis that appears to offer strong possibilities of being profitable.

3. Total net loss for the year is $3,000,000. (See Exhibit 1—Simplified Financial Statements).

4. The analysis of the distribution channel structure showed that customer traffic in existing retail outlets (jewelry stores, department store jewelry departments) is decreasing. In fact, some watches manufactured by competing firms are no longer being sold in department store jewelry departments; rather, some lower-priced watches are being displayed in other departments such as men's furnishings. Only the "prestige" watches, such as "Accutron" by Bulova, remain in the same departments. National's watches are among those getting minimal exposure and promotional effort.

5. Several retailers of National watches voiced complaints that the National watches did not "move" as well as others. It was requested that National change some of the more conventional styles or reduce prices in order to speed up turnover.
6. During 1969, seven of National's salesmen retired and two others left the company. Even more disturbing was the fact that National is experiencing difficulty in hiring capable college graduates for the sales force.

Generally, the executives are disappointed by the decline which had continued in 1969, but they are not discouraged. They feel that National sells a quality product which, if marketed aggressively, will return a substantial profit. However, they feel that some action must now be taken to get to the roots of the problems and then to solve them. Thus, they resolved to call in a consultant group to further analyze the firm and to recommend action.

QUESTIONS

1. What factors seem to be most responsible for the declining fortunes of the firm? What other factors may have contributed to the present condition?
2. Are all of the factors influencing the firm's success or failure controllable by the firm? Which factors are and which are not? Why?
3. As a consultant presented with the available facts described above, outline a program of action for National.

EXHIBIT 1
Simplified Financial Statements

I. *Income Statements**

| | Year Ended | | |
	1967	1968	1969
Net sales	$61,500	$55,400	$52,970
Cost of goods sold	43,000	41,800	40,750
Selling expenses	4,350	4,432	4,630
General and administrative expenses	9,100	9,100	9,600
Advertising	900	900	1,000
Net profit (loss) after taxes	$ 4,150	($832)	($3,010)

II. *Consolidated Balance Sheet**

Assets	Dec. 31, 1968	Dec. 31, 1969
Cash and marketable securities	$ 9,200	$ 2,300
Receivables, net	7,300	10,200
Inventories	16,600	19,100
Net properties (less depreciation)	4,900	4,200
Total assets	$38,000	$35,800
Liabilities		
Accounts payable	$ 8,300	$10,400
Bank loan	9,000	7,000
Accruals	2,600	3,300
Total liabilities	$19,900	$20,700
Equity		
Capital stock (5,000,000 shares, $1 par)	$ 5,000	$ 5,000
Paid-in surplus	5,000	5,000
Earned surplus	8,100	5,100
Total equity	$18,100	$15,100
Total liabilities and equity	$38,000	$35,800

*In thousands of dollars.

78.

The Heritage Manufacturing Company

Competing in the Fashion Industry

The Heritage Manufacturing Company is a medium-sized, family-owned firm which manufactures and wholesales men's and boys' apparel. Its home office is in a large Midwestern city and its factories are located in nearby rural communities. It has 1,680 employees, 90 percent of whom are unionized production workers. Its products are distributed nationally.

Company History

Three brothers and a former business associate bought the Heritage Manufacturing Company from its previous owners in 1916. These men were energetic and aggressive. They procured from the estate of Robert Louis Stevenson the rights to the author's name and the names of Jim Hawkins and Long John Silver as brand names. They expanded their product lines rapidly, selling shirts for men under the Robert Louis Stevenson label and a wide line of apparel for boys under the Jim Hawkins brand name. All products were considered to be in the popularly priced middle quality range.

Promotion was used extensively in relation to the size of the firm. For instance, many full page ads were purchased and appeared nationally in the *Saturday Evening Post*. From 1925 through the Second World War, the brand name "Jim Hawkins" was a household word with mothers of young boys.

From the beginning, products were distributed through the company's own national sales organization which sold directly to retail stores. The company followed the strategy of selling to one of the two or three best stores in a market area on an exclusive basis. This strategy was common in the industry. It was particularly advantageous when a major department store would carry a manufacturer's full line, also on an exclusive basis. In time, however, many retailers found that this arrangement was not in their best interest. Therefore, when the retailers began to buy from several manufacturers, Heritage found it had to reverse its own policy in the late 1950s. Since their exclusive account strategy had resulted in all but the established accounts being ignored, other buyers had the ready excuse "My needs are already covered," for not buying Heritage's products. Although the validity of the excuse was questioned by some executives, the problem of finding new accounts continued to plague the company even into the late 1960s.

By the end of World War II, the founders of the firm were all in their late fifties. Over the next ten years, they proceeded to turn over control of the firm to their two sons and two of their nephews.

During this transitional period, the company followed a more conservative marketing policy. This was possible because defense production during the war and the boom after the war had resulted in production at full capacity. The only product addition during this period was the Long John Silver line of apparel for young men. Promotional outlays were cut due to the increased cost of media space and the prevalent opinion that national advertising was of limited effectiveness in the apparel industry. Changes also occurred in the sales force. Many of the firm's most able salesmen reached retirement age. New men added to the sales force did not always have the experience or the ability of the men they replaced.

In the late 1960s, it became obvious that the company was experiencing some difficulties. Key income statement figures appear in Exhibit 1. In spite of the high cost, it was decided by the officers of the firm to call in outside help. In 1969, a respected management consulting firm made a thorough study and analysis of Heritage's problems. The following discussion covers some of the major factors that were analyzed.

Organization

Standard marketing functions were divided between two major departments. The sales department, headed by one of the firm's vice-presidents, was responsible for management of the sales force, advertising and promotion, and miscellaneous other problems which were related to the actual selling of the product to the retailer.

The merchandising department was headed by the president of the firm. Under him were four product managers and two stylists. These men were responsible for product planning functions such as style development, maintenance of quality, price determination, and sales forecasting. Exhibit 2 presents a diagram of this organization.

In spite of this separation of marketing responsibilities, good working arrangements existed between the two departments. Major decisions were made only after interdepartmental agreement. Many decisions of lesser importance were also made jointly.

Product Lines

The company was unique in its industry in that it produced an extremely wide line of products. Most competing firms specialized in either men's or boys' apparel; Heritage made both. Perhaps even more significant, most competitors produced either furnishings (shirts, pajamas, etc.), clothing (slacks, suits, sport coats), or outerwear. Heritage produced the full range of these products.

The products were divided into four branded lines which were usually purchased separately by the retailer. Some thought had been given in 1968 to adding a new special fashion line which would capitalize on the current trends in clothing such as the sudden shift to "mod" clothing in both the men's and boys' markets. It would be called the "Swinger" line and would include a wide range of products. The new line would not prevent existing lines from following style trends as they had in the past. A decision on the proposed line was postponed.

The Jim Hawkins juvenile line was for boys in the one-to-four age group. This line included most types of furnishings and clothing products made by the firm; however, it was styled separately. It accounted for 20 percent of the boys' apparel business done by the firm.

The regular Jim Hawkins line was for boys to age fourteen. This was the most widely accepted of Heritage's lines and had the widest assortment of all the firm's products.

The Long John Silver line had been in existence for about fifteen years. It was aimed at the teen and college man markets and contained all the firm's products except pajamas. Special design effort was involved in preparing this line for its style-conscious market. It represented 80 percent of the firm's men's shirt business and about 30 percent of the firm's total business.

The Prestige line, until a year before the consultants were called in, had been the Robert Louis Stevenson line of dress and sport shirts for mature men. The name had been changed because Robert Louis Stevenson shirts had been sold exclusively to small town retailers for a number of years, and the name seemed to acquire a "hayseed" connotation with major retailers in large cities. It was hoped that the name change would allow the product to be reintroduced into major department stores. At the time of the consulting firm's investigation, the declining sales trend had not, however, been reversed.

Aside from its regular product lines, the firm also did some private labeling for major retail chains. This business was usually handled by an officer of the firm, and contracts were negotiated well in advance of the regular selling season. The primary advantage of these contracts was that they allowed Heritage to run its factories in the off season.

Sales by product class, but not by brand, were computed annually by the firm. The dollar sales figures appear in Exhibit 3, along with unit sales figures for 1968. Sales were totaled in this fashion because they were believed to be more meaningful to the firm. The company had eight factories, each of which was capable of producing only one type of product. Since costs and profits were tied to sales as a percent of factory capacity, the totals in Exhibit 3 were judged to be very relevant. In late 1968, none of the company's eight factories were operating at capacity.

The Consumer Market

The user of most of Heritage's products was the young man between the ages of five and nineteen. The size of this market is indicated in Exhibit 4.

The Jim Hawkins line was generally purchased by the user's mother. The Long John Silver line, with the exception of gifts, generally was purchased by the teen man himself with occasional guidance from a parent.

The Retail Market

Generally, retailers purchase 75 percent of their lines of apparel prior to the start of the season. Manufacturers like to receive these orders three to four months before the delivery date. Retailers, however, often delay to the last minute, forcing manufacturers to build large inventories prior to the start of each season. Heritage had always carried these inventories.

The principal outlets for men's and boys' clothing are general merchandise retail stores and more specialized apparel and accessory stores. These retailers can be divided into several groupings according to their buying or distribution methods. Each group represents a different channel involving different marketing considerations for a manufacturer. Sears, Roebuck & Co. and J. C. Penney Co. are examples of national chains that carry primarily their own brands. Other national chains such as Federated Department Stores and the May Company carry both their own brands and other nationally advertised brands. They represent a separate group. Discounters are less interested in brand name apparel. They buy on a price basis and often purchase distress merchandise. Basement stores, while not always representing a different retail establishment, do represent a separate apparel market. Their requirements are similar to the discounters'. Mail order houses represent another market for manufacturers. They often have special packaging and warehousing requirements.

Heritage primarily solicited the business of better grade "upstairs" department stores in cities and the highest quality stores in small towns. Eighty to ninety percent of the firm's total sales were to these outlets.

The Merchandising Function

The merchandising department controlled all aspects of product planning which involved a number of activities. The various styles had to be developed; fabrics and supplies had to be selected and purchased; and the total size of the line as well as the quality of each item in the line had to be determined. These functions were carried out by each of the product managers, one of whom was responsible for boys' furnishings, one for men's shirts and two for clothing. They made frequent trips to New York where piece goods manufacturers are located and where market information can be readily obtained. The composition of the product line was greatly influenced by this information. On the other hand, product advice offered by salesmen was often ignored. Most of the salesmen's ideas were derived from recognition of local fads in each salesman's territory. Only if expected volume from a new style idea was greater than fifty dozen was it seriously considered.

Other style changes originated among the company's stylists, who were considered to be among the best in the industry. They attempted to improve or adapt existing styles or develop new styles. Several innovative ideas had been developed by them and built into the product line, but generally they had not gained widespread consumer acceptance.

Pricing was also a function of the merchandising department. The general policy was to aim for the middle price range at the retail level. Boys' shirts and pajamas were priced to retail at $3.00, $4.00, and $5.00. Men's shirts were priced to retail at $4.00, $5.00, and $6.00. Boys' slacks were expected to retail at $4.00 to $8.00. All other items were priced to conform to the same image presented by the prices above.

The actual process of pricing the line was straightforward, but was often very time consuming. Rigid retail price lines existed for most of the firm's products. Further, retailers expected a mark-up of 40 to 45 percent on the retail selling price. The greater the mark-down potential, the higher was their expected mark-up. Another factor which limited the company's pricing freedom was that there were certain expected wholesale price lines. These, however, were more flexible than the retail price lines. For instance, a shirt that would retail for three dollars would normally wholesale for from $21.90 to $22.50 per dozen.

The price of a given item was determined in the following way. After the item had been styled and a piece goods price obtained, the design was given to the production department. This department developed an operation sheet and from it determined the production cost based on raw materials, labor, and the actual prior years' factory overhead per unit of production. These costs, plus the company's standard mark-up, determined the minimum standard wholesale price. This was followed up by a subjective evaluation as to whether the particular item warranted the price that had been determined. If it did, it became part of the line. If not, the design was changed to cut costs or, if this was not feasible, the item was no longer considered to be a potential part of the line.

Competitive Strategies

Generally, all firms in the industry followed one of two marketing strategies. Smaller companies and a few of the large ones emphasized style and price. They did not attempt to create a brand image and, in many cases, produced under a wide variety of labels. They usually did not produce staple products, such as white dress shirts, as the marketing of these items required a constant inventory. (Heritage, for instance, did 20 percent of its business in staple items.) The strategy of these firms was to identify new fads and then manufacture and sell these fads before the larger companies were ready to take the necessary risks.

A second major strategy was that practiced by brand name producers, including Heritage. Some commonly known names in this classification were: Savada Brothers, Robert Bruce, Elder, Levinson, Levi Strauss, Farah, Billy the Kid, H.I.S., Arrow, Van Heusen, and Pendleton. These companies generally relied on service, style, brand names, and promotional aids for the retailer to sell their product. They generally carried large inventories. It was the judgment of a Heritage vice-president that firms manufacturing boys' apparel did not put a major emphasis on national advertising to the consumer.

The Sales Force

Heritage had forty-eight salesmen in four national sales regions. Each of these regions had regional sales managers who supervised the sales force in the field.

Salesmen were classified by the lines they carried. Prior to 1967, all salesmen carried the full line of Heritage's products. In contrast, salesmen for competing firms carried a more restricted line. For example, a salesman sold either furnishings or clothing; or he would carry either men's or boys' clothing, but not both. The Heritage lines were so extensive that the policy involved several disadvantages. In order to show the full line, several large cases were necessary to carry it. The sheer bulk of the cases encouraged salesmen to sometimes leave some items at home. In addition, buyers were sometimes reluctant to give Heritage's salesmen the time required to show all lines.

Although Heritage's ability to service a major part of a retailer's needs with the general line was considered to be an important success factor for the company, the disadvantages of general line selling caused Heritage to divide its products into a furnishings line and a clothing line for most territories. Thus, since 1967, only a few salesmen have continued to sell the general line where the nature of their territories made the new system less feasible.

Under the new arrangement, each salesman traveled in a one-to-three state area with either a clothing or a furnishings line. Traveling separately in the same territory was another salesman with the complementary line of Heritage's products. Although cooperation was encouraged, each salesman operated relatively independently of the other, often not knowing basic information about the products his "partner" was carrying. Although the selling time problem was corrected by this organization, it was found that many salesmen continued to leave samples which they considered to be poor sellers, at home.

It was found, upon reviewing company records, that the target sales per salesman per territory were $300,000 a year. The high man in the sales force had sold $420,000 worth of merchandise in the prior year. As for the rest of the sales force, twenty men had sold more than $200,000 worth of goods and twenty-seven had sold less than $200,000. It was difficult to measure the relative success of the salesmen, particularly since at least twelve of those in the lower sales classification operated in "marginal" territories in which salesman turnover had been high for several years.

Customer records showed that Heritage salesmen called on over 6,000 customers in the United States. In analyzing shipments, however, it was found that 80 percent of the purchases were made by 10 percent of the customers.

Each salesman received a 6 percent direct commission on net sales in his territory. No other payments in the form of salaries or bonuses were distributed.

National sales meetings were held whenever possible at the home office. In the last three years, there had been one meeting each year. These meetings served to introduce the new Spring and Summer lines and to pass on new selling ideas to the salesmen. The meetings also gave the sales manager the opportunity to confer with individual salesmen. No formal training was given during these sessions. Because there was a new Fall line each year—and only one national sales meeting—the Fall line was introduced to salesmen in the field at meetings held by the regional sales managers.

When the company hired salesmen who had either worked for other companies in the industry or who had sales backgrounds, the new employees went directly into the field. Others were hired as trainees and spent several months as shipping clerks in the warehouse before taking out a line of products. During the first two or three weeks that a trainee or a new salesman was on the road, his regional sales manager or some other company executive would travel with him. This process was not formalized in any way and no other training, formal or informal, existed.

It appeared to some of the executives that morale of the sales force was relatively low. Part of this was attributed to salesmen's uncertainty about the company's future course due to the declining sales and profit picture.

Advertising and Promotion

It was the philosophy of the firm that if the product line could be "sold" to leading retailers, the retailers themselves would take care of consumer promotion. In line with this philosophy, nearly all company promotional efforts involved an attempt to obtain retailer acceptance of the line. Exhibit 5 shows the promotion budget (as developed prior to the beginning of each fiscal year) and the actual amount spent for promotion for the last three years.

It is clear from analysis of the budget that emphasis was placed on cooperative dealer advertising. Heritage offered to pay a portion of the advertising cost of all its retailers. The offer covered newspapers, catalogues, and newspaper supplements, subject to certain restrictions on use of brand names in ads, size of ads, and time periods. The company was enthusiastic about this approach because it provided a means of reaching the consumer while serving as a potentially strong selling tool for the company's salesmen. Despite the general enthusiasm of the firm's executives, retailer response had been somewhat disappointing. Thus, actual cooperative expenditures were considerably less than the amount budgeted. The firm spent $42,000 in 1965, $28,000 in 1966, and $29,000 in 1967 for cooperative advertising.

Although it was generally known that industry advertising expenditures amounted to less than one percent of net sales, the exact distribution of the industry's promotional dollar could not be determined. Several firms in men's wear such as Arrow and H.I.S. did some consumer advertising on their own. One Heritage executive did not feel, however, that this was the primary reason for their success. Although nearly all firms, including Heritage, placed advertisements from time to time in national magazines, many of these were subsidized by fiber producers or piece goods manufacturers.

Consultants' Report

After reviewing all functions of the business, the consultants pointed out two alternative courses of action for the company.

First, the company could cut from its line all products which could not be marketed profitably due to low volume. This would enable the firm to sell or convert to other uses the factories which produced these goods and concentrate on the manufacture and sale of only the most profitable items. This would bring about an immediate sizable profit and allow the present owners to sell out profitably in a few years if they desired. The main drawback to this alternative was that many manufacturing and office employees, as well as salesmen, would have to be dismissed due to the smaller scale of operations.

The second alternative was to take aggressive marketing action to build up consumer demand and production levels to the point that all products would be profitable. Roughly, this would entail generating sales of at least $18 million at current market prices. It was felt that this alternative was only feasible if this needed volume could be attained in three years or less.

An informal sampling of opinion indicated that the officers of the company favored the second alternative. This was also the recommendation of the consultants.

QUESTIONS

1. Do you agree with the consultants' evaluation of the alternatives open to the Heritage Company?
2. Evaluate the firm's condition, identifying its most serious problems.
3. Outline a program for reversing the downward trend of company sales and profits.
4. Discuss the effectiveness of present company policies regarding selling and promotion.

EXHIBIT 1
Selected Income Statement Information
(in Thousands of Dollars)

	1965	*1966*	*1967*	*1968*
Gross sales	14,527	15,408	13,821	14,678
Returns and allowances	500	640	408	421
Net Sales	14,027	14,768	13,413	14,257
Cost of goods sold	11,238	12,048	10,990	12,019
Gross profit	2,789	2,720	2,423	2,238
Profit net sales (%)	19.8%	18.4%	18.1%	15.4%
Commissions	622	650	609	604
Net profit to retained earnings	142	130	63	107

Net Sales
1957-1964

1957	$14,672	1961	$13,913
1958	$13,723	1962	$12,380
1959	$13,903	1963	$14,719
1960	$14,034	1964	$15,776

EXHIBIT 2
Heritage Manufacturing Co.—Organization

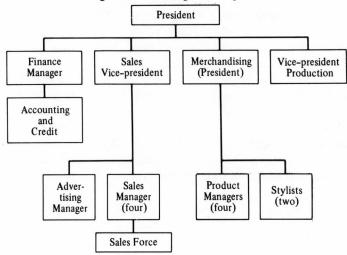

EXHIBIT 3
Sales by Product Class

	Dollars (000's)				Dozens
	1965	1966	1967	1968	1968
Men's dress shirts	225	258	303	290	11,253
Men's sport shirts	611	659	740	771	24,889
Bowling shirts*	178	94	46	43	1,626
Clothing	1,891	2,017	2,075	2,116	16,583
Boy's sport and dress shirts	4,297	4,179	4,176	4,259	199,538
Pants and slacks	1,657	1,520	1,096	989	31,007
Pajamas	489	502	471	461	13,777
Knit shirts	1,772	1,476	1,082	958	9,219
Outerwear	955	855	610	833	7,979
Special departments†	2,452	3,848	3,222	3,958	186,131
Total	14,527	15,408	13,821	14,678	502,002

*Company is in process of phasing out this product due to distribution problems and decreasing demand.
†Private label business.

EXHIBIT 4
Male Population, 5 to 19 Years of Age

	1940	1950	1960	1964	1968
Total (in millions)	17.6	18.2	25.0	28.0	30.2
Average annual rate of increase		0.3%	3.7%	3.0%	1.9%

Source: U.S. Bureau of the Census, *Statistical Abstract of the United States*, 1968.

EXHIBIT 5
Promotional Budget

	1966	1967	1968
Trade publications	$ 20,300	$ 23,700	$ 29,000
Mat book and catalog	6,000	5,000	5,000
Mats	1,500	1,800	1,500
Postage for direct mail	2,500	3,500	3,000
Other direct mail expense	6,000	4,000	4,000
Display cards	2,000	2,000	2,000
Salesmen shows	300	1,000	600
Unassigned	5,700	5,000	5,000
Miscellaneous ads	700	500	500
Promotional gifts	8,500	7,500	8,000
Cooperative advertising	60,000	69,000	66,400
Other	14,000	2,000	------
Total budgeted	127,500	125,000	125,000
Total actual expenditures	53,756	69,148	88,333

79.

Anheuser-Busch, Inc.

Creative Marketing and Management Science

Mr. Edward H. Vogel, Vice-president of Marketing, Anheuser-Busch, Inc., with headquarters in St. Louis, Missouri, described the company's marketing policies and strategies in the following paper at the XV International Meeting of the Institute of Management Sciences, in Cleveland, Ohio, September 15, 1968.

"Creative Marketing" can be characterized briefly as the systematic questioning of the assumptions behind marketing strategy and tactics and the use of the best available technology in doing so. My company has been in a particularly good position to engage in such marketing because it is involved in selling to both consumers and industry. Such involvement gives us an opportunity to learn about marketing at a level of generality that is not available to many companies.

Some of the differences in marketing to consumers and industry are very obvious, but others are very subtle. I will only be concerned here with some of the more subtle differences.

It is commonly assumed that industrial purchasing is essentially rational and that consumer purchasing is not. It is apparent that in industrial buying, for example, relevant data about the product and its producer are usually systematically collected, that decisions usually involve several well-informed purchasers, and that objective evaluation of delivered products and services are common. It is generally assumed, however, that many, if not most, consumer purchases are irrational, emotional, and impulsive. This assumption enables the marketer to blame his failures on the unpredictability of the consumer. After all, how can one predict irrational, emotional, and impulsive behavior?

It is here that we have learned one of our most important lessons from the use of the management sciences in the development of marketing policies. Consumer marketing problems are not solved by assuming the consumer is irrational and the marketer is rational, but just the opposite.

Rational in the Long Run

Consumers may behave irrationally in the short run, but not in the long run. They learn fast. Marketers who claim consumers are irrational really mean that they do not understand consumers and either don't know how to acquire such understanding or don't want to. Now mind you, I am not saying consumers are conscious of what they are doing or why. They can be rational even if they don't understand themselves. It is our job to find out why they do what they do, even if they don't know.

One brief and familiar example. Most marketers of gasoline assume consumers buy on the basis of brand preferences. Policies based on this assumption have uniformly failed. Studies have shown that consumers do not have gasoline brand preferences, and for good reason: they can't tell the difference between the performances of competing brands. And again for good reason: there isn't any significant difference between them. It turns out, however, that consumers pick service stations, not brands, and they do so in such a way as to minimize the amount of time they lose in buying gasoline. This is completely rational behavior under the circumstances.

In our own work we have found that consumer preferences for different kinds of alcoholic beverages are not irrational but are based on different functions that different beverages perform well under different environmental, economic, and physiological conditions.

We must not only develop understanding of the consumer and do so by at least starting with the assumption that he is rational, but we must also start with the assumption that most of our marketing errors and failures are due to our own irrationality. It is the irrationality of marketing rather than the rationality of consumption that I want to address first.

To become rational and effective marketers we must come to understand each aspect of marketing: advertising, pricing, sales effort (manpower), point-of-sales displays, and communications. Understanding means knowing what causes produce what effects.

For example, in general, the more advertising a company does, the larger are its sales. It is commonly assumed, therefore, that to sell more one must advertise more. This is irrational for two reasons. First, most companies set their advertising budgets as a fixed percentage of forecast sales. This means that increased forecasts cause increased advertising, not that increased advertising causes increased sales. Secondly, advertising is a stimulus and purchasing is a response. In psychology, no instance has been found in which responses increase linearly or even continuously with increases in stimulation.

Agencies' Income

This irrationality is perpetuated by advertising agencies, and for good reason. Their income increases as advertising does. There is no more irrational way for marketers to pay advertising agencies. Can you imagine paying your auditor a percentage of the taxes you pay the government? Would you expect them, if so compensated, to minimize your tax bill?

I would like to point out some of the marketing questions we have been asking and applying research to, questions which we didn't ask before, and which most companies are still not asking. If they are, few are willing to support the research effort required to find the answers. True, we have found research to be time-consuming and costly; but the returns from it have justified it many times over. Here are some of the questions we have been asking and getting answers to:

1. How much should we spend on advertising?
2. How should this be allocated to different media?
3. How should our expenditures be spread across the year; that is, how should they be timed?
4. How can the effectiveness of a message be measured?
5. How can more effective messages be written by using what we learn about why a consumer does what he does?
6. How can advertising and pricing be combined to get the best results possible in each individual marketing area?

By considering these and many other related questions we have managed to get some startling results. In 1962 we were spending $1.89 per barrel of Bud sold, in advertising. Today we are spending eighty cents per barrel. Exhibit 1 shows what has happened to the sales of Bud and its share of market in the intervening period.

Answers to such "how" questions as I have identified depend on answers to more basic "why" questions.

There are two aspects to finding answers to the "why" questions that I would like to point out. First, when we ask someone who does not know why something is happening to indicate what variables he thinks may be responsible for what is observed, he will play it safe and name everything that comes into his mind. It turns out that when we really do understand something very few variables are required to explain it. For example, one gasoline marketer was using an equation with 35 variables in it to predict service station sales, and the predictions were not very good; a group of operations researchers developed another equation which explained the sales of a station, not merely described it, and this equation had only four variables in it. It predicted three times as well as the equation with 35.

Secondly, since most purchasers do not know why they do what they do, nor for that matter do they usually know what they are doing, there is little point in asking them. Further, since most marketers do not know why they do what they are doing, there is no point in asking them either. Reliance on the questionnaire as the principal source of marketing data has been more responsible for misconceptions in marketing than any other single factor.

Market research often gets out on a limb by assuming that a large number of opinions must be right on the average. At Anheuser-Busch we prefer to analyze what people do, rather than what they say.

For example, some time ago we were faced with deciding whether to use plastic or paper for our six-pack carriers. The market researchers went to wholesalers, retailers, and consumers with both types of carriers and asked which they preferred. Eighty percent preferred the paper carrier.

Not being satisfied with this opinion poll, I asked that the two packs be placed in a sample of stores, side-by-side, and that we watch what choice consumers make. It turned out that they preferred the plastic carrier—a complete reversal of the earlier study. People often react differently than they say they will. This is particularly true when they are asked about something they have not experienced in their normal environment.

We must learn to distinguish between opinions and facts. This is as true of the past as it is of the future. In most cases marketers do not know whether a past decision had the desired effect or not. Sure, they have opinions; but different marketers always have different ones. And so we learn only slowly from experience. Every marketing decision can and should be experimentally evaluated. It is this fact that has had the greatest impact on our style of marketing management. We no longer go into the field with decisions unless we have a way of determining whether or not they work.

Commercially available marketing research services cannot be relied upon. They should be evaluated before use. For example, we employed one of the most widely used services for rating the quality of television commercials. Our management scientists designed an experiment to determine whether the ads that were rated as "superior" by this service resulted in more sales—for that's what counts, not rating points—than ads rated as "inferior." There was no difference in the effects on sales. We are still trying to find out how to get a meaningful rating of ads, so we know how difficult it is to do so.

Much has been written and expounded about the Nielsen ratings of television programs. Advertisers are prone to judge the competency of their work by these standards. The same is true for printed circulation. Audience and/or reader-mix, not number, is the really important ingredient. For example, the leading attraction at Madison Square Garden is the Ringling Bros. Circus. But the smallest amount of beer is sold at it because the audience is composed primarily of children below the legal drinking age.

Behavior and Beer

We are in the midst of an intensive study of beer-drinking behavior, a study which consists of a very complicated social-psychological analysis of who drinks beer, where, when, and why. Unless we understand the logic of beer consumption, we must use a shot-gun approach to influencing consumers rather than zeroing in on a specific target. This is economically wasteful. We have already learned from this study that most beer advertising is addressed to the wrong audience and that they are given the wrong reasons for drinking beer.

Most of the marketing problems I have discussed are current. What is equally important is long-range market planning. Every company is concerned with the future and what it will bring. Some are only slightly concerned for they feel secure in the beliefs that they can respond to whatever changes the future brings and that they can do well enough to survive. And for many companies nothing is more important than survival. Others are greatly concerned with the future but for different reasons. One group feels that it is not good enough to respond to changes after they have occurred; they want to prepare for and be ready for the changes.

These companies, therefore, tend to be preoccupied with forecasting the future. Often they are still trying to predict it when it is past. Another and smaller group are not so much interested in forecasting the future as they are in creating it. For these companies the objective is not to predict but to control the future. Thus there are three attitudes toward the future which, ordered from the most to least prevalent, are:

1. wait and see;
2. predict and prepare; and
3. make it happen.

One cannot grow and profit at a faster rate than one's competitors merely by responding to a future that others create. Those who benefit most from the future are those who have helped create it. One may be able to survive and even prosper without making the future, but one cannot pull away from the pack without doing so.

Now, obviously, we cannot completely control the future. But we can play an important, if not critical, role in shaping it. We may not be able to affect greatly what will happen, but we can significantly affect when and how it will happen. Put another way, by analyzing the present and the past we can see what must happen in the future: what is inevitable. Then we can plan to exploit the opportunities that inevitable changes will bring about and accelerate the coming of these changes in a way in which we and our consumers can most benefit.

Operations research has helped us develop a perception of the future, and it will help us exploit it to the benefit of the consumer and our company. Operations research has proven it can solve many shorter-range tactical problems with relative ease and at low cost. But, in my opinion, it can yield as large, if not larger, payoffs in the strategic area.

A Good Marriage

I first introduced operations research to my company in 1959. The use of such research has long since become an integral part of what might be called our style of management and operations. Today hardly a decision of any consequence is made that does not involve our researchers in one way or another. This blending of research and management did not occur over-night. It developed slowly under careful guidance.

Acceptance and exploitation of the management sciences resulted from the application of a few obvious principles to which much lip-service is given, but which are little practiced.

The key to acceptance of research is involvement: involvement of company personnel at every level. From the very start we saw to it that our research consultants met frequently with our management and discussed their formulation of our problems, the assumptions underlying their attack on them, the logic of their attack, their data collection procedures, and their methods of analysis. Management was brought along each step of the way and from the beginning contributed significantly to the research process.

Differences of opinion were thrashed out along the way, not after results were obtained. When results were obtained and recommendations were extracted, they seldom came as a great surprise and hence were implemented without great fuss. The necessary face-saving had taken place gradually before decisions had to be made.

We did not try to impose recommendations as though we suddenly had gained possession of the ultimate truth. Applications of recommendations were usually initiated on a small scale with close controls imposed on them. As confidence in the results developed, applications were extended.

No matter how general the acceptance of a research result by management, it was never applied without a well-designed control system to tell us whether the recommendations were working as expected. We have learned as much from the feed-back provided by such controls as we have from the research that produced the initial recommendations.

Designed Controls

More important, perhaps, is the fact that we now design controls for evaluation of decisions reached by management without the benefit of research. This enables us to learn more rapidly and accurately from experience, and it has indoctrinated management with an experimental approach to decision making.

Involvement of management is not enough; involvement of personnel at all levels is required. We have regularly scheduled sessions at which our operations researchers and field marketing personnel meet for several days to review the research in process and to allow those who will be affected by it to criticize it and make their own inputs.

In addition we periodically report on and discuss what is happening in research with our independent wholesalers. I have set up a mechanism by which they can express their points of view on our research and the policies derived from it.

Finally, and very important, our advertising agencies are involved regularly in our research planning and evaluation. Their research departments now work closely and directly with both our internal and external management science groups. They have conducted, and are conducting, many joint studies.

We began our exploration of the management sciences in 1959 by using external aid, the Operations Research Group at Case Institute of Technology, and later moved with most of that group to the Wharton School at the University of Pennsylvania. With the help of this group, we have developed several inside teams which work closely with each other and with our outside group. It is hard to tell them apart without a program. There is hardly a working day in which some of our people are not at Penn or some of their people are not at our offices. Communication between managers and these groups is continuous.

Whom Do We Trust?

It is only through continuous interaction of the sort I have described that mutual trust and friendship can develop. Without the trust that friendship breeds, research results will always be regarded with suspicion. Trust and respect cannot be legislated, it must be cultivated.

Our managers and researchers communicate well, but the burden for this has rested with our researchers. They must make even their most technical excursions understandable to management. I am convinced that until they can do so, they do not understand what they are talking about

286

no matter how impressive is the jargon with which they can conceal their lack of understanding.

Just as researchers must share all their thinking with managers, managers must do the same with researchers. We make it a point to have our researchers participate in management's discussions of its problems, whether or not they are working on them. Researchers must be as integral a part of the organization as managers are. Unless management scientists are taken into management's councils, they cannot perceive the needs and pressures placed upon managers and be responsive to them.

Outside the In Group

Unlike most companies that use operations research extensively, we continue to use an external group even after having developed a considerable internal capability. We plan to continue to do so because I think we have a fruitful division of labor between internal and external groups. The external group has increasingly been concerned with the "why" questions whose answers require extended research and often excursions into basic research. Our internal groups are primarily concerned with shorter-run problems of the "what" and "how."

Our internal groups have responsibility for maintaining solutions developed externally as well as internally. The reason this works well is that the "why" questions often require a wider range of disciplines than can be brought to bear on them inside the company. The University can call on these disciplines as they are needed.

In less than ten years after introducing operations research to my company, it is hard to imagine its operating without it. But its future, like that of management, is never assured. Management's task is to keep the research creative and productive. To do this we need creative and productive managers. Operations research has helped us create them; the interdependence is complete.

One final observation. Intelligence, competence, creativity, productivity, and communication skills are not enough in either management scientists or managers. Another essential ingredient is required: guts. Without the courage to face strong opposition and even personal abuse, and the willingness to risk one's status and even security, significant break-throughs will not be obtained. Management scientists who do not have guts may produce research that they are proud to report, but not progress that companies are proud to report.

My company has pulled away from the pack. I believe that its having done so is impressive evidence of what managers and management scientists can do together as managers learn to think more like management scientists, and management scientists learn to think more like managers.

287

QUESTIONS

1. Evaluate Anheuser-Busch's marketing program. What are its strengths? Are there any weaknesses?
2. What strategies and techniques are used at Anheuser-Busch to keep the research creative and productive?
3. Explain the role of management science in both short-range and long-range planning at Anheuser-Busch.
4. "At Anheuser-Busch we prefer to analyze what people do, rather than what they say," states vice-president Vogel. What evidence does he cite to support this statement? Is management justified in placing more faith in experimentation than in conventional marketing research surveys?
5. While advertising expenditures for Budweiser have been drastically cut from 1962 through 1968, sales have doubled. Also, during this period, share of market for Budweiser has gone up from 8.14 percent to 12.94 percent. How can you explain these surprising results? What marketing mix was used by management to increase sales and market share?

EXHIBIT 1
Budweiser's Share of the Malt Beverage Market

Year	Barrel Equivalent Sales	Share of Market
1962	$7,427,320	8.14%
1963	7,451,344	7.94
1964	8,342,129	8.46
1965	9,666,892	9.63
1966	11,294,141	10.83
1967	12,892,299	12.05
1968	14,386,000	12.94*

*Estimated

APPENDIX

CROSS INDEX TO MARKETING TEXTBOOKS
(Chapter Numbers)

(Case Numbers)

Shaw Willenborg, Stanley,	Beckman, Davidson	Buskirk	Converse, Huegy, Mitchell	Cundiff, Still	Grayson, Olsen	Kerby	Kotler	Lazer	McCarthy	Phillips, Duncan	Stanton	Staudt, Taylor	Sturdivant	Taylor, Shaw
1-6	28	3,5,22	23	5,6,7,22	6	5,6,7,8,9	1,9,22	7,16,17,18,19,20	4,6,8	22	3,4	5,6,8	1,6	3,4,5,18
7-14						2	2,5		5	1	27	5,6 32		
15-22	17	9,10,11	26,27	8,9,10,11	7,8	10,11,12	13,14	10	10,11,12,13,14	23	9,10,11	11,12,13,14	7	19
23-20	9,10,11	12,13,14,15,16	13,14,15,16,17	12,13,14,15	14,15	13,14,15,16	16,17	12,13	15,16,17,18,19	24,26	12,13,14,15,16,17	15,16,17,18,19,20,21	11,12,13	6,7,8,9,11,14,24
30-40	18,19	17,18	29	19,20,21	9	21,22,23	15	11	23,24,25,26,27	29,30,31	18,19,20,21	27,28,29	9	20,21,22
41-54	21,22	19,20,21	30	16,17,18	10,11,12,13	17,18,19,20	18,19	14,15	20,21,22	27,28	22,23,24	22,23,24,25	8	23
55-60			22					10	12		25			10
61-73	3	24,25	11	23	5	24	20	21,22,23	3	32	2,29,30		3	15
74-79				24					28,29		2,28	4	15	

Related Texts

Theodore N. Beckman, and William R. Davidson, *Marketing*, 8th Edition (New York: The Ronald Press Company, 1967).

Richard H. Buskirk, *Principles of Marketing*, 3rd Edition (New York: Holt, Rinehart and Winston, Inc., 1970).

Paul D. Converse, Harvey W. Huegy, and Robert V. Mitchell, *Elements of Marketing*, 7th Edition (Englewood Cliffs, New Jersey: Prentice-Hall, Inc., 1965).

Edward W. Cundiff and Richard R. Still, *Basic Marketing*, 2nd Edition (Englewood Cliffs, New Jersey: Prentice-Hall, Inc., 1971).

Robert A. Grayson and Reynold A. Olsen, *Introduction to Marketing* (New York: Appleton-Century-Crofts, 1971).

Joe Kent Kerby, *Essentials of Marketing Management* (Cincinnati: South-Western Publishing Company, 1970).

Philip Kotler, *Marketing Management* (Englewood Cliffs, New Jersey: Prentice-Hall, Inc., 1967).

William Lazer, *Marketing Management* (New York: John Wiley & Sons, Inc., 1971).

E. Jerome McCarthy, *Basic Marketing*, 4th Edition (Homewood, Illinois: Richard D. Irwin, Inc., 1971).

Charles F. Phillips and Delbert J. Duncan, *Marketing Principles and Methods*, 6th Edition (Homewood, Illinois: Richard D. Irwin, Inc., 1968).

William J. Stanton, *Fundamentals of Marketing*, 3rd Edition (New York: McGraw-Hill Book Company, 1971).

Thomas A. Staudt and Donald A. Taylor, *A Managerial Introduction to Marketing*, 2nd Edition (Englewood Cliffs, New Jersey: Prentice-Hall, Inc., 1970).

Frederick D. Sturdivant and Others, *Managerial Analysis in Marketing* (Glenview, Illinois: Scott, Foresman and Company, 1970).

Weldon J. Taylor and Roy T. Shaw, *Marketing*, 2nd Edition (Cincinnati: South-Western Publishing Company, 1969).

Alphabetical List of Cases